Essential Figures
in the Bible

Essential Figures in the Bible

Ronald L. Eisenberg

Jason Aronson
Lanham • Boulder • New York • Toronto • Plymouth, UK

Published by Jason Aronson
A wholly owned subsidiary of The Rowman & Littlefield Publishing Group, Inc.
4501 Forbes Boulevard, Suite 200, Lanham, Maryland 20706
www.rowman.com

10 Thornbury Road, Plymouth PL6 7PP, United Kingdom

British Library Cataloguing in Publication Information Available

Library of Congress Cataloging-in-Publication Data

Eisenberg, Ronald L.
  Essential figures in the Bible / Ronald L. Eisenberg.
    p. cm.
  Includes bibliographical references.
  ISBN 978-0-7657-0939-4 (cloth : alk. paper) — ISBN 978-0-7657-0940-0 (ebook)
  1. Bible. O.T.—Biography—Dictionaries. I. Title.
  BS570.E37 2013
  220.9'2—dc23

                                                                    w2012021305

©™ The paper used in this publication meets the minimum requirements of
American National Standard for Information Sciences—Permanence of Paper
for Printed Library Materials, ANSI/NISO Z39.48-1992.

Printed in the United States of America

To Zina Leah, Avlana Kinneret, and Cherina Carmel, who beautify, nurture, and uplift my life's journey and joyously share in my love of Torah.

Contents

Preface

Once when searching for information about a biblical figure, I realized this was not necessarily an easy task. Finding either encyclopedic volumes giving detailed descriptions of the nearly 3,000 people named in the Bible, or shorter books providing only brief identification, I decided to develop *Essential Figures in the Bible* to present manageable amounts of information about the more than 250 individuals I found to be most important to an understanding of the text.

In addition to those biblical figures familiar to readers of the Five Books of Moses, I also included the twelve Israelite tribal chieftains who made identical offerings for the dedication of the Tabernacle, individuals associated with Joshua's conquest of the Promised Land or the reign of King David, including all his wives and lesser-known sons, and all of the so-called minor prophets and kings of Judah. Keeping in mind the issues that I had encountered in my own research, I tried to make the book thorough, yet efficient and accessible. Each entry contains a summary of the relevant narrative with illustrative quotations from the text and cross-references to other entries in the book. When appropriate, there is also supplementary material from the Talmud, Midrash, and other rabbinic literature.

In addition, several appendices are included to aid the reader. A table charting the first biblical mention of each figure provides a handy chronological framework. There is also a list of the abbreviations of the biblical and rabbinic works cited in the text, as well as a glossary of terms that includes a brief synopsis of the tractates of the Mishnah and other rabbinic writings.

The Bible is the core text in Judaism and the foundation of the religious faith of millions of people throughout the world. *Essential Figures in the Bible* is designed for a broad audience of Bible readers of all denominations—to anyone who is fascinated, as I am, with the people in the Book.

Acknowledgments

In preparing the English translations from the Bible and rabbinic literature, I consulted several superb references that I would like to acknowledge. These include the Jewish Publication Society Tanach, the CD version of the Soncino edition of the Babylonian Talmud (Davka), and the Schottenstein editions of the Babylonian Talmud and Jerusalem Talmud (Mesorah).

I also want to express special thanks to my wife, Zina Schiff, for her continual encouragement and constant enthusiasm in reading and thoughtfully editing my writing, which were so vital to the publication of this book.

Abbreviations

Ar.	Arachin
ARN	Avot d'Rabbi Nathan
Av. Zar.	Avodah Zarah
Avot	Pirkei Avot
BB	Bava Batra
B.C.E.	Before the Common Era
Bek.	Bechorot
Ber.	Berachot
Betz.	Beitzah
Bik.	Bikurim
BK	Bava Kama
BM	Bava Metzia
C.E.	Common Era
Chron.	Chronicles
Dem.	Demai
Deut.	Deuteronomy
Deut. R.	Deuteronomy Rabbah
Eccles.	Ecclesiastes
Eccles. R.	Ecclesiastes Rabbah
Eduy.	Eduyot
Er.	Eruvin
Esth.	Esther
Esth. R.	Esther Rabbah
Exod.	Exodus
Exod. R.	Exodus Rabbah
Ezek.	Ezekiel
Gen.	Genesis
Gen. R.	Genesis Rabbah
Git.	Gittin
Hab.	Habbakuk

Hag.	Haggai (Bible)
Hag.	Hagigah (Talmud)
Hal.	Hallah
Hor.	Horayot
Hos.	Hosea
Hul.	Hullin
Isa.	Isaiah
Jer.	Jeremiah
Jon.	Jonah
Josh.	Joshua
JT	Jerusalem Talmud
Judg.	Judges
Ker.	Keritot
Ket.	Ketubot
Kid.	Kiddushin
Kil.	Kilayim
Lam.	Lamentations
Lam. R.	Lamentations Rabbah
Lev.	Leviticus
Lev. R.	Leviticus Rabbah
Mak.	Makot
Mal.	Malachi
Mech.	Mechilta
Meg.	Megillah
Men.	Menacot
Mic.	Micah
Mid. Ps.	Midrash Psalms
Mik.	Mikva'ot
MK	Mo'ed Katan
Nah.	Nahum
Naz.	Nazir
Ned.	Nedarim
Nid.	Niddah
Num.	Numbers
Num. R.	Numbers Rabbah
Obad.	Obadiah
PdRE	Pirkei de-Rabbi Eliezer
PdRK	Pesikta de-Rabbi Kahana

Pes.	Pesachim
Pes. Rab.	Pesikta Rabbati
Prov.	Proverbs
Ps.	Psalms
RH	Rosh Hashanah
Ruth R.	Ruth Rabbah
Sam.	Samuel
Sanh.	Sanhedrin
Sem.	Semachot
Shab.	Shabbat
Shek.	Shekalim
Shev.	Shevu'ot
Song R.	Song of Songs Rabbah
Soph.	Sopherim
Sot.	Sotah
Suk.	Sukkah
Taan.	Ta'anit
Tam.	Tamid
Tanh.	Tanhuma
Tos.	Tosefta
Yev.	Yevamot
Zech.	Zechariah
Zeph.	Zephaniah
Zev.	Zevachim

A

Aaron, son of Amram and Jochebed, great-grandson of Levi, brother of Miriam and Moses, and the first high priest of Israel.

When Moses complained that he was "slow of speech" and lacked the eloquence to persuade the Israelites to follow his lead, God told Moses that his brother Aaron would be his spokesman. "You shall speak to him and put the words in his mouth—I will be with you and with him as you speak, and tell both of you what to do—and he shall speak for you to the people" (Exod. 4:15–16). When the brothers appeared before the ruler of Egypt, it was Aaron who "cast down his rod in the presence of Pharaoh and his courtiers, and it turned into a serpent" (Exod. 7:10). After the Egyptian magicians and sorcerers duplicated this feat, "Aaron's rod swallowed their rods" (Exod. 7:12). At the command of Moses, Aaron stretched out his rod to bring on the first three plagues of blood, frogs, and lice (Exod. 7:19; 8:1; 8:12). When the Amalekites attacked the tired Israelites fleeing Egypt, Aaron joined Hur in supporting the hands of Moses so the Israelites were victorious (Exod. 17:9–14). A *midrash* says that this was the result not of their military prowess, but of their faith in God as their eyes gazed heavenward toward Moses' outstretched hands (RH 29a).

When the people feared that Moses was so long in coming down from Mount Sinai, they gathered around Aaron and demanded, "Come, make us a god who shall go before us" (Exod. 32:1–35). Thinking that greed would quell this uprising, Aaron said to them, "Take off the gold rings on the ears of your wives, sons, and daughters and bring them to me." The people immediately complied, and Aaron took the gold, "cast it in a mold and made it into a molten calf." The Israelites exclaimed, "This is your god, O Israel, who brought you out of the land of Egypt!" When Aaron saw their reaction, he announced, "Tomorrow shall be a festival of the Lord!" "Early on the next day, the people offered up burnt offerings and brought sacrifices of well-being; they sat down to eat and drink, and then rose to dance."

God urged Moses to hurry down the mountain. As he witnessed the shameful episode of the Golden Calf, Moses angrily flung the tablets to the ground, shattering them. He took the molten image and burned it, grounding it to powder, and threw it on the water that he made the Israelites drink.

Confronting Aaron, Moses asked: "What did this people do to you that you have brought such great sin upon them?" Aaron replied, "Let not my lord be enraged. You know that this people is bent on evil." Recounting what had transpired, Aaron concluded, "They gave it [the gold] to me and I hurled it into the fire, and out came this calf!" Only the intercession of Moses saved Aaron from the Divine plague that smote the people.

According to a *midrash*, seeing the mob kill Hur for rebuking their idolatrous intentions and realizing that he also would be killed for resisting their demands, Aaron preferred to commit a sin himself rather than have the Israelites collectively condemned for a second murder (Exod. R. 41:7). "Aaron intended only to delay them until Moses came down [from Mount Sinai], though Moses thought that Aaron was collaborating with them and was incensed against him" (Exod. R. 37:2). The Rabbis used Aaron's reply to teach: "A person should always be careful when responding [to a question], because from Aaron's answer heretics found a basis for their false beliefs and were able to deny God ['I cast it into the fire and this calf emerged (by itself)' giving the impression that the calf, and other idolatrous gods, had divine power]" (Meg. 25b).

When the tribe of Levi was set apart for priestly service, Aaron was arrayed in the robes of his office and instructed in its specific duties. Ironically, on the day of his consecration as high priest, his sons, Nadab and Abihu, were consumed by Divine fire for having offered "alien fire" before the Lord (Lev. 10:1–2). Yet "Aaron was silent" (Lev. 10:3); according to the *aggadah*, "Silence is a sign of being comforted" (ARN 14).

Following the Korach rebellion against the leadership roles of Moses and Aaron, each of the princes of Israel wrote his name on a rod, which was placed overnight in the Tent of Meeting. The next day, "The staff of Aaron of the house of Levi had budded, blossomed, and produced ripe almonds" (Num. 17:23). This miracle unequivocally demonstrated the prerogative of the Levites in being responsible for the sacred service, with the descendants of Aaron being in charge of the sanctuary and the altar (Num. 18:1–7).

Like his brother, Aaron was not permitted to enter the land of Canaan. In the principal account of his death (Num. 20:22–29), Aaron, his son Eleazar, and Moses ascended Mount Hor "in the sight of the whole community." After Moses stripped Aaron of his priestly vestments and put them on Eleazar, "Aaron died there on the summit of the mountain . . . and all the house of Israel cried bitterly for Aaron for thirty days."

In the rabbinic literature, Aaron was known as the great peacemaker. "He loved peace and pursued it, loved people and drew them close to Torah" (Avot 1:12). When Aaron encountered a wicked person, he greeted him. The next day, when that person wanted to commit a sin, he thought back to

Aaron's greeting and how ashamed he would be before Aaron if he followed his sinful desire. When two people quarreled, Aaron would go and sit down with one of them, saying how ashamed the other was because he had sinned against him. Then Aaron would go to the other and say the same thing. In this way, Aaron would "dispel any ill feeling in the heart" of both. When the two friends later met, "they embraced and kissed each other." It was said that "there were thousands in Israel who were called by the name of Aaron, for if not for Aaron, they would not have come into the world. [Aaron] made peace behind husband and wife so that they came together; and they named the child [that was born] after him" (ARN 12:3).

"In one year, three righteous people died: Moses, Aaron, and Miriam. Three precious gifts that had been given through the merit of each were canceled": the manna (Moses), the pillar of cloud (Aaron), and the well (Miriam). "All of them were removed in the same month" (Sifrei Deut 305).

The Rabbis said, "Moses and Aaron are equivalent to one another" (Gen. R. 1:15); "The merit of Moses and Aaron was enough to redeem Israel" (Exod. R. 15:3); and "The world exists only for the sake of Moses and Aaron" (Hul. 89a). *See also* Hur; Korach; Miriam; Moses.

Abel, second son of Adam and Eve, and the younger brother of Cain (Gen. 4).

The source of Abel's name is uncertain, though it may be related to the Hebrew word *hevel*, meaning "breath, vapor, or futility." Used extensively in the Book of Ecclesiastes, Abel's name was symbolic of his tragically short life.

Abel was the first shepherd and brought an offering to God from "the choicest of the firstlings of his flock," while his brother Cain, a "tiller of the soil, . . . brought an offering to the Lord from the fruit of the ground." Without giving a reason, God accepted Abel's offering but rejected Cain's. Searching for an explanation, the Rabbis noted that Abel brought the choicest firstlings of his flock, whose wool had not been shorn, while Cain offered merely "an offering" of parched grain and flax plants (left over food), far from the best of his agricultural produce (PdRE 21). Angered by this rejection and unassuaged by God's assurance that Divine acceptance depended on proper intention, Cain attacked his brother. According to legend, as the two men grappled, Abel overcame Cain, who fell beneath him. When Cain begged for mercy, Abel let him go. Immediately, Cain "rose up against Abel his brother and slew him."

In response to God's asking, "Where is your brother Abel?" Cain replied: "I do not know. Am I my brother's keeper?" Shocked by Cain's murderous act, God exclaimed: "Your brother's blood cries out to Me from the ground." The word "blood" appears in the plural in the text, meaning that Cain had killed not only Abel but also all his potential descendants. As punishment for his crime, Cain was doubly cursed—the ground would no longer yield any return for his labor, and he would "become a ceaseless wanderer on earth."

The *aggadah* embellishes the terse story in the text. Abel was stronger than Cain and overpowered his brother. As he lay beneath Abel, Cain begged for mercy: "We are the only sons in the world. What will you tell Father if you kill me?" Filled with compassion, Abel let him go, whereupon Cain rose up and killed him. According to another *midrash*, the murder resulted after Cain proposed that he and Abel divide the world between them, with Cain receiving all the land (real property) and Abel all the chattel (movable, personal property). As soon as Abel agreed, Cain accused him of walking on the land, which belonged to him. In response, Abel claimed that Cain was clad in garments made of animal skins, which belonged to him. In the ensuing quarrel, Cain killed Abel with a stone (Gen. R. 22:7). In one version of the tale, Cain's motivation was not merely jealousy at God's having accepted Abel's offering. Both Cain and Abel had twin sisters whom they were to marry. However, Abel's twin sister was more beautiful, and Cain desired to get rid of his brother so that he could have her as his wife (PdRE 21; Gen. R. 22:7).

At the time, human beings had no knowledge of burial. As Abel was the first person to die, his corpse remained unburied for some time. So God sent two turtledoves, which landed near Adam and Eve. After one bird died, the other dug a hollow place to push the body. Seeing this behavior, the first couple did the same to the body of Abel (PdRE 21).

Tales of rivalry between the nomadic shepherd, with his flocks and herds, and the settled farmer cultivating his land were a staple of popular literature throughout the ancient Near East, dating back as early as the second millennium B.C.E.

Abiathar, one of the two chief priests of King David.

When King Saul ordered the massacre of the priests of the village of Nob because they had aided David during his flight, Abiathar alone escaped. Hearing of the slaughter, David asked Abiathar to join him as his priest. Upon becoming king, David established both the descendants of Abiathar and Zadok as the priestly lines of the royal court (2 Sam. 8:17). When David was forced to flee Jerusalem during Absalom's revolt, the king sent Abiathar and Zadok to the capital to inform him of the developing intrigues in the rebel court (2 Sam. 17:15).

During the struggle for succession to the throne after the death of David, Abiathar supported Adonijah (1 Kings 1:7), while Zadok championed Solomon. Consequently, when Solomon emerged as the new king, he anointed Zadok as high priest, banishing Abiathar and his descendants to Anatot and taking away their privileges to serve as priests in Jerusalem. The prophet Jeremiah, described as descending from the priests of Anatot (Jer. 1:1), may thus have been a descendant of Abiathar.

Abidan, son of Gideoni and chieftain of the tribe of Benjamin.

Abidan made the ninth of the twelve identical offerings for the dedication of the Tabernacle in the wilderness (Num. 7:60–65).

Abigail, wife of Nabal the Carmelite and later of King David.

When fleeing from Saul, David sent ten of his men to the wealthy Nabal, asking for food and drink to sustain the fugitives (1 Sam. 25:2–42). After the miserly Nabal refused the request, his beautiful and prudent wife learned that the angry David was approaching with a large force of armed men. She rushed to take food and drink to the approaching soldiers and begged David to spare her worthless husband and his servants, lest he (the future king) shame himself by shedding blood without cause. David was impressed by Abigail's wisdom and courage and, after Nabal's death ten days later, sent for Abigail and married her. She bore him a son, Chileab (1 Sam. 3:3), who was also called Daniel (1 Chron. 3:1).

The Talmud lists Abigail as one of four women of surpassing beauty (the others being Sarah, Rahab, and Esther) (Meg. 15a) and one of the seven prophetesses (Meg. 14). It adds that a king is forbidden from having more than eighteen wives, "even if they are like [i.e., as virtuous as] Abigail" (Sanh. 21a). The *aggadah* relates that when David was determined to kill her husband immediately, Abigail calmly asked: "Does one judge cases involving capital punishment at night [i.e., and yet you are condemning Nabal to death]?" When David retorted that it was not necessary to formally try Nabal, since he was a rebel against the king, Abigail replied: "Saul is still alive, and the world does not yet know that you were anointed king," which she knew through her gift of prophecy. David then said, "Blessed is your discretion and blessed are you who have kept me from incurring blood guilt" (Meg. 14a–b). *See also* Nabal.

Abihu, second son of Aaron and Elisheba.

Together with his brother, Nadab, Abihu met an untimely and mysterious death after offering "strange fire" before the Lord (Lev. 10:1–3). Because both Abihu and Nadab "left no sons" (Num. 3:4), their priestly lines became extinct. *See also* Nadab.

Abijah, son of Rehoboam, grandson of Solomon, and the second king of Judah (914–911 B.C.E.).

Constantly at war with Jeroboam, the king of the Northern Kingdom of Israel, Abijah was described as a wicked ruler "who followed the sinful ways of his father" (1 Kings 15:3). Later in the Bible, however, Abijah was lauded for defeating the northern army and seizing a large amount of territory from his rival (2 Chron. 13:17–19). (*See* Nadab.)

Abimelech, heathen ruler of Gerar and subject of the first dream mentioned in the Bible.

Fearing for his safety while temporarily dwelling in Gerar, Abraham introduced Sarah as his sister, and she was brought into the royal household. Instead of inflicting a severe plague on the king, as had been the punishment of Pharaoh in a previous similar incident (Gen. 12:14–20), God "came to Abimelech in a dream by night and said to him, 'You are to die because of the woman you haven taken, for she is a married woman'" (Gen. 20:3). When Abimelech protested his innocence, arguing that he was unaware of the true situation, God accepted his contention, indicating that He had stopped Abimelech from sinning by preventing him from touching Sarah (Gen. 20:6). A similar incident with Abimelech was reported in connection with Isaac and Rebecca, in which the king again complained of the perfidy of a patriarch (Gen. 26:1–11).

"The shepherds of Abimelech and Abraham quarreled, each arguing that a disputed well was theirs. Abraham's shepherds suggested, 'The well belongs to the one for whom the water rises to water his sheep.' When the water saw Abraham's flock, it immediately ascended" (Gen. R. 54:5). After later disputes over wells, Abraham and Isaac each entered into covenants of peace with Abimelech at Beersheba (Gen. 21:27–31; 26:28–33).

The Midrash regards Abimelech as a righteous gentile (Mid. Ps. 34), whose attempted seizure of Sarah reflected that he was childless and hoped to be blessed with offspring by marrying such a pious woman (PdRE 26). Among the punishments for his sin were that "ruffians entered his house and attacked him all night," "boils erupted on his body" (Gen. R. 64:9), and his household became barren (BK 92a). Commenting on the biblical verse, "Behold it is for you a covering of the eyes" (Gen. 20:16), the *aggadah* relates that Abimelech said to Abraham: "You covered my eyes [i.e., deceived me by saying that Sarah was your sister], therefore the son that you will sire will be of covered eyes [i.e., blind]," a prophecy that was fulfilled in Isaac's old age (BK 93a; Gen. R. 52:12). Remembering his previous punishment, Abimelech left Rebecca alone, even though he had heard of her great beauty. However, once Isaac had become so wealthy that people kept saying, "Rather the dung of Isaac's mules than Abimelech's gold and silver," the latter became jealous and claimed that Isaac's wealth (lit., "the strength you have acquired"), "was it not [derived] from us? Originally you had but one sheep, while now you have many" (Gen. R. 64:7).

Abimelech, son of Gideon, born to his Shechemite concubine (Judg. 8:31).

Although his father had seventy sons from various wives, Abimelech claimed power over Shechem and was determined to gain control by force (Judg. 9). Supported by his mother's family, Abimelech hired "some worthless and reckless fellows" who joined him in murdering all but one of his half-brothers to eliminate any potential rivals for power. After ruling for three years, "God sent an evil spirit between Abimelech and the men of Shechem," but Abimelech defeated his enemies, destroying the city and killing its inhabitants. While besieging the neighboring fortress of Thebez, Abimelech's skull was crushed by a millstone thrown by a woman. Realizing that he was mortally wounded, Abimelech ordered his armor-bearer to kill him at once with his sword, lest his enemies say, "a woman slew me."

Although Abimelech was not considered among the judges or credited with saving Israel from its oppressors, his story probably was included in the Book of Judges because of the prominence of his father, Gideon.

Abiram, son of Eliab.

Abiram joined his brother Dathan in the rebellion against Moses (Num. 16:1). *See also* Dathan.

Abishag, unmarried Shunnamite girl brought to minister to the aged and infirm King David.

David's servants hoped that through her fresh beauty, "the king may become warm [i.e., revive his failing body and mind]" (1 Kings 1:4). According to the *aggadah*, although Abishag was "only half as beautiful as Sarah," her beauty was such that she merited the rank of queen (Sanh. 39b). After Solomon succeeded his father, his older brother Adonijah, who had tried to usurp the kingship while David was still alive, asked Solomon's mother, Bathsheba, to arrange for him to wed Abishag. Correctly interpreting this request as another attempt by Adonijah to seize the throne, since according to ancient tradition the concubine of a man became the inheritance of his heir, Solomon ordered the execution of his brother (1 Kings 2:13–25).

The Talmud relates that Abishag suggested that David marry her, but the king replied that he already had his permitted number of eighteen wives. Aware of David's prior philandering, she taunted him about his impotence: "When courage fails the thief, he becomes virtuous" (Sanh. 22a).

Abishai, son of King David's sister, Zeruiah, and the brother of Joab and Asahel.

One of David's "mighty men" (2 Sam. 23:18–19) and second in command to Joab, Abishai led the army that defeated the Edomites in the Valley of Salt, where 18,000 of the enemy were killed (1 Chron. 18:12). During one of David's battles against the Philistines, Abishai saved the king's life from a giant (Ishbi-benob) who carried a spear with the weight of "300 shekels of bronze" (2 Sam. 21:15–17).

However, Abishai had a cruel and impulsive streak. When he and David made their way into Saul's camp one evening, Abishai would have killed the king who had been relentlessly pursuing David ("God has delivered your enemy into your hand this day; now let me strike him, I beg you"; 1 Sam. 26:8). However, David restrained his nephew: "As the Lord lives, the Lord shall strike him; or his day shall come to die; or he shall descend into battle, and perish. God forbid that I should lay a hand against the Lord's anointed" (1 Sam. 26:10–11). Abishai later joined Joab in treacherously murdering Abner in revenge for Abner having caused the death of their brother Asahel (2 Sam. 3:30).

The Talmud elaborates on the story of how Abishai saved the life of David. Satan once appeared before David disguised as a deer. David repeatedly shot arrows at the deer, but they did not reach him. As he followed the animal, David unwittingly entered the land of the Philistines. When Ishbi-benob saw David, he realized that it was he who had killed his brother Goliath. "So he bound David, bent him over, and cast him under an olive press [to crush him]; but a miracle occurred and the ground softened under David" (Sanh. 95a).

Meanwhile, when Abishai was washing his hands before the Sabbath, he saw bloodstains in the bowl. Others say a dove came and beat its wings before him, scratching his face. Reasoning that Israel was likened to a dove (Ps. 68:14), Abishai concluded that David must be in trouble. Unable to find David in his house, Abishai took David's mule (the danger of the moment outweighing the rule that one may "not ride upon his [a king's] horse, nor sit upon his seat, nor use his scepter"), hoping that the animal's instinct would lead it to his master. The way was miraculously shortened for him, as it was for Eliezer returning with Rebecca to marry Isaac, and for Jacob when fleeing to escape his brother Esau. When he passed by Orpah (Ishbi-benob's mother) spinning, she threw the spindle at Abishai, intending to kill him. Pretending that it had merely fallen out of her hand, she asked Abishai to retrieve it, but instead he threw it on the top of her head and killed her. Seeing what had transpired, Ishbi-benob "threw David up [in the air] and stuck his spear [into the earth], saying, 'Let him fall upon it, and perish.'" However, Abishai pronounced the Divine Name, which kept David suspended between heaven and earth. "Why did David not pronounce it himself?—Because a prisoner cannot free himself from prison." Abishai then pronounced the Divine Name again and brought David down safely, at some distance from where Ishbi-benob stood (Rashi).

The enraged giant, described in a *midrash* as equal to 70,000 men of Israel (Mid. Ps. 17:4), pursued David and Abishai. Although afraid, they eventually decided to make a stand and fight him. They taunted Ishbi-benob: "Go and find your mother, Orpah, in the grave!" Hearing that his beloved mother was dead at Abishai's hand, "the giant's strength failed and they slew him."

Abital, wife of King David.

Abital was the mother of Shephatiah, the fifth son of David, who was sired by the king during his rule in Hebron (2 Sam. 3:2–4; 1 Chron. 3:1–3).

Abner, son of Ner the Benjaminite, cousin of King Saul, and the "captain of his host" (1 Sam. 14:50–51).

Abner joined Saul in the pursuit of David. At court, Abner occupied the seat of honor next to Jonathan, Saul's son and the heir apparent (1 Sam. 20:25). When David once slipped into Saul's camp unnoticed, he taunted Abner for failing to properly guard the king. "As the Lord lives, you deserve to die, because you did not keep watch over your master, the Lord's anointed. Look around and see where are the king's spear and water jar that were at his head [both of which David had removed!]" (1 Sam. 26:14–16).

After the death of Saul and three of his sons on Mount Gilboa, Abner made Saul's son Ishbosheth king over the northern tribes of Israel, with his capital at Mahanaim in Transjordan, while Judah broke away and elected David as their king in Hebron (2 Sam. 2:8–11). When fleeing the scene after his forces were defeated by David's troops at Gibeon, Abner was pursued by Asahel, the brother of Joab. After pleading unsuccessfully with Asahel to cease the bloodshed, Abner killed him in self-defense. Joab finally agreed to blow the shofar, which ended the battle (2 Sam. 2:12–29). When accused by Ishbosheth of conspiring against him to seize the throne, the furious Abner switched sides and eventually convinced the leaders of Saul's own tribe of Benjamin to offer David the crown of a reunited kingdom (2 Sam. 3:11–19). However, Abner was then murdered by Joab, the commander of David's forces, to avenge the death of his brother Asahel (2 Sam. 3:27–30). Shocked by this treacherous deed, David cursed Joab and his house, lamenting: "A prince and a great man has fallen this day in Israel" (2 Sam. 3:31–39). Solomon later fulfilled David's deathbed charge to avenge Abner's murder (1 Kings 2:5, 32).

The *aggadah* describes Abner as a giant of extraordinary strength (Eccles. R. 9:11) and the son of the Witch of En Dor (PdRE 33:13). According to the Talmud, when Doeg argued that, as the descendant of a Moabite woman (Ruth), not only was David prohibited from becoming king of Israel but could not even be admitted "into the assembly of the Lord" (based on Deut. 23:4), it was Abner who refuted the argument by saying that the biblical prohibition used the masculine gender and thus applied only to a Moabite and not to a Moabitess (Yev. 76b).

Abraham, son of Terah, husband of Sarah, father of Ishmael and Isaac, and the first patriarch of Israel.

Initially called Abram (exalted father), God subsequently changed his name to Abraham (father of a multitude of nations; Gen. 17:5) when making the covenant symbolized by the rite of circumcision. Born in Ur of the Chaldees, Abraham moved with his family to Haran, where his father died. There God appeared to Abraham, saying: "Go forth from your land, and from the place of your birth, and from the house of your father to a land that I will show you. I will make of you a great nation, and I will bless you; I will make your name great, and you shall be a blessing" (Gen. 12:1–2). So Abraham, together with his wife and his nephew Lot, traveled to Canaan, where God promised that all the land he could see in every direction would be given forever to him and his offspring, who would become as uncountable as the dust of the earth (Gen. 13:14–17).

After a journey to Egypt during a time of famine, where Sarah was briefly abducted into Pharaoh's household (Gen. 12:10–20), and a military campaign to rescue Lot (Gen. 14:1–23), God again came to Abraham in a vision and promised that his descendants would inherit the land of Canaan and become as numerous as the stars in the heavens (the "covenant between the pieces"; Gen. 15:1–21). Since Sarah "had borne him no children," she gave Abraham her maidservant Hagar, so that "perhaps I shall have a son through her" (Gen. 16:1–2). This union resulted in the birth of Ishmael. When Abraham was ninety-nine years old, he was visited by three angels who announced that within a year the aged Sarah would bear a child (Gen. 18:1–15), who was born at the appointed time (Gen. 21:2). The angels also related that God intended to destroy the wicked cities of Sodom and Gomorrah. Boldly questioning the Divine justice of collectively punishing both sinners and righteous alike, Abraham bargained with God to spare Sodom if it contained ten righteous men, but that number could not be found (Gen. 18:22–32). This became one source for ten constituting a *minyan* (quorum) for prayer.

The most serious trial of Abraham's life was God's command to offer up Isaac as a burnt offering (Gen. 22:1–19). Without any hesitation, Abraham obeyed the Divine request and took his son to be sacrificed on Mount Moriah. With his son bound to an altar (*akedah*, the binding of Isaac), Abraham picked up the knife to slay his son, but was suddenly stopped by an angel of the Lord, who again promised that Abraham's descendants would be "as numerous as the stars of heaven and the sands on the seashore."

When Sarah died, Abraham purchased the Cave of Machpelah in Hebron as her burial site (Gen. 23:1–20). After sending his servant Eliezer to his family in Haran to find a suitable wife for Isaac (Gen. 24:1–61), Abraham died at age 175 and was buried by his sons Isaac and Ishmael next to Sarah in the Cave of Machpelah (Gen. 25:7–10). According to legend, "On the day when Abraham our father departed from the world, all the great ones of the nations of the world stood in a line [the custom for those who come to offer comfort to mourners] and said, 'Woe to the world that has lost its leader! Woe to the ship that has lost its pilot'" (BB 91a–b).

The Talmud (Ber. 26b) attributes the institution of the morning (*Shacharit*) prayer to Abraham, based on the verse that he "rose up early in the morning and hurried to the place where he had stood [in the presence of the Lord]" (Gen. 19:27).

The Rabbis invoked analogies and parables relating to the ten "trials/tests" of Abraham to explain why God inflicts suffering on the righteous.

> The potter does not test cracked [glass] vessels, for he need only strike them once and they break. But if he tests sound vessels, he can strike them many times without their breaking. Similarly, God does not try the wicked, but the righteous. If a farmer has two cows, one strong and one weak, on which does he place the yoke? Obviously, on the strong. In like manner, God tests the righteous. (Gen. R. 55:2)

Isaac and Ishmael were engaged in a controversy of who was the most beloved. Ishmael argued that he fit that description, since he was circumcised at age thirteen when he could have protested, whereas Isaac was circumcised at eight days when he could not complain. Isaac exclaimed, "O that God would appear to me and order me to cut off one of my limbs! Then I would not refuse." God said, "Even if I command you sacrifice yourself, you will not refuse." In another version, Isaac retorted to Ishmael, "All you gave to God was three drops of blood. Now I am thirty-seven years old, yet if God desired that I be slaughtered, I would not refuse." Immediately, God declared: "This is the moment!" and, as the Torah related, "God tested Abraham" (Gen. R. 55:4). *See also* Ephron; Isaac; Ishmael; Lot, Melchizedek; Nimrod; Terah.

Absalom, third son of King David.

Born in Hebron, the mother of Absalom was Maacah, the daughter of Talmai, king of Geshur (2 Sam. 3:2). Strikingly handsome and with a charismatic personality, Absalom was described as having "stolen the hearts of the men of Israel" (2 Sam. 15:6). After his full sister, Tamar, had been raped and then cast away by David's eldest son, his half-brother Amnon, Absalom swore to avenge the deed (2 Sam. 13). The opportunity presented itself two years later, when Amnon was "merry with wine" during a sheep-shearing feast. Absalom ordered his servants to kill Amnon, but fearing David's wrath at the death of his firstborn son, Absalom fled. After three years, Joab, the commander of the royal army, convinced David to allow Absalom to return to his house and family (2 Sam. 14). Although initially forbidden to appear before the king, eventually Absalom reconciled with his father. However, the ambitious

Absalom then plotted against his father and conspired with Ahithophel, one of David's most honored advisers, to overthrow the king (2 Sam. 15). As the rebellion grew, David was forced to flee Jerusalem and seek refuge beyond the Jordan. Absalom entered the capital, occupied the royal palaces, and even took over the king's harem on the advice of Ahithophel (2 Sam. 16–17). Ahithophel urged Absalom to immediately pursue David. However, Hushai, a loyal friend of David who remained at court, advised caution, recommending that Absalom strengthen his forces and lead them himself. In the climactic battle, Absalom was defeated (2 Sam. 18). Although David had ordered that Absalom not be killed, when his son fled on horseback through the woods, his long hair became tangled in the branches of a tree. The Talmud considered this poetic justice, for just as by his long hair (as a lifelong Nazirite, whose vow prohibited him from cutting his hair; Naz. 4b) Absalom had "entangled the people to rebel against his father, [so] by it did he himself become entangled, to fall victim to his pursuers" (Sot. 1:8). Despite the king's explicit instructions, Joab thrust three darts through the treacherous Absalom's heart. David's mourning was far greater for Absalom than for Amnon (2 Sam. 19), until Joab was compelled to point out to the king that Absalom's own evil deeds had led to his death. "And Absalom in his lifetime had taken the pillar which is in the king's valley and set it up for himself, for he said, 'I have no son to keep my name alive' and named the pillar after himself. And it is called Absalom's monument to this day" (2 Sam. 18:18).

The Talmud relates how a subtle difference in the wording of a farewell greeting led to a dramatic change in fate. "When a man takes leave of his fellow, he should not say to him, 'Go in peace,' but 'Go to peace.' Moses, to whom Jethro said, 'Go to peace' (Exod. 4:18), went up and prospered, whereas Absalom, to whom David said, 'Go in peace' (2 Sam. 15:9), went away and was hung" (Ber. 64a; MK 29a). The Rabbis considered Absalom's conduct toward his father so abhorrent that he was listed as among those who have no share in the World to Come (Sanh. 103b).

Using the relationship between David and Absalom as an example, the Rabbis taught that when a father refrains from chastising his son for disobedience, the son will fall into evil ways and eventually come to hate his father. Not rebuking his son when appropriate ultimately led to Absalom attempting to kill his father, forcing David to flee Jerusalem barefoot and weeping. In consequence of David's parental failing, many thousands of Israelites were killed and other cruel afflictions befell the king (Exod. R. 1:1). *See also* Tamar.

Achan, son of Carmi of the tribe of Judah.

Achan "took of the devoted things [spoils reserved for God]," resulting in "the anger of the Lord being kindled against the people of Israel" (Josh. 7:1). In defiance of the ban (*cherem*) imposed on Jericho, Achan admitted that when he saw "a fine garment of Shinar [Babylonia], 200 shekels of silver, and a wedge of gold of 50 shekels weight, I coveted and took them" and buried them in the ground under his tent. Achan's crime brought immediate Divine retribution, with the Israelites suffering a crushing defeat in the battle of Ai—an example of collective responsibility, with the entire people punished for the sin of one man. When lots were cast among the tribes to discover the family guilty of violating the ban, they fell upon Achan, who subsequently confessed his sin publicly before the Lord. Then Achan and his family were stoned to death in the Valley of Achor (trouble). They and their possessions were burned, and "a great heap of stones" was placed over the ashes.

The Talmud also accuses Achan of transgressing the majority of the Torah commandments, including desecrating the Sabbath, obliterating evidence of his circumcision (the sign of the Abrahamic covenant), and committing adultery with a betrothed maiden (Sanh. 44a). Nevertheless, the Mishnah deems him a model of the penitent sinner, for his public confession and subsequent punishment saved him from eternal doom in Gehenna (Sanh. 6:2).

Achish, Philistine king of Gath during the time of Kings David and Solomon.

On two occasions, David sought asylum with Achish while fleeing from Saul. The first time, David arrived incognito but was soon recognized. "Is not this David the king of the land? Did they not sing one to another of him in dances, saying, 'Saul has killed his thousands, and David his ten thousands?'" Fearing for his life, David feigned madness—"scratched on the doors of the gate, and let his spittle run down upon his beard"—until he was able to escape (1 Sam. 21:11–16). The second time, when David arrived with 600 men, Achish welcomed him as a supposed enemy of Saul. He gave him the city of Ziklag and its surroundings, where David remained for sixteen months (1 Sam. 27:1–7). Achish even made David his bodyguard when organizing his forces to attack Saul (1 Sam. 28:1–2). Against his will, Achish was forced by the Philistine princes to move David and his men to the rear, for they feared that David would support his own people during the battle (1 Sam. 29).

Adah, one of two wives of Lamech, and the mother of Jabal and Jubal (Gen. 4:19–21).

According to a *midrash*, in the immoral generation before the Flood, it was customary for a man to marry two wives—one to bear children to perpetuate the race and the other for indulgence in sexual pleasure. In the household of Lamech, Adah assumed the former role, abused by her husband or ignored and left mourning like a widow. His other wife, Zillah, was the pampered mistress of the family who controlled her husband's actions (Gen. R. 23:2). It was to these two wives that Lamech recited his song, the first one recorded in the Bible (Gen. 4:23–24).

Adah was also the name of a Hittite native of Canaan who became the wife of Esau (Gen. 36:2).

Adam, first man, husband of Eve, father of Cain, Abel, and Seth, and progenitor of the human race.

In the Bible, the term *adam* is usually used in a generic sense for human being. However, when referring to the first man, the name was explained as deriving from God having "formed man from the dust of the ground [*adamah*] and breathed into his nostrils the breath of life, and man became a living being" (Gen. 2:7). Adam was created at the end of the sixth day. "And God said, 'Let us make man in our image, after our likeness'" (Gen. 1:26), with the first person plural suggesting that God was surrounded by a multitude of angels in a heavenly court.

God gave the first human being dominion over the earth and commanded him to "be fruitful and multiply" (Gen. 1:28)—the first mitzvah in the Torah. God "placed man in the Garden of Eden, to till it and tend it" (Gen. 2:15), allowing him to eat the fruit from any tree but the Tree of Knowledge of Good and Evil (Gen. 2:17). As an indication of the rabbinic sensitivity to environmental concerns, a *midrash* relates that when God created Adam, He led him around the Garden of Eden and pointed out the beauty and excellence of all His works: "For your sake I created it. See to it that you do not spoil and destroy My world, for if you do, there will be no one to repair it after you" (Eccles. R. 7:13).

To provide a fitting companion, God fashioned woman (Eve) from Adam's rib/side. When Eve was persuaded by the snake to eat of the forbidden fruit and then shared it with Adam, "the eyes of both of them were opened and they perceived that they were naked; and they sewed together fig leaves and made themselves loincloths" (Gen. 3:7). The punishment decreed for disobeying the Divine commandment was explicitly stated: "For on the day you eat from it, you shall surely die" (Gen. 2:17). Since Adam lived to the age of 930, it is clear that he was not to die as soon as he ate the fruit. Instead, he would become *subject to* death, whereas if he had never sinned, his holiness would have let him live forever. Adam received the additional punishment of becoming forced to work to sustain himself: "By the sweat of your brow shall you eat bread" (Gen. 3:19). The ultimate punishment for Adam and Eve was their expulsion from the Garden of Eden (Gen. 3:23–24).

Why was only a single man created first? To teach that, "Whoever destroys a single soul is as if he destroys a whole world; while whoever saves a single soul is as if he saves a whole world." Moreover, no race or class may claim a nobler ancestry by saying "my father is greater than yours," and everyone can assert that "the world was created for my sake" (Sanh. 37a). The creation of a single man also proclaimed the greatness of God, for each person is unique: "When a mortal man stamps many coins from a single mold, they are all alike; but the King of kings fashioned all men from the mold of Adam [the first man], and not one of them is like his fellow. Therefore, every person is obliged to say, 'For my sake was the world created'" (Sanh. 4:5).

The Rabbis considered each individual person as a microcosm of the entire world: "All that God created in the world, He created in man." Among numerous examples of this ideal: the hair of a human being was said to correspond to forests, the teeth to doors, the lips to walls, the fingers to nails, and the neck to a tower (ARN 31).

Why was Adam the last being created? To teach him humility, for even the lowly fly preceded him in the order of creation. Another reason was that Adam could begin his life by performing the mitzvah of observing the Sabbath. R. Meir related the tradition that "the dust of the first man was gathered from all parts of the earth." Rav taught "[The earth for] Adam's trunk [which ranks lower than the spirit] came from Babylonia [a low-lying country], his head [the most distinguished part of the body] came from the Land of Israel [the most exalted of lands], and his limbs from other lands." R. Aha added that his private parts came from Akra di Agma, a town near Pumbedita that was notorious for the loose morals of its inhabitants (Sanh. 38a–b).

There was a rabbinic opinion (Er. 18b; Gen. R. 8:1) that God originally created Adam as a "double-faced" hermaphrodite and then split that one being into two separate bodies. This concept was based on the verse, "Male and female He created them, and He blessed them and called *their* name Adam on the day they were being created" (Gen. 5:2).

In the biblical description of the creation of Adam, there is the unusual appearance of two consecutive *yuds* in the word "*vayitzer*" (He formed), relating to God fashioning Adam "from the dust of the earth" (Gen. 2:7), rather than the single *yud* in standard Hebrew grammar. From this, the Rabbis deduced that the extra *yud* was inserted to indicate that each human being possesses two inclinations—toward good and evil (Ber. 61a). The consensus was that the inclination toward evil is present at birth, whereas the inclination toward good only manifests at age thirteen, a time at which the moral conscience develops and each person becomes responsible for his or her actions.

According to a *midrash*, Adam had a busy first "day," which was divided into twelve hours: "In the first hour, his dust was gathered; in the second, it was made into a shapeless mass; in the third, his limbs were shaped; in the fourth, a soul was infused into him; in the fifth, he arose and stood on his feet; in the sixth, he named all the animals; in the seventh, Eve became his mate; in the eighth, two went up onto the bed and four came down [from the bed; this refers to the birth of Cain and his twin sister; Abel and his twin sister were born after Adam and Eve sinned]; in the ninth, he was commanded not to eat of the Tree [of Knowledge of Good and Evil]; in the tenth, he sinned [by eating from it]; in the eleventh, he was judged, and in the twelfth he was expelled [from the Garden of Eden] and went on his way." Initially Adam reached from one end of the world to the other, but when he sinned God "diminished him" (Sanh. 38b).

According to the Talmud, as darkness fell at the end of the first Sabbath, Adam became frightened, for he knew that he and Eve would now have to leave Eden and face the dangers outside the protected Garden. God then taught them how to strike two flints together to make fire, and they uttered a blessing over it. From this arose the custom of kindling fire in the form of a candle at the Havdalah ceremony at the end of the Sabbath (Pes. 54a). *See also* Eve.

Adonijah, fourth son of King David, by Haggith.

After the death of Absalom, Adonijah as the eldest surviving son claimed to be the rightful heir to the throne, even though the infirm David was still alive (1 Kings 1:5–53). Adonijah's attempted coup was supported by Abiathar the priest and by Joab, the commander of David's army. However, it was opposed by Zadok the priest, Benaiah, Nathan the prophet, and David's "mighty men," all of whom were not invited to Adonijah's solemn sacrifice and "coronation feast" at Ein Rogel. When Nathan and Bathsheba, the mother of Solomon, informed David of the plot and reminded the king of his formal pledge that Solomon would succeed him, David immediately ordered that Solomon be anointed king. Upon learning what had transpired, Adonijah and his followers fled in terror, with Adonijah seeking sanctuary by grabbing hold of the horns of the Altar. Solomon agreed to spare Adonijah's life: "If he will show himself a worthy man, there shall not a hair of him fall to the earth; but if wickedness shall be found in him, he shall die." After David's death, Adonijah asked Bathsheba to arrange for him to wed Abishag, the concubine who had been the king's companion in his last days. Regarding this request as a treasonous ploy to seize the throne and thus a violation of their agreement, Solomon ordered Benaiah to kill Adonijah, thus eliminating this potential rival for the crown.

The Talmud numbers Adonijah among those "who set their eyes upon that which was not proper for them; what they sought was not granted to them, and what they possessed was taken from them" (Sot. 9a). It interprets the biblical verse, "And he [Adonijah] was born after Absalom" (1 Kings 1:6) as indicating that, although the two had different mothers, they are mentioned together since both rebelled against the king (BB 109b). The verse "[Adonijah] exalted himself, saying, 'I will be king'" (1 Kings 1:5) was said to mean that Adonijah attempted to try on the royal crown but it would not fit him. According to an *aggadah* quoted by Rashi, a golden rod passed through the hollow of the crown, from one end to the other, which fitted into a cleft or indentation in the skull, an anatomic peculiarity of some in the house of David. Only one whom the crown fitted was considered worthy of being king (Sanh. 21b).

Adoni-Zedek, king of Jerusalem at the time of the Israelite conquest of Canaan.

Alarmed by how the Israelites had defeated Jericho and Ai and cowed the inhabitants of the "great and mighty" city of Gibeon to make peace with them, Adoni-Zedek organized and led a coalition of neighboring Amorite kings (Hoham of Hebron, Piram of Jarmuth, Japhia of Lachish, and Debir of Eglon) to oppose any further invasion of their land. When the kings besieged Gibeon, Joshua came to the defense of his new allies and defeated their forces. The five kings fled from both their pursuers and intense hailstorms, taking refuge in a cave at Makkedah. When the kings were found, Joshua ordered his troops to "roll great stones upon the mouth of the cave, and set men by it to guard them." In this way they trapped the kings while the Israelites destroyed their armies. Then the kings were brought out of the cave, and Joshua "slew them, and hanged them on five trees . . . until the evening," before throwing their bodies back into the cave in which they had hidden (Josh. 10:26).

Agag, king of the Amalekites.

As revenge against the people who had perpetrated a cowardly attack on the rear of the Israelite column after the Exodus from Egypt (Deut. 25:17–19), Samuel transmitted a Divine command to King Saul: "Go and strike Amalek, and completely destroy all that belongs to him; spare no one, but kill both men and women, infants and sucklings, oxen, and sheep, camels and donkeys" (1 Sam. 15:3). However, after defeating the Amalekites, "Saul and the people spared Agag, the best of the sheep, the oxen, the fatlings, the lambs, and all else that was of value. They would not completely destroy them; but every thing that was cheap and worthless, that they destroyed completely" (1 Sam. 15:9). Samuel was furious, deeming this clemency mere defiance of the Divine will and not accepting Saul's excuse that the property they spared was for sacrifices to God. "Does the Lord delight in burnt offerings and sacrifices as much as obedience to the Lord's command? Surely, obedience is better than sacrifice, and compliance is better than the fat of rams. For rebellion is as the sin of witchcraft, and defiance is like the sin of idolatry. Because you have rejected the Lord's command, He has rejected you as king" (1 Sam. 15:22–23). When Agag was brought before him, Samuel said: "As your sword has made women childless, so shall your mother be childless among women. [Then] Samuel cut Agag in pieces before the Lord in Gilgal" (1 Sam. 15:33).

According to the *aggadah*, the delayed execution of Agag was to prove a serious danger to the Jewish people. Had Saul immediately killed Agag on the day of his capture, the king of Amalek would not have been able to sire an heir and thus become the progenitor of Haman, the arch-enemy of Israel (Meg. 13a).

Ahab, seventh king of Israel (871–852 B.C.E.).

The son of Omri, who established the Israelite kingdom at Samaria, Ahab entered into a political marriage with Jezebel, the daughter of the king of Sidon, to secure Israel's peace with a powerful neighbor and enhance the economic conditions in his land (1 Kings 16:28–31). However, Jezebel was a corrupting influence on Ahab, pressuring him to tolerate and even support the worship of Baal in his kingdom. She also convinced her weak husband to have Naboth killed illegally for refusing to sell Ahab a vineyard that the king coveted (1 Kings 21). As punishment for both these nefarious acts, Elijah the prophet foretold Ahab's gruesome death: "In the very place where the dogs licked up the blood of Naboth, there the dogs will also lick up your own blood" (1 Kings 21:19). However, the execution of this sentence was postponed when Ahab responded by tearing his clothes, putting on sackcloth, and repenting: "Because he has humbled himself before Me, I will bring the disaster in his son's time" (1 Kings 21:27–29). Ahab was killed in battle after being seriously wounded, though he had continued fighting all day propped up on his chariot. "Then they washed the chariot in the pool of Samaria; and the dogs licked up his blood; and the harlots bathed in it; in accordance with the word of the Lord" (1 Kings 22:38).

Ahab continued his father Omri's policy of cultivating peaceful relations with the Kingdom of Judah, a pact sealed by the marriage of his daughter Athaliah to Jehoram, the son of King Jehoshaphat of Judah (2 Kings 8:18; 2 Chron. 18:1). According to the Talmud, Ahab was one of three men (with Ahasuerus and Nebuchadnezzar) "who ruled over the whole world" (Meg. 11a).

The Talmud depicts Ahab as an enthusiastic champion of idolatry, one of three kings who have no portion in the World to Come (Sanh. 10:2). On the gates of Samaria he had inscribed the words "Ahab has denied the God of Israel," and it was said that "there was not a furrow in Israel on which Ahab did not place an idol and bow down to it" (Sanh. 102b). The Rabbis taught, "One who sees Ahab in a dream should worry about punishment" (Ber. 57b). Nevertheless, his wife Jezebel was blamed as the major instigator of Ahab's crimes (BM 59a). Based on their relationship, Rav said: "He who follows his wife's counsel will descend [fall] into Gehenna." In view of a seemingly contrary saying: "If your wife is short, bend down and hear her whisper!," the Rabbis indicated that there was no contradiction: "The one [former] refers to general matters; the other to household affairs. Another version: the one [former] refers to religious matters, the other to secular questions" (BM 59a).

Despite his long list of transgressions, the Talmud accords Ahab some positive qualities. As a reward for using some of his vast wealth to support scholars of the Torah (which was written with twenty-two letters), Ahab was permitted to rule for twenty-two years (Sanh. 102b). *See also* Jezebel; Naboth.

Ahasuerus, king of Persia in the Purim story.

Known to the Greeks as Xerxes, Ahasuerus is the Hebrew form of the Persian king who ruled from 486–465 B.C.E. According to the Book of Esther, Ahasuerus "reigned over a hundred and twenty-seven provinces from India to Ethiopia" and had his capital in Shushan. In the third year of his rule, Ahasuerus gave a series of banquets for all the nobles and governors of the provinces to "display the vast riches of his kingdom and the splendid glory of his majesty." On the seventh day, "when the king was merry with wine," he ordered his beautiful Queen Vashti to appear before the assembled guests "wearing [only] a royal diadem," but she refused to come. Incensed, Ahasuerus asked his trusted counselors for advice as to "what shall be done, according to the law?" They replied that the queen had committed an offense not only against the king, but also against all the peoples in all of the provinces of the realm. "The queen's behavior will make all wives despise their husbands . . . and there will be no end of scorn and provocation!" They convinced the king to issue a royal edict prohibiting Vashti from ever appearing before the king, and to "bestow her royal state upon another who is more worthy than she," so that "all wives will treat their husbands with respect, high and low alike" (Esth. 1).

When Esther was selected as the new queen, she hid the fact that she was Jewish and related to Mordechai. Haman, the grand vizier of the kingdom, bribed Ahasuerus to issue an edict ordering the massacre of Jews, the people of Mordechai who blatantly refused to bow down to his exalted personage. In a dramatic banquet scene, Esther revealed her identity as a Jewess and accused Haman of attempting to kill her and her people. The furious Ahasuerus ordered the execution of Haman on the gallows he had prepared for Mordechai. Esther and Mordechai urged Ahasuerus to send an edict throughout his kingdom countermanding Haman's previous dispatch to destroy the Jews. Although Ahasuerus replied that "an edict that has been written in the king's name and sealed with the king's signet may not be revoked," the king did issue an order that permitted the Jews to fight against their enemies and destroy them (Esth. 8:8–14). The Jews were victorious and Ahasuerus named Mordechai as second-in-command in the royal court.

According to the Talmud, "Three men ruled over the whole world: Ahab, Ahasuerus, and Nebuchadnezzar" (Meg. 11a). "One opinion was that he was a clever king. Another was that he was a foolish king" (Meg. 12a) and "his stupidity made him a laughingstock of the world" (Esth. R. 4:12). The Talmud relates that "Ahasuerus had four good points: he spent three years without a crown or a throne; he waited four years to find himself a suitable wife; he made no move before taking counsel; and he recorded every favor that anyone did for him" (Esth. R. 1:15).

Ahasuerus had an abiding love for Esther, who was "as precious to the king at all times as at the first time" (Yoma 29b). When Esther appeared before him unbidden, a crime punishable by death, the king "was furiously angry that she had broken his law by coming before him without being called. But God saw and had mercy on his people, and gave her grace in [the king's eyes]. He ran to Esther, embraced her, put his arm around her neck, and said: 'Why are you so afraid? This law that we have made does not apply to you, for you are my beloved and my companion'" (Esth. R. 9:1).

The *aggadah* relates that Ahasuerus clad himself in robes of state that once belonged to the high priests in Jerusalem and desecrated Temple vessels while drinking at the feasts he made for nobles throughout his kingdom, even though he knew the disaster that had happened to Belshazzar for similar conduct (Meg. 11b). It also states that Ahasuerus "hated Israel more than the wicked Haman" (Esth. R. 7:20), but the king feared suffering a fate similar to other enemies of the Jews. *See also* Esther; Haman; Mordechai; Vashti.

Ahaz, eleventh king of Judah (735–719 B.C.E.).

The son of Jotham and father of Hezekiah, Ahaz was one of the kings who "did not do that which was right in the sight of the Lord his God" (2 Kings 16:2), Ahaz practiced idolatry and participated in pagan sacrifices, even offering his own son to Molech (2 Kings 16:3–4). Based on a verse from Isaiah (8:16), who was forced to teach in secret—"Bind up the testimony, seal the law among my disciples"—the Rabbis accused Ahaz of ending the sacrificial service and threatening the very existence of the Jewish religion by "sealing the Torah" (i.e., closing the schools and houses of worship so that no instruction would be possible) (Sanh. 103b). After a series of military defeats and loss of territory, Ahaz turned for protection to the king of Assyria, Tiglath-Pileser III, bribing him with extensive gifts from the Temple treasury (2 Kings 16:7–8).

According to the *aggadah*, the ministering angels complained, "Woe [to the world] that Ahaz rules!" However, God replied: "He is the son of Jotham, and since his father was righteous, I cannot do anything to him" (Gen. R. 63:1). Similarly, because Ahaz was placed between two righteous people, Jotham and Hezekiah, Ahaz was not counted among those who have no share in the World to Come (Sanh. 104b). Nevertheless, the Talmud praises Hezekiah for having "dragged his father's bones [corpse] on a rope bier [i.e., giving him a pauper's funeral rather than showing him the honor due to a king, as atonement for Ahaz's sins]" (Pes. 56a). Also to atone for his sins, "the day on which Ahaz died consisted of only two hours," so that there was no time for funeral honors and eulogies. The ten lost hours were later returned to Hezekiah when he recovered from his illness (Sanh. 96a).

Ahaziah, sixth king of Judah (842–841 B.C.E.).

"He followed the practice of the house of Ahab, for his mother [Athaliah] counseled him to do evil" (2 Chron. 22:3). A supporter of the king of Israel, Ahaziah was caught and slain during the rebellion instigated in the Northern Kingdom of Israel by the prophet Elisha (2 Kings 9). A shameless sinner, Ahaziah was said to have erased the Name of God from every passage where it occurred in the Holy Scripture, inserting the names of idols in its place.

Ahiezer, son of Ammishaddai and chieftain of the tribe of Dan.

Ahiezer made the tenth of the twelve identical offerings for the dedication of the Tabernacle in the wilderness (Num. 7:66–71).

Ahimaaz, son of Zadok the priest.

When David fled with the Ark of the Covenant during Absalom's rebellion, he begged both the priests Zadok and Abiathar to remain in Jerusalem, where they could learn what was happening and have that information relayed to the king by their sons—Ahimaaz and Jonathan, respectively (2 Sam. 15:24–37).

After Absalom's defeat and death, Ahimaaz begged Joab to allow him to bring the news to David, but Joab sent another messenger instead. However, Ahimaaz persisted, and Joab reluctantly permitted Ahimaaz to also announce the victory. Running at top speed, Ahimaaz arrived first and told David of the great triumph, but was noncommittal as to Absalom's fate. Therefore, it fell to the other messenger to relay the bad news of Absalom's death, which sent David into intense mourning (2 Sam. 18:19–32).

Ahimelech, son of Ahitub, great-grandson of Eli, and high priest of Nob (1 Sam. 21).

When David arrived in Nob after fleeing from Saul, Ahimelech sensed that something was amiss and asked, "Why are you alone, and no man is with you?" David responded with a vague and ambiguous reply: "The king has commanded me with a matter." When the famished David asked for bread, Ahimelech replied that only "consecrated bread" was available. According to the *aggadah*, when Ahimelech hesitated to give up the showbread, David informed the priest that when a man is starving, all food was permitted to him (Men. 95b). Then David asked if there was any weapon available, and he was given the sword that had belonged to Goliath. When Saul learned what had occurred, he ordered that Ahimelech and all the priests of Nob be put to death (1 Sam. 22). Abiathar, the only son of Ahimelech, was the sole priest to survive the massacre.

One explanation of the dispute between Ahimelech and Saul (1 Sam. 22:12–19) was based on Ahimelech's action in consulting the *Urim* and *Thumim* on David's behalf. Saul argued that it was a capital offense, since it was a privilege reserved for the king. Ahimelech maintained that the *Urim* and *Thumim* could be consulted when affairs of state were involved, and this certainly applied to David in his position as a general of the army. Abner and Amasa supported Ahimelech's argument, but Doeg did not. Consequently, Saul assigned Doeg the task of executing Ahimelech (Yalkut Shimoni, Samuel 131).

Ahinoam, daughter of Ahimaaz, wife of Saul, the first king of Israel (1 Sam. 14:50), and mother of Jonathan.

Ahinoam, Jezreelite woman captured by King David while he was at war with Saul (1 Sam. 25:43).

Though already married to Abigail, David took Ahinoam as his wife (2 Sam. 2:2). Subsequently taken captive by the Amalekites, she was soon rescued by David (1 Sam. 30:5, 18). After Saul's death, Ahinoam returned with David and Abigail to Hebron, where she gave birth to Amnon, David's first son (2 Sam. 3:2).

Ahira, son of Enan and chieftain of the tribe of Naphtali.

Ahira made the final of the twelve identical offerings for the dedication of the Tabernacle in the wilderness (Num. 7:78–83).

Ahithophel, native of Giloh in the Judean highlands and a major adviser of King David.

The *aggadah* deems Ahithophel to be "a man, like Balaam, whose great wisdom was not received in humility as a gift from heaven, and so became a stumbling-block to him" (Num. R. 22). He was described as one of those "who set their eyes upon that which was not proper for them; what they sought was not granted to them and what they possessed was taken from them" (Sot. 9b) and as one of "four commoners who have no share in the World to Come" (Sanh. 10:2).

Although a trusted confidant of David, Ahithophel played a key role in Absalom's conspiracy to seize the throne from his father (2 Sam. 15–17). He urged Absalom to take possession of the royal harem to solidify his position as the new king. Ahithophel recommended that Absalom immediately pursue David and his forces, but his wise military advice was rejected in favor of the cautious approach advocated by Hushai, who had remained loyal to David. "And when Ahithophel saw that his advice had not been followed [and realizing that the reprieve given to David would be fatal to Absalom and his supporters], he saddled his donkey and went home to his native town. He set his affairs in order and then hanged himself" (2 Sam. 17:23).

According to the *aggadah*, Ahithophel was the grandfather of Bathsheba (Sanh. 69b). He mistakenly interpreted astrologic signs to mean that he was destined to become the king of Israel. If Absalom were to seize the throne and kill his father, Ahithophel thought that he could convince the people that the usurper merited death for his crime, thus becoming king himself. However, the astrological signs actually had indicated that his granddaughter, Bathsheba, would become queen (Sanh. 101b).

In another Talmudic legend, David excavated so deeply for the foundations of the Temple that floods broke forth and nearly inundated the earth. David asked whether it was permissible to write the Divine Name on a shard and throw it into the deep to make the waters keep to their own region, but Ahithophel remained silent in the hope that the flood would carry David away. When none of the wise men replied, the king uttered a curse against anyone who had the answer and refused to speak. Ahithophel reasoned that, if for the sake of restoring harmony between husband and wife, the Torah permitted the Name of God solemnly inscribed in the scroll to be blotted out in the ordeal prescribed for the allegedly unfaithful wife (*sotah*; Num. 5:12–26), it certainly could be done to preserve the safety of the entire world! Ahithophel so counseled the king, and when the shard containing the Divine Name was thrown into the waters, they immediately subsided (Mak. 11a).

According to the Rabbis, "Ahithophel advised his sons to do three things: do not take part in dissension; do not rebel against the kingdom of the House of David; and if the weather on the Festival of Sukkot is clear, sow wheat [because fine weather at that season is an indication of a good wheat harvest for that year]" (BB 147a).

Amalek, son of Eliphaz, and the grandson of Esau (Gen. 36:12).

The name Amalek later became associated with a nomadic tribe living in the Sinai Desert and southern Negev, which perpetrated a cowardly and unprovoked attack upon weary stragglers at the rear of the Israelite column as they wandered in the wilderness soon after the Exodus from Egypt (Exod. 17:8–16). Amalek became the epitome of evil, leading to the Divine command to "blot out the remembrance of Amalek from under heaven; do not forget!" (Deut. 25:19). This passage is read as the *maftir* portion in synagogue on the Sabbath immediately preceding Purim, most appropriate at this time since, according to the Book of Esther, the archvillain Haman was a direct descendant of Agag, the king of the Amalekites.

According to one Talmudic account, Timna (the mother of Amalek) was a royal princess who wanted to become a proselyte. When Abraham, Isaac, and Jacob did not accept her, "she became a concubine to Eliphaz the son of Esau, saying, 'I had rather be a servant to this people than a mistress of another nation.' From her was descended Amalek, who afflicted Israel. Why so?—Because they should not have repulsed her" (Sanh. 99b). Rashi had a different interpretation of the story, maintaining that Timna was so anxious to marry a descendant of the renowned Abraham that she said to Eliphaz, "If I am unworthy to become your wife, let me at least be your concubine!"

Amalek once asked his father, Eliphaz the Yemenite, "Who will inherit this world and the World to Come?" Eliphaz replied, "The Children of Israel. Go out and dig wells and fix roads for them. If you do so, your share will be with the lowly among them, and you will enter the World to Come." However, Amalek did not follow his father's advice and instead set out to conquer the world (Yalkut Shimoni, Beshalach 268). *See also* Agag.

Amasa, nephew of King David.

Amasa was the military commander of the army of Absalom when he rebelled against his father, David (2 Sam. 17:25). After Absalom's revolt was crushed, David proposed that Amasa become the leader of his forces instead of Joab, who had aroused the king's anger by killing Absalom (2 Sam. 19:4). However, Joab treacherously killed Amasa (2 Sam. 20:9–10), an act that infuriated the king. In his last days, David ordered Solomon to take revenge on Joab (1 Kings 2:5, 32).

Amasa, together with Abner, refused Saul's command to slay the priests of Nob: "What do you hold over us—the weapons and uniforms that you have given us? Here, take them back [lit., 'they are at your feet']" (JT Sanh. 10:2). He defended the legitimacy of David to be king despite his descent from Ruth the Moabitess, citing a tradition that the biblical exclusion of Moabites from the congregation of Israel did not apply to women since the male gender was used (Yev. 76b). Ironically, Amasa's piety indirectly led to his death. When challenged by Solomon at court to explain why he had killed Amasa, Joab replied that Amasa had disobeyed the order (lit., "rebelled against the throne") to gather an army within three days (1 Sam. 20:4–5), a crime punishable by death. Amasa's reason for the delay was that he did not want to interrupt his men from studying a recently begun tractate. He believed that the obligation to study God's law was more important than the will of a king, so that fulfilling the royal command could wait until the men had finished their Divinely mandated activity (Sanh. 49a).

Amaziah, eighth king of Judah (800–771 B.C.E.).

Beginning his twenty-nine-year reign at a turbulent period after the murder of his father, Joash, Amaziah succeeded in returning quiet to the land. After consolidating his hold on the throne, Amaziah executed the men who had killed his father. However, Amaziah spared their children, in accordance with the Torah command that a person should only be put to death for his own sin (Deut. 24:16). The Bible (2 Chron. 25:14) relates that, after vanquishing Edom, Amaziah "brought the gods of the children of Seir and set them up to be his gods, bowing down himself before them and burning incense unto them" (2 Chron. 25:14). Commenting on this verse, R. Papa said: "Weep for him who knows not his fortune, laugh for him who knows not his fortune. Woe to him who knows not the difference between good and bad" (Sanh. 103a). Amaziah attacked the Northern Kingdom of Israel but was soundly defeated, and the king's worship of alien gods led his enemies to murder him.

According to the *aggadah*, Amaziah was a brother of Amoz, the father of Isaiah (Meg. 10b).

Ammon, son of Abraham's nephew Lot and his unnamed younger daughter, who became the ancestor of the tribe bearing his name.

After fleeing the destruction of Sodom, Lot's daughters reasonably feared that this devastation had extended to the entire world and that they were the only ones remaining. "And the older one said to the younger, 'Our father is old, and there is not a man on earth to consort with us in the way of all the world [to propagate the human race]. Come, let us make our father drink wine, and let us lie with him, that we may maintain life through our father'" (Gen. 19:31–32). This relationship resulted in the birth of a son, Ammon, whose name presumably derived from the Hebrew *ben-ammi* (son of my people; Gen. 19:38). Because her intentions were purely motivated, the Torah does not explicitly condemn Lot's daughter or label the relationship as incestuous. Indeed, she merited being the ancestress of Naamah, the queen of Solomon and the mother of Rehoboam, the first king of Judah following the death of his father.

Nevertheless, biblical law explicitly states that "an Ammonite and a Moabite shall not be admitted into the congregation of the Lord forever" (Deut. 23:4). However, the Mishnah later restricted this prohibition to males, noting that the biblical proscription used the masculine gender (Yev. 8:3). Eventually, the restriction was completely abolished when Judah, an

Ammonite proselyte, asked whether he was permitted to enter the assembly by marrying a Jewess. The Rabbis acceded to this request, noting that the current inhabitants of these countries were not descended from the Ammonites and Moabites of biblical times, since Sennacherib (king of Assyria) had long ago "mixed up all the nations" (Ber. 28a).

Despite Abraham having saved their ancestor Lot, the Ammonites and Moabites repeatedly committed hostile acts against Israel, such as hiring Balaam to destroy Israel and waging open war against them at the time of Jephthah and Jehoshaphat. When Jeremiah prophesied the destruction of Jerusalem, the Ammonites and Moabites rushed to report his words to Nebuchadnezzar and persuade him to attack the capital (Sanh. 96b). While the heathens entered the Temple and sought its gold and silver treasures, the Ammonites and Moabites seized the Scroll of the Law to erase the decree against them (Yev. 16b). *See also* Lot.

Amnon, firstborn son of King David and Ahinoam, the Jezreelite woman.

Amnon was infatuated by his half-sister Tamar, the full sister of Absalom, and lusted for her. Feigning illness, Amnon lured Tamar into his chamber on the pretext of needing her to prepare him food (2 Sam. 13). Thereupon Amnon overpowered and raped Tamar, but once his desire was satisfied, he "had a great loathing for her" and threw her out. Although angered by Amnon's actions, David failed to punish his son. However, Absalom swore to avenge his sister's honor. Two years later, Absalom invited Amnon, along with all of David's other sons, to a sheep-shearing celebration. When "the heart of Amnon was merry with wine," Absalom ordered his servants to kill him. Following this event, Absalom fled to Talmai, the son of the king of Geshur.

The Rabbis used the tragic story of Amnon and Tamar as justification for their rule forbidding a man from being alone with any woman other than his wife (Sanh. 21a–b).

Amon, fourteenth king of Judah (642–640 B.C.E.).

Amon continued the idolatrous practices of his father, Manasseh, "burning the Torah and allowing spider webs to cover the Altar [through complete disuse]" (Sanh. 103b). Indeed, the Book of Chronicles considered Amon even worse than Manasseh. Whereas the former "pleaded with the Lord his God, and humbled himself greatly before the God of his fathers [i.e., repented]" (2 Chron. 33:12–13), Amon "did not humble himself before the Lord" (2 Chron. 33:23) before being murdered by his own servants (2 Kings 21:23).

The Talmud relates that Amon even consorted with his mother, which prompted her to ask: "Do you derive any pleasure from the place out of which you came?" Amon replied, "I do it only to anger my Creator!" (Sanh. 103a).

Despite his iniquity, Amon was permitted to enjoy the World to Come, to spare his righteous son Josiah from disgrace (Sanh. 104a).

Amos, third of the minor prophets.

A shepherd and dresser of sycamore trees from Tekoa, in the hills of Judah, around 750 B.C.E., Amos went to sell his animals in Bethel, the principal religious center of the Northern Kingdom of Israel. There he cried out against the injustice and poverty of the masses under King Jeroboam II, attacking the wealthy minority who feasted while most of the people went hungry. The prosperity of the elite had led to a collapse of moral standards, with the rich oppressing the poor and rejecting the biblical ideal of justice and loving kindness. Amos rejected those who believed that sacrifice and ritual were the paths leading to the Creator: "Even though you offer Me your burnt offerings and cereal offerings, I will not accept them. And to the peace offerings of your fatted beasts I will pay no heed. Spare Me the sound of your hymns, and let Me not hear the music of your harps. But let justice well up like waters, and righteousness like a mighty stream" (Amos 5:22–24).

Amos called for justice for all humanity and was the first to see God as the universal Lord of all the nations. Although he sorrowfully predicted that the punishment of Israel would be its destruction by Assyria, Amos dreamed of a future golden age of peace, when the exiles of Israel would return home, rebuild their wasted cities, replant vineyards, and "nevermore be uprooted from the soil I have given them" (Amos 9:14–15).

The Talmudic passage (Mak. 24a) detailing various attempts to condense the 613 commandments to their essence observes that Amos reduced them to one: "Seek Me and live" (Amos 5:4).

Amram, son of Kohath, and the grandson of Levi.

The father of Moses, Aaron, and Miriam (Num. 26:58–59), Amram was initially described only as "a certain man of the house of Levi" (Exod. 2:1). The Rabbis offered several reasons why neither the names of Amram nor his wife Jochebed (who was also his aunt, making a union that would have been prohibited by later biblical law) were mentioned until much later. One explanation was that their decision to marry was not their own, but rather was Divinely determined. Another was that it taught that any Jewish parents can have a child who will accomplish great deeds. For this reason, at every circumcision a chair is set aside for Elijah the prophet, the herald of the Messiah, implying that perhaps this boy will be the awaited one.

According to the *aggadah*, Amram and Jochebed already had two children, Miriam and Aaron, when Pharaoh decreed that all newborn Israelite males would be cast into the Nile. Amram divorced his wife, arguing that there was no point having another child only to see him killed. As "leader of the Sanhedrin and the greatest man of his generation," all the other Israelite men followed his example. Miriam then accused her father of being worse than Pharaoh: "Pharaoh decreed only against the males; you have decreed against the males and the females. Pharaoh only decreed concerning this world; you have decreed concerning this world and the World to Come [i.e., the drowned infants would live again in the future world, but unborn children are denied that bliss]." She added that there was a possibility that Pharaoh's decree might not be carried out, whereas "though you are righteous, it is certain that your decree [not to have children] will be fulfilled." Amram saw the wisdom of his daughter's words and reunited with his wife, and soon afterward Moses was born (Sot. 12a).

Asa, third king of Judah (c. 911–870 B.C.E.).

A loyal adherent of the worship of God, Asa instituted reforms to rid the land of heathen deities and practices. Consequently, he is described in the Bible as doing "what was right in the eyes of the Lord" (1 Kings 15:11). However, "in his old age he suffered from a foot disease" (1 Kings 15:23)—either gout or gangrene. The Talmud (Sot. 10a) attributes this to Divine punishment for Asa conscripting *all* of Judah and forcing them to march off to forced labor or war, including "disciples of the sages" and newly married husbands (in direct violation of Deut. 20:7). The Bible condemns Asa because "he did not seek guidance of the Lord but resorted to physicians" (2 Chron. 16:11). Nevertheless, Asa received the honor of being buried in the City of David (2 Chron. 16:14).

Asahel, son of Zeruiah, the sister of King David, and brother of Abishai and Joab, the commander in chief of David's army.

One of the "thirty mighty men of David" (2 Sam. 23:24) and as "fleet-footed as a wild gazelle" (2 Sam. 2:18), the *aggadah* claims that Asahel was so speedy that he outraced deer. When he ran over a field of ripening corn, the ears of grain did not even bend, remaining upright as if untouched (Eccles. R. 9:11). After the defeat of Saul's son, Ishbosheth, in the battle at Gibeon, Asahel pursued Abner but was killed by the latter in self-defense (2 Sam. 2:17–23). Although David made peace with Abner, Joab avenged his brother by treacherously murdering Abner at Hebron (2 Sam. 3:22–30).

Asaph, ancestor of one of the principal families of singers in the Temple.

Generally considered the son of Korach, Asa is described by the *aggadah* as an example of how the son of a wicked person can become righteous through the study of Torah (Song R. 4:4). Listed among the levitical singers who participated in bringing the Ark up to Jerusalem (1 Chron. 15:17, 19), Asaph is best known as one of the ten elders whose works were incorporated by King David in the Book of Psalms (BB 14b), with Psalms 50 and 73–83 having the caption "of Asaph." It is related that Asaph sang while the Temple was burning, justifying his action by declaring: "I am singing because God has poured out His wrath on only wood and stones [rather than on the people of Israel]" (Lam. R. 4:14).

Asenath, wife of Joseph.

Daughter of Potiphera, an Egyptian priest of On, Asenath was given by Pharaoh to Joseph when he became viceroy of Egypt after successfully interpreting the monarch's dreams (Gen. 42:45). Noting the similarity between their names, the Rabbis determined that Potiphera was actually Potiphar. By allowing his own daughter to marry Joseph, Potiphar clearly indicated that he did not believe the false charges made by his wife that Joseph had attacked her (Gen. 39:14–19).

According to rabbinic legend, Asenath was the daughter born to Dinah after she had been raped by Shechem. When her brothers learned of the birth of an illegitimate child in their family, they wanted to kill her. But Jacob disagreed, hung a metal amulet engraved with the Name of God on her neck, and placed her under a thorn bush (*sneh* in Hebrew, from which derived her name). The angel Michael took the infant down to Egypt to the house of Potiphar, whose childless wife adopted Dinah as her own daughter (PdRE 38).

Another *midrash* tells a different story. Potiphar wanted to kill Joseph after his wife's false accusation until Asenath came secretly to Potiphar's house, told him the truth, and swore to it. In response to Asenath's actions, God said: "Just as you have spoken on Joseph's behalf, so I will have the tribes that descend from him come through you" (Yalkut Shimoni, Vayeishev 146).

Asher, Jacob's eighth son (in order of birth) and second son by Zilpah, the handmaid of Leah (Gen. 30:12–13).

According to the biblical text, the name derived from Leah's exclamation after his birth: "What fortune [*Be-oshri*]! Women will deem me fortunate [*ishruni*]" (Gen. 30:13). However, some scholars believe that the origin of the name was related to the male counterpart of the goddess Asherah, especially since Zilpah's other son, Gad, was also named after a pagan deity. The *aggadah* suggests two other possibilities. Leah selected the name Asher (praise) because she believed that all would praise her since, though already blessed with Jacob's children, she unselfishly permitted her handmaid to have a second child with her husband. An alternative is that Leah prophesied that in the future the sons of Asher would praise God for their bountiful possessions in the Land of Israel. His flag was the fiery red of beryl, on which an olive tree was embroidered, based on the verse: "Asher's bread shall be rich, and he will provide royal delicacies" (Gen. 49:20).

After the conquest of the Promised Land, the tribe of Asher was allotted territory in the hills of Upper Galilee, a fertile area rich in olive trees that supplied oil to all of Israel. Moses said of Asher: "Most blessed of sons be Asher; may he be the favorite of his brothers, may he dip his foot in oil [i.e., have a great abundance of crops]" (Deut. 33:24). His tribe supplied the others with large amounts of appetizing food, even in a Sabbatical Year (Men. 85b). The daughters of Asher were renowned for their beauty; many married high priests and kings, who were anointed with sacred oil. Asher himself was described as inheriting palaces throughout the world (more castles than Judah inherited lands), so that he never was forced to spend a night in an inn (Gen. R. 71:10).

Athaliah, queen of Judah (841–835 B.C.E.).

Daughter of King Ahab and Jezebel of Israel, Athaliah was the wife of Jehoram and mother of Ahaziah. She introduced Baal worship into Judah, corrupting the reigns of both her husband and son. A *midrash* relates that, during the reign of Athaliah, the Name of God left the mouths of the people so that they no longer greeted each other in the Name of the Lord ("The Lord be with you"), which had been the custom since the time of Boaz (Ruth R. 4:4–5).

Following the death of Ahaziah, Athaliah seized power and killed virtually all the members of the royal Davidic line who might prove to be her rival. However, Jehoash, the infant son of Ahaziah, was saved and hidden by his aunt Jehosheba (wife of the high priest Jehoiada; 2 Kings 11:1–3). When Jehoash was seven years old and about to be crowned the legitimate king, Athaliah hurried to the Temple to prevent the ceremony from taking place. However, Jehoiada ordered her to be seized and killed (2 Kings 11:4–20).

The *aggadah* describes Athaliah as one of four women (including Jezebel; Semiramism, the wife of Nebuchadnezzar of Babylon; and Vashti, the wife of Ahasuerus) who "wielded the scepter" (i.e., ruled) in the world (Esth. R. 3:2).

Azariah. *See* Hananiah, Mishael, and Azariah.

B

Balaam, son of Beor from Pethor, a Mesopotamian town along the Euphrates (Num. 22:5).

A soothsayer of great renown, Balaam received messengers from Balak, king of Moab, offering him vast riches to curse the Israelites threatening his territory. God initially ordered Balaam to refuse this invitation: "Do not go with them. You must not curse that people, for they are blessed" (Num. 22:12). When Balak sent more distinguished messengers, Balaam replied that even if the Moabite king were to offer him a "house full of silver and gold," he could not "do anything, big or little, contrary to the command of the Lord my God" (Num. 22:15–18). However, this time God permitted Balaam to go, with the understanding, "Whatever I command you, that you shall do" (Num. 22:20). Nevertheless, God was angry at Balaam and placed an angel with drawn sword in his path three times. Invisible to the seer Balaam, his donkey saw the angel and stubbornly refused to go forward, despite being beaten. Miraculously given the power of human speech, the donkey asked why his master continued to strike him. "Then the Lord uncovered Balaam's eyes" (Num. 22:31), and after repenting the seer was allowed to proceed.

When Balaam met Balak, he warned the king: "I can utter only the word that God puts into my mouth" (Num. 22:38). On four separate occasions (Num. 33–34), Balaam blessed Israel. When he saw Israel dwelling according to their tribes, which the Talmud (BB 60a) said "indicates that he saw that the doors of their tents did not exactly face one another [i.e., affording each family privacy]," Balaam exclaimed, "Worthy are these that the Divine Presence should rest upon them!" His declaration "How goodly are your tents, O Jacob, your dwelling places, O Israel" (Num. 24:5) is the source of the *Mah Tovu* prayer that is recited daily upon entering the synagogue for the morning service. Balaam even predicted the defeat and destruction of Moab (Num. 24:17).

The *aggadah* observes, "All that Israel enjoys in the world comes from the blessings of Balaam" (Deut. R. 3:4). In addition, "The blessing that Balaam gave Israel is better than the blessings that Jacob gave the tribes and the blessings that Moses gave [Israel]. When Jacob blessed the tribes, he rebuked them; even Moses did not bless [Israel] before he had rebuked them. But when Balaam blessed them, his blessings were consistent and without blemish" (Yalkut Shimoni, Balak 771).

The Rabbis maintained that, although unable to "curse" the Israelites, Balaam (frequently labeled "the wicked" in the Talmud) was responsible for the shameful incident at Shittim. There the people engaged in idol worship and licentious behavior ("whoring with the Moabite women"), which so incensed God that He sent a plague that killed 20,000 of them (Num. 25:1–5, 9). As the wicked Balaam advised Balak: "The God of the Israelites hates lewdness, and the Israelites are very partial to linen [garments, which were worn by the wealthy and noble]. Set up tents enclosed by hangings and seat harlots in them, an old one outside and a young one inside to sell them linen garments." Gradually the Israelites were lured from buying linen to idolatry and immorality (Sanh. 106a). The Talmud noted that it was fortunate that God "did not exercise the Attribute of Anger during the days of the wicked Balaam, for had He done so, not a trace would have remained [of Israel]" (Ber. 7a).

According to the *aggadah*, the donkey that spoke to Balaam was created on the sixth day of Creation. Jacob gave the animal to Balaam so that he would not advise Pharaoh to enact an evil decree against his sons. Nevertheless, Balaam advised Pharaoh that the Israelites be put to work making bricks. He also recommended that Pharaoh slaughter the Jews and bathe in their blood so that he would be healed of his leprosy. Only the wicked Balaam was able to determine the precise moment in time (*rega*) when God was angry, which the Talmud defined as one 53,848th of an hour, based on the verse that Balaam "knows the knowledge of the Most High [Num. 24:16]" (Ber. 7a; Av. Zar. 4a).

When the Torah was given to Israel, a sound rang out from one end of the world to the other. All the heathen kings, who were seized with trembling in their palaces, gathered around the wicked Balaam. They asked the seer the source of this tumultuous noise, fearing a devastating flood that would destroy the world. Balaam replied, "God has a precious treasure [the Torah] in His storehouse, which was hidden for many generations before the world was created, which He wants to give to His children" (Zev. 116a).

The Talmud declares that Balaam was one of "four commoners" who have no share in the World to Come (Sanh. 90a). According to *Pirkei Avot*, "An evil eye, a haughty spirit, and a lusting soul [are signs of] the disciples of the wicked Balaam" (5:2). *See also* Balak.

Balak, son of Tzipor, and the king of Moab.

Alarmed by the number and power of the Israelites, who had handily defeated the Amorites under Sihon and Og, Balak remarked: "Now this horde will lick clean all that is about us, as an ox licks up the grass of the field"

(Num. 22:3–4). Consequently, Balak engaged the seer Balaam to curse the advancing Israelites. However, acting under Divine direction, Balaam could only praise Israel and predict their glorious victories. Ironically, Balaam ended up cursing Balak's own people: "A star rises from Jacob, a scepter comes forth from Israel; it smashes the brow of Moab" (Num. 24:17).

According to the Talmud, as a reward for the forty-two sacrifices that he offered during his attempts to have Balaam curse the Israelites, Balak merited being the progenitor of Ruth (Naz. 23b; Sot. 47a). *See also* Balaam.

Barak, son of Abinoam of the tribe of Issachar.

The prophetess Deborah asked Barak (Hebrew for "lightning") to lead the Israelite tribes against King Jabin of Hazor, promising him victory in the name of the Lord (Judg. 4). However, as a condition of his acceptance, Barak insisted that Deborah join him. She agreed, but not before warning him: "The course you are taking will not give you any glory; for the Lord will deliver Sisera into the hand of a woman."

Barak mustered his forces on Mount Tabor and advanced to meet the Canaanite king. In the ensuing battle, Barak and his men routed the army led by Sisera, Jabin's military commander. In thanksgiving for God's deliverance of their people, Barak joined Deborah in singing a glorious hymn of triumph to the Lord (Judg. 5). *See also* Jael.

Baruch, secretary and confidant of the prophet Jeremiah.

A member of a distinguished family, Baruch was the son of Neriah and the brother of Seraiah, a high official in the court of King Zedekiah (Jer. 51:59). Jeremiah dictated to Baruch all the words that God had spoken to him (Jer. 36). Because "I am imprisoned and cannot go to the House of the Lord," Jeremiah sent Baruch as a messenger with the potentially dangerous task of reading these prophetic words in the Temple before the people of Judah. King Jehoiakim demanded that the scroll be brought and read to him. Despite the pleas of his courtiers, the furious monarch tore up the leaves of the scroll and burned them in the fireplace. He ordered the arrest of Jeremiah and Baruch, "but the Lord hid them." Jeremiah then redictated the first scroll to Baruch, adding that because of his actions Jehoiakim would have no descendants sitting on the throne of Judah. "His dead body will be left exposed to the heat by day and the cold by night." Moreover, God "will punish him, his seed, and his servants for their iniquity; and I will bring on them, the inhabitants of Jerusalem, and the men of Judah all the disasters that I have warned them—but they would not listen."

In the final siege of Jerusalem (586 B.C.E.), Baruch witnessed the prophet's purchase of his ancestral estate in Anatot, convinced that God would redeem the Israelites and allow them to return to their land (Jer. 32). After the murder of Gedaliah, Baruch was carried off with Jeremiah to Egypt.

The apocryphal Book of Baruch was attributed to this scribe, as were various other versions that related Baruch's experiences before and after the destruction of Jerusalem and his subsequent journey through the heavens. Some scholars have asserted that Baruch was the redactor of the Five Books of Moses, who wove together the four major strands of literary tradition, according to the "Documentary Hypothesis" (Friedman).

Bathsheba, wife of King David, and the mother of King Solomon.

Bathsheba was the wife of Uriah the Hittite (2 Sam. 11:3), one of David's warriors. According to the *aggadah*, Bathsheba was bathing on the roof of her house behind a wickerwork screen when Satan appeared outside it disguised as a bird. David shot an arrow at the bird, but instead it struck and split the screen, thus revealing Bathsheba to David in all her beauty. Charmed by this captivating woman, the king ordered that Bathsheba be brought to the palace (Sanh. 107a).

When David discovered that Bathsheba was pregnant with his child, he attempted to recall Uriah from the battlefield so that the child would be considered as her husband's. However, after Uriah refused to leave his fellow soldiers, David ordered his military commander to station Uriah in the front line opposite the enemy at a point where the battle was fiercest, thus leaving Uriah to meet his death (2 Chron. 11:15). After Bathsheba's period of mourning for her husband was completed, David called her to the palace and she became his wife.

David's actions displeased the Lord, and the prophet Nathan came to the palace to rebuke the king (2 Sam. 12). Nathan related a parable about two men—a rich man with many flocks and herds and a poor man who had nothing except for one little lamb. When a traveler once came to the house of the rich man, the latter took the poor man's only lamb to prepare a meal for his guest, since he was too miserly to use one of his own animals. When David expressed his anger against the rich man, saying that he deserved to die, Nathan calmly informed David that he was that man. David immediately realized that he had committed a grievous sin and repented for his actions. The child died soon after birth, in punishment for David's sin. Nine months later, however, Bathsheba bore David a son and named him Solomon.

When Adonijah attempted to seize the throne, Bathsheba and Nathan approached the dying David and reminded him of his pledge that Solomon would be his successor. David immediately ordered that Solomon be crowned as king (1 Kings 1:13).

According to the *aggadah*, Bathsheba was the granddaughter of Ahithophel, whose belief in a prophecy foretelling his ascent to royal status actually applied to her (Sanh. 101b). Bathsheba was destined to marry David since the six days of Creation, but his sin was taking her before the appointed time (Sanh. 107a). Bathsheba was not guilty of adultery since the soldiers in David's army customarily gave their wives conditional bills of divorce that would become effective were they killed in battle, as was Uriah (Ket. 9b).

Further developing Nathan's parable of the lamb, the Talmud concludes that David's punishment for committing adultery and instigating the murder of Uriah was similar to the fourfold restitution the Bible required for stealing a sheep (Exod. 21:37). Thus his first child with Bathsheba, as well as three later children (Amnon, Tamar, and Absalom), all died during David's lifetime. In this way, David paid four of his "lambs" for the one he had unrighteously taken from its master (Yoma 22b). *See also* Ahithophel.

Benaiah, son of Jehoiada, and one of King David's "mighty men."

Renowned for a series of heroic feats (2 Sam. 20–23; 1 Chron. 11:22–25), Benaiah sided with Solomon (along with Zadok the priest and Nathan the prophet) in opposing Adonijah's attempt to seize the throne (1 Kings 1:5). After carrying out the executions of Adonijah, Joab, and Shimei—who had rebelled against the establishment of Solomon's kingdom—Benaiah was rewarded by being appointed commander of the army in place of Joab (1 Kings 2:25–46).

According to a *midrash*, when the king of Persia was dying, the doctors said his only hope for a cure was to drink the milk of a lioness. The king asked for help from Solomon, who summoned the brave Benaiah to go to a den where a lioness was nursing her cubs. Benaiah approached her slowly, throwing a goat for her to eat. He repeated this for seven days, each time coming a little closer, until finally she allowed him to play with her and even take some of her milk, which he brought to Solomon to cure the king (Mid. Ps. 39:2).

Benjamin, youngest son of Jacob and Rachel, and the only son of Jacob born in the land of Canaan.

His mother, who died soon after giving birth, named him "Ben-oni" (son of my sorrow) (Gen. 35:18), but his father called him "Benjamin" (son of the right hand). The flag of the tribe of Benjamin was a combination of twelve colors and embroidered with the image of a wolf, based on Jacob's final blessing: "Benjamin is a ravenous predatory wolf; in the morning he consumes the foe, and in the evening he divides the spoils" (Gen. 49:27).

As the youngest son, Benjamin was forbidden by Jacob from joining his brothers when they went down to Egypt to purchase food during the famine. However, when Joseph insisted that Benjamin must also be present, Jacob reluctantly agreed and Judah assumed responsibility for him. Overcome with emotion at seeing his only full brother, Joseph fled to a private room and wept. He invited his brothers to dine and favored Benjamin with extra portions. Attempting to test how his brothers would act on this occasion when his father's favorite son was threatened, Joseph instructed his steward to conceal a silver goblet in Benjamin's sack, overtake the brothers on their journey home, and accuse him of stealing it. When Judah declared himself ready to sacrifice his liberty in exchange for Benjamin's release, in order to spare their father from grief if his beloved youngest son failed to return, Joseph finally revealed his identity to his brothers and invited the entire family to settle in Goshen (Gen. 42–45).

Of the brothers, Benjamin alone did not participate in the sale of Joseph. Therefore, he was rewarded by having the Temple built in the territory of his tribe (Gen. R. 99:1). When Joseph saw his youngest brother, the text stated that he "embraced Benjamin [lit., 'fell upon his neck'] and wept" (Gen. 45:14). The Talmud interprets this as weeping over the two Temples in the territory of Benjamin, which were destined to be destroyed (Meg. 16b). Untainted by sin (Shab. 55b), when Benjamin died, his body was never attacked by worms (BB 17a).

Many of Benjamin's descendants were mighty and fearless warriors. Rashi maintained that "the morning" in Jacob's blessing (see above) referred to King Saul, who rose as the champion of the people during the early years of Israel's history, when the nation began to flourish and shine. In the national "evening" of decline, when the people were exiled to Babylonia and Persia, Benjamin's offspring would triumph over Israel's enemies and divide the spoils of victory. This was an allusion to Mordechai and Esther, of the tribe of Benjamin, who defeated Haman and were awarded his estate.

Bethuel, son of Milcah and Nahor, the brother of Abraham, and the father of Rebecca and Laban (Gen. 24:15).

During Eliezer's bridal negotiations for Rebecca, Bethuel disappeared from the text, leading to the assumption that he died suddenly. According to one *midrash*, as king of Aram-Naharaim, Bethuel demanded the right to cohabit with every maiden on her wedding night before returning her to her husband. All his subjects agreed to submit themselves to this outrageous action as long as he would do the same with his own daughters. When Bethuel appeared willing to exercise this right on Rebecca, God caused the death of her father to spare his daughter from shame. Another *midrash* relates that when Bethuel saw the treasures that Eliezer brought with him as gifts, he placed food containing a deadly poison before the servant of Abraham. However, the angel traveling with Eliezer switched the dishes so that Bethuel ate the poisoned food and died (Yalkut Shimoni, Genesis 109).

Bezalel, chief architect of the Tabernacle.

A member of the tribe of Judah, Bezalel was appointed by Moses to head the skilled artisans who constructed and decorated the Tabernacle in the wilderness according to a plan detailed to Moses on Mount Sinai (Exod. 31:1–6; 35:30). Bezalel was perfectly suited for the task, for God had "endowed him with a Divine spirit of skill, ability, and knowledge in every kind of craft, to make designs for work in gold, silver, and copper, to cut stones for setting and to carve wood" (Exod. 31:3–5). The Talmud relates that "Bezalel knew how to combine the letters by which the heaven and earth were created" and had a degree of wisdom and understanding similar to that with which God had created the universe (Ber. 55a).

In the late genealogical lists, Bezalel was described as "the son of Uri, the son of Hur" (2 Chron. 1:5). According to the *aggadah*, which considered Hur to be the son of Miriam and Caleb, Bezalel would have been the great-grandnephew of Moses (Exod. R. 48:3–4).

During Talmudic times, certain local officials were appointed by the heads of the Jewish community—the patriarch in the Land of Israel and the exilarch in Babylonia. The most important requirement was that their choices met with public approval. As R. Isaac said, "We must not appoint a leader over a community without first consulting it." He offered a *midrash* based on the verse, "See, the Lord has called by name Bezalel, the son of Uri [to be the lead architect for the Tabernacle]" (Exod. 35:30). When God asked Moses if he considered Bezalel suitable, Moses replied: "Sovereign of the Universe, if he is acceptable to You, surely he must also be to me!" But God persisted, "All the same, go and consult the people" (Ber. 55a). Similarly, all laws must be generally acceptable: "No law may be imposed on the people unless a majority of the community can endure it [i.e., is able to comply with its terms]" (Hor. 3b).

Bilhah, Rachel's handmaid, and the mother of Dan and Naphtali.

"When Rachel saw that she had borne Jacob no children, she became envious of her sister [the fruitful Leah]" and demanded that Jacob "give me children or I shall die" (Gen. 30:1). Consequently, she gave him Bilhah as a concubine so that Jacob could cohabit with her "so that she may bear on my knees and through her I also may have children" (Gen. 30:3–4). In ancient times, this action was tantamount to adoption, so that Bilhah would be a surrogate mother whose offspring Rachel would accept as her own.

Later, Reuben (Jacob's firstborn son by his wife Leah) "went and lay with Bilhah, his father's concubine; and Israel [Jacob] found out [lit., 'he heard']" (Gen. 35:22). This action may be explained by the regular practice among ancient Near Eastern heirs-apparent to take possession of their father's wife, so as to assert their right to the throne and become identified with the late ruler's personality in the eyes of the people. However, this incestuous act earned the unending wrath of his father and resulted in Reuben forfeiting his privilege as the firstborn (Gen. 49:4). *See also* Dan; Reuben.

Bithiah, daughter of Pharaoh (1 Chron. 4:18).

According to the *aggadah*, the name Bithiah (daughter of God) was given to her as a reward for her devotion in treating Moses as her own child after saving the infant from the Nile (Lev. R. 1:3). Every morning, Bithiah went to bathe in the water to cleanse herself from the idolatrous customs of her father, who regarded the Nile as a god to be worshiped (Sot. 12b). Since immersion is part of the ceremony of conversion, it was assumed that she became a proselyte to Judaism. Some Rabbis said that Bithiah knew Moses was a Hebrew child because of his circumcision (Sot. 12b). Others maintained she was aware that the child radiated a Divine aura as soon she realized that, upon touching the basket, she was healed of the scabs and boils that afflicted all Egyptians (Exod. R. 1:23). According to the *aggadah*, her handmaidens tried to counsel her against saving the baby and defying the royal decree, but they were killed (lit., "pressed into the ground") by the angel Gabriel (Sot. 12b).

The Egyptian princess called the child Moses, not only because she had "drawn" him out of the water, but because she saw through Divine inspiration that he would "draw" the children of Israel out of Egypt. Although Moses had many names, God called him only by the name Bithiah gave him (Exod. R. 1:25). All female, as well as male, Egyptian firstborns in Egypt died during the tenth plague except for Bithiah, since she had Moses as her advocate with God (Exod. R. 18:3).

The Bible relates that Bithiah was the wife of Mered (meaning "rebel"), who the Rabbis said was Caleb. "Just as he rebelled against the counsel of the ten princes sent to spy out the Promised Land, so she rebelled against the counsel of her father, who decreed that all the male Hebrew infants be killed." As one sage declared, "He saved the flock [Israel]; she saved the shepherd [Moses]" (Lev. R. 1:3). According to legend, Bithiah was one of the nine who entered the Garden of Eden during their lifetimes (Derech Eretz Zuta 1). *See also* Caleb.

Boaz, second husband of Ruth.

A wealthy Judean landowner living in Bethlehem, Boaz was a kinsman of Elimelech, the late husband of Naomi and father-in-law of Ruth (Ruth 2:1). Seeing the reapers in his fields, he greeted them, "The Lord be with you!" and they responded, "The Lord bless you!" (Ruth 2:4). Therefore, the Rabbis considered Boaz to be the first to use the Divine name in greeting his fellow men, a practice that received the approval of Heaven (Mak. 23b).

Seeing a new woman gleaning, he asked the reapers about her identity and learned that she was the daughter-in-law of Naomi, recently arrived from Moab. Learning of the poverty of Ruth and her loyalty to Naomi, Boaz protected Ruth and ordered his workers to deliberately leave grain for her to glean in his fields. Unlike the other women gleaners who flirted with the harvesters, Ruth remained reserved; rather than gleaning between the sheaves like the others, Ruth gathered only from that which was definitely abandoned. Instead of bending over to glean like the other women, she sat down due to modesty (Ruth R. 4:9).

At mealtime, Boaz said to Ruth, "Come over here and partake of the meal, and dip your morsel in the vinegar" (Ruth 2:14). According to the Rabbis, the phrase "Come over here" was a hint from Boaz (under the influence of the Holy Spirit) that the kingdom of the House of David would come forth from her, while "Dip your morsel in the vinegar" was a hint that one of her descendants would be the wicked king Manasseh, whose deeds would be sour as vinegar. The description that Ruth "sat beside the harvesters," separated her from Boaz, was a hint that the kingdom of David that would issue from both of them would eventually be split into two (Shab. 113b).

At Naomi's urging, one night Ruth "went over stealthily [to the place where Boaz slept] and uncovered his feet and lay down. In the middle of the night, the man was startled and pulled back—there was a woman lying at his feet!" (Ruth 3:7–8). According to the one *aggadah*, Boaz asked who she was and why she was there. Ruth replied, "To fulfill the [verse in the] Torah (Lev. 25:25): 'If your brother becomes poor and has to sell some of his possessions, his closest kinsman [lit., 'nearest redeemer'] shall come and redeem what his brother has sold" (Tanh. Behar 3). Boaz explained that he wanted to marry her, but that there was a closer relative who first would have to renounce his right to marry her before Boaz could act as the redeemer. As Ruth lay near him, the evil inclination distressed Boaz all night. "You are single and seeking a wife; she is single and looking for a husband. Consort with her and she will become your wife." But Boaz repulsed his evil inclination. "As God lives, I shall not touch her [because of the closer redeemer with the right to marry her]." To Ruth he said, "Lie down until morning" (Sifri Beha'alotcha 88).

When the closer kinsman refused to marry Ruth and redeem Elimelech's estate, Boaz and Ruth were married. As R. Isaac stated, "The wife of Boaz died on the very day when Ruth the Moabitess came to the Land of Israel," to which he applied the popular maxim, "Before a person dies, the master of his house is appointed" (BB 91a).

According to the *aggadah*, Boaz was eighty years old and had never sired children, but as soon as the righteous Naomi prayed for him, he immediately sired a son. Ruth was forty years old and had never conceived, but as soon as the righteous Boaz prayed for her, she immediately conceived (Ruth R. 6:2). Their child, Obed, became the father of Jesse and the grandfather of King David (Ruth 4:22).

C

Cain, first son of Adam and Eve, born after they were banished from the Garden of Eden.

Cain's name in Hebrew (*Kayin*) and other Near Eastern languages (Aramaic and Arabic) means "smith," though the biblical text indicates that Eve selected it because she "gained [*kaniti*, meaning 'I produced'] a male child with the help of the Lord" (Gen. 4). As the Bible related, "Cain became a tiller of the soil . . . [and] brought an offering to the Lord from the fruit of the soil," while his brother Abel "brought the choicest of the firstlings of his flock." Without giving a reason, God accepted the offering of Abel but rejected Cain's. Searching for an explanation, the Rabbis noted that Abel brought "the choicest" of his animals, while Cain offered merely "an offering," not necessarily the best, from his agricultural produce. A *midrash* compares Cain to "a bad tenant, who eats the first ripe figs [esteemed as a special delicacy] but honors the king with the late figs" (Gen. R. 12:5). Angered by this rebuff and unmoved by God's assurance that Divine acceptance depended on proper conduct, Cain killed his brother. For this Cain merited double punishment—the ground would no longer yield any return for his labor, and he would "become a ceaseless wanderer on earth." Cain complained, "My punishment is too great to bear," and that as a wanderer "anyone who meets me may kill me." Indeed, according to legend, "the cattle, beasts, and birds assembled to demand justice for Abel." However, as the Rabbis explained, Cain would be spared the punishment given to other murderers, since without any example from which to learn, he had no idea of the enormity of his crime (Gen. R. 12:12).

So God "put a mark [*ot*] on Cain"—not as a sign of disgrace, but rather as an indication of Divine protection: "If anyone kill Cain, sevenfold vengeance shall be taken on him." The *aggadah* offers various suggestions as to the precise nature of this sign: "God made the sun shine upon him [as a sign of Divine benevolence]; He caused Cain to develop *tzara'at* [flaky white skin disease, mistranslated as leprosy, which would cause others to avoid him]; He gave him a vicious dog [to scare away anyone who would attack him]; and He made Cain a sign to others [a warning to murderers and an indication of the saving power of repentance]. In addition, God suspended the punishment of Cain until [some future time when] the Flood came and drowned him" (Gen. R. 22:12). Another explanation is that "God took one of the twenty-two letters [*aleph-bet*] from which the Torah was written and placed it on Cain's arm, so that he would not be killed" (Yalkut Shimoni, Genesis 38).

Nevertheless, Cain "settled in the land of Nod, east of Eden," where he had a son Enoch, after whom he named a city he had built. Among Cain's descendants were Lamech (the first to take two wives) and his three sons, who were responsible for material development and social progress—Jabal (who established the nomadic style of life), Jubal (the inventor of music), and Tubal-cain ("who forged all implements of copper and iron"). According to legend, God caused a horn to sprout on Cain's forehead to protect him. When the blind Lamech was hunting in the fields, with his young son holding him by the hand, the child saw something that looked like the horn of a wild beast. Lamech shot an arrow in that direction and killed his great-grandfather Cain (Tanh. Gen. 11).

According to Midrash Tanhuma, "Cain's offering consisted of the seed of flax and that of Abel of the firstlings of his sheep." The disastrous consequence that resulted has been suggested as the underlying reason for the biblical prohibition against the wearing of a garment containing both vegetable and animal fibers, such as wool and linen (*sha'atnez*) (see Lev. 19:19; Deut. 22:11). *See also* Abel.

Caleb, son of Jephunneh and leader of the tribe of Judah.

Caleb was one of the twelve "spies" sent by Moses to "scout the land of Canaan" (Num. 13:1). Ten of the spies admitted the richness of the land, which "flowed with milk and honey," but they argued: "We cannot attack that people, for it is stronger than we. . . . The country that we traversed and scouted is one that devours its settlers. All the people that we saw in it are men of great size . . . and we looked like grasshoppers to ourselves, and so we must have looked to them" (Num. 13:31–33). Rather than contradict the facts presented by the other scouts, Caleb vehemently disagreed with their defeatist conclusion. "Let us by all means go up, and we shall gain possession [of the land], for we shall surely overcome it" (Num. 13:30). However, the Israelites were fearful of the majority report and determined to return to Egypt. Caleb, along with Moses and Joshua (the twelfth scout), argued with them, but to no avail. Disgusted with the people, God decreed that all those who were aged twenty or older, except for Caleb and Joshua, would be prohibited from entering the Promised Land. The Israelites were condemned to wander forty years in the wilderness, one year for each day the spies scouted the land, while the ten who "spread calumny about the land died of plague" (Num. 14:26–38). After entering Canaan, Caleb requested the city of Hebron for himself and his descendants. Joshua agreed in recognition of Caleb's brave conduct during the episode of the spies and "because he fully followed the Lord, God of Israel" (Josh. 14:6–15).

Rava interpreted the difference in pronouns in the verse, "And *they* went up by the South and *he* came unto Hebron" (Num. 13:22), as meaning that Caleb paid a special visit to the grave of the patriarchs and prostrated himself upon it, asking them to "pray on my behalf that I may be delivered from the evil intentions [conspiracy] of the spies" (Sot. 34b). Caleb was the one who insisted that the spies take with them samples of the superb fruit of the land to show the people (Num. R. 16:14). Seeing how the Israelites had shouted down Joshua when he defended Moses, Caleb pretended to agree with the other spies, so that he would be permitted to address the people. However, Caleb also was shouted down once he began to support Moses (Sot. 35a). As a reward for their conduct, the portions for Joshua and Caleb in the Land of Israel were determined by Divine command rather than by lots, and they received portions that originally had been intended for the other spies (JT BB 8:3).

The *aggadah* relates that Caleb had two wives. His first marriage was to Miriam, the sister of Moses, making him the progenitor of the House of David (Sot. 11b, 12a). He also married Bithiah (daughter of God), the name given by the Rabbis to the daughter of Pharaoh as a reward for her devotion in treating Moses as her own child and thus disobeying her father's decree to kill all the newborn Hebrew males. The only female firstborn spared in Egypt (Exod. R. 18:3) and a convert to Judaism, Bithiah married Caleb (also known as Mered, meaning "to rebel") because just as she had rebelled against her father, so he would rebel against the evil report of the spies (Meg. 13a; Sanh. 19b).

Canaan, son of Ham, and the grandson of Noah.

After Ham acted disrespectfully toward his drunken and naked father (Gen. 9:22), it was Canaan who was cursed as "the lowest of the slaves," who would serve his uncles, Shem and Japheth (Gen. 9:25–27). The sages suggested several reasons why Canaan had to suffer for the sins of his father. Some maintained that it was Canaan who saw Noah and raced to tell his father, Ham, while others claimed that Canaan castrated Noah so that he could have no more progeny. However, God had already blessed Noah and his sons (Gen. 9:1), and there cannot be a curse where a blessing has been given.

On his deathbed, Canaan was said to have urged his sons: "Love one another, love robbery, love lewdness, hate your masters, and do not speak the truth" (Pes. 113b). The concept of the accursed Canaanites as forever morally corrupt led the patriarchs to forbid their children from marrying them. In one *midrash*, when Noah divided the earth, he assigned the Land of Israel to the descendants of Shem. Rejecting this allocation, Canaan took possession of it, so that when the Israelites conquered the Promised Land, it reverted to its rightful owners.

According to the Talmud, "Canaan had many descendants who were worthy of rabbinic ordination [as scholars], such as Tabi, the slave of Rabban Gamaliel, but the guilt of their ancestor caused them [to lose their chance and forced them to remain as slaves]" (Yoma 87a).

Chileab, second son of King David, born to Abigail in Hebron (2 Sam. 3:3).
Elsewhere, his name was given as Daniel (1 Chron. 3:1).

Cozbi, Midianite princess and daughter of Zur (Num. 25:15).
Along with her lover, Zimri, Cozbi was slain by Pinchas at the conclusion of the shameful episode of apostasy and licentiousness at Shittim (Num. 25:1–9).

D

Dan, fifth son of Jacob and the firstborn of Bilhah, the handmaid of Rachel.

Rachel named him Dan because "God has vindicated me (*dananni*); He has heeded my plea and given me a son" (Gen. 30:6). The *aggadah* states that Bilhah called her first son Dan because the Hebrew word means "judge," praying that his descendant, Samson, would be one of the judges of the Israelites in their land.

On the blue flag of the tribe of Dan was embroidered a serpent, based on the verse, "Dan shall be a serpent by the road, a viper by the path, that bites the horse's heels so that his rider is thrown backward" (Gen. 49:17–18). Known for its fighting men, including Samson, the tribe of Dan was allotted the fertile area between Judah and the Mediterranean Sea in the south of Canaan (Josh. 19:40–48). Unable to establish themselves in the coastal plain because it was occupied by the Philistines and Amorites, the Danites moved farther north and conquered Laish, a town near the headwaters of the Jordan River, which they renamed Dan (Josh. 19:47). This was considered the northernmost limit of the Land of Israel, whose north-south span was described by the popular phrase, "from Dan to Beersheba" (Judg. 20:1).

Daniel, prophet from the tribe of Judah.

Together with three other young men of aristocratic stock (Hananiah, Mishael, and Azariah), Daniel was carried off to Babylonia and educated in the court of Nebuchadnezzar, where he was trained for the king's service. At a great royal banquet where 1,000 Babylonian lords drank wine from gold and silver utensils from the vanquished Temple, a mysterious hand suddenly appeared and silently wrote four strange words across the palace wall: *Mene mene tekel upharsin* (Dan. 5). When asked to interpret this eerie event, Daniel foretold that it presaged the downfall of King Belshazzar, whose arrogant actions had earned the wrath of God. That very night, the king was killed and Darius became ruler of the land.

Despite a royal decree prohibiting anyone from presenting a petition to any god or man other than the king, Daniel continued to pray and give thanks to God three times a day (Dan. 6:11). Based on the preceding verse describing Daniel as having "windows made in his upper chamber looking toward

Jerusalem," it became *halachic* requirements that a synagogue must have windows and that all Jews pray facing the site of the Jerusalem Temple. As punishment for disobeying the king, Daniel was cast into a den with seven famished lions, miraculously remaining there unharmed for six days.

According to the *aggadah,* "If all the wise men of other nations were in one scale of the balance, and Daniel, the greatly beloved, in the other, would he not outweigh them all?" (Yoma 77a). While living in the royal court, Daniel instituted the prohibition against eating the oil of an idolater (Av. Zar. 36a). He was prepared to sacrifice his life rather than omit the thrice-daily recitation of the statutory praises or worship an idol (Song R. 7:9).

Some Rabbis suggested that Daniel was thrown into the lion's den because he advised Nebuchadnezzar that by giving charity he could postpone the punishment of a descent into madness (BB 4a). Others believed that it was only to show that God would make wonders and miracles for him and thus sanctify His Name in the world (Sifri Ha'azinu 306). Although Daniel was described as "occupying himself with acts of lovingkindness, outfitting and gladdening the bride, escorting the dead, and giving money to the poor" (ARN 4), the Talmud notes that even he was not rescued from the lion's den because of his own merits, but rather through those of Abraham (Ber. 7b).

The last half of the Book of Daniel, written in Hebrew (the rest is in Aramaic), contains mystical revelations about the end of days, the Day of Judgment when the wicked world powers will be destroyed and the Jewish people will be restored to their homeland. *See also* Hananiah, Mishael, and Azariah.

Dathan, son of Eliab, who joined his brother Abiram in the rebellion against the leadership of Moses.

As descendants of Reuben, Jacob's firstborn son and the original leader of the tribes, they resented Moses and charged him with usurping the leadership of the people. Contradicting Moses' claim that the Promised Land was one "flowing with milk and honey," they maintained that this description actually belonged to the fertile land of Egypt, from which Moses had taken the people only to die in the wilderness (Num. 16:13). As punishment for their lying words, Abiram and Dathan, along with Korach, were miraculously swallowed up by the earth and "went down alive into Sheol, with all that belonged to them" (Num. 16:32–33).

According to the *aggadah,* Dathan and Abiram repeatedly conspired against Moses. They were identified as the two Israelites whose quarrel led to Moses fleeing from Egypt (Exod. 2:13–15), as well as the pair who attempted to incite the people to return to the land of bondage, both at the Sea of Reeds (Exod. 14:11–12) and when the spies returned from scouting out the land of Canaan (Num. 14:39–45). Described in the Talmud as being "wicked from beginning to end" (Meg. 11a), their names were interpreted allegorically to indicate that Dathan violated God's law while Abiram refused to repent (Sanh. 109b). They were said to have become leaders of the rebellion against Moses and Aaron under the influence of Korach, whose camp was next to theirs, causing the Rabbis to state: "Woe to the wicked, woe to his neighbor" (Num. R. 18:5).

David, youngest son of Jesse, great-grandson of Ruth and Boaz, and the second king of Israel (1010–970 B.C.E.).

Born in Bethlehem of the tribe of Judah, David watched his father's sheep. The *aggadah* relates that David's tender and loving care of his animals indicated that "he understands how to pasture sheep; therefore he shall become the shepherd of My flock Israel" (Mid. Ps. 78:70; Exod. R. 2:2). King Saul, who was depressed by an "evil spirit from God," asked his servants to find someone who could lift his spirits by playing the lyre. They recommended the son of Jesse, "who knows how to play, is a fine warrior and prudent in speech, a handsome person, and the Lord is with him." Brought to court, "David took a lyre, and played it with his hand; so Saul was refreshed, and was well, and the evil spirit departed from him" (1 Sam. 16:14–23). Indeed, today David is best known as the "sweet singer of Israel," the author of the Psalms (*Tehillim*).

David developed a deep friendship with Jonathan, the son of King Saul. When Goliath taunted and challenged the Israelite army, David killed the Philistine giant with a stone from his slingshot (1 Sam. 17). David distinguished himself in battle, and Saul gave him his daughter, Michal, as a wife. However, the king became jealous of David's popularity and repeatedly tried to kill him, forcing David to flee for his life. The fury of Saul was vented at the priests of Nob, who innocently had aided the fugitive. With the exception of Abiathar, all were executed as traitors (1 Sam. 21–22). On one occasion, David had an opportunity to kill Saul, but spared the king's life, "for who can stretch forth his hand against the Lord's anointed and be guiltless?" (1 Sam. 26:9). Seeking refuge, David even volunteered to serve Achish, the king of the Philistines (1 Sam. 27).

After Saul and three of his sons were killed at the battle of Gilboa (1 Sam. 31), the men of Judah anointed David as their king at Hebron (2 Sam. 2:4). At the same time, Abner, Saul's general, had Saul's son Ishbosheth crowned king of northern Israel (2 Sam. 8–10). Seven and a half years later, David's forces under Joab vanquished Abner (2 Sam. 4), and David united all the Israelite tribes into a single kingdom (2 Sam. 5). David captured Jerusalem from the Jebusites and made it his capital, the center of worship, and the holy city of religious pilgrimage. With music and rejoicing he brought the Ark of the Covenant to Jerusalem, which later became known as the City of David (2 Sam. 6). A brilliant military hero, during his forty-year reign David expanded the boundaries of Israel to an area never again attained, except for a short period under the Hasmoneans.

Yet David was not immune to controversy and tragedy. To marry Bath-sheba, he arranged for the death of her husband, the innocent Uriah (2 Sam. 12). He failed to properly punish his eldest son Amnon for raping and then casting away his half-sister Tamar, which resulted in Absalom killing Amnon to avenge his full-sister's honor (2 Sam. 13). When Absalom rebelled, David was forced to flee Jerusalem until the tide of battle reversed and his son was killed (2 Sam. 15–18). Even on his deathbed, David had to withstand his son Adonijah's attempt to usurp the throne before proclaiming Solomon his royal heir (1 Kings 1).

According to the *aggadah*, King David was destined to live only three hours. But when Adam learned that this was the fate of such a noble soul, he volunteered to give David seventy of the 1,000 years of life that he originally had been granted (PdRE 19). The Talmud relates that in answer to his plea, "Lord make me know my end" (Ps. 39:5), David was informed that his death would occur on a Sabbath. Therefore, after each Sabbath, King David would celebrate because he was assured of life for at least one more week. This may be the origin of the *melaveh malkah* (escorting the Queen), the farewell feast in honor of the departing Queen Sabbath. David spent every Sabbath studying Torah, so that the Angel of Death could not seize him. But one day the angel caused a loud noise in the royal palace. When David stopped for a moment and climbed a ladder to see what had caused the sound, it broke under him and the king fell dead (Shab. 30a–b).

In the Psalms, David requested, "Let me dwell in Your tent forever" (61:5). Rather than believing that he could achieve eternal life, the *aggadah* interprets his words as a plea to God that his songs and hymns of praise be uttered in synagogues and houses of study forever (JT Ber. 2:1, 4a). *See also* Abigail; Abishag; Abishai; Abner, Absalom; Achish; Ahimelech; Ahithophel; Bath-sheba; Goliath; Hushai; Jonathan; Michal; Nabal; Nathan; Samuel; Shimei; Solomon; Uriah.

Debir, king of Eglon.

He joined the coalition of five Amorite kings that was defeated by Joshua at Gibeon (Josh. 10:3). *See also* Adoni-Zedek.

Deborah, sole female judge of Israel and third of the seven prophetesses.

Her home and seat of justice was at the southern extremity of the hill country of Ephraim, between Bethel and Ramah, under the "palm-tree of

Deborah" (Judg. 4:5). The Rabbis offered several explanations why Deborah judged under the palm tree. First, as a woman and to prevent scandal, she was required to teach or judge only in the open air (not in private, and a palm tree is not leafy), where all could assemble. Second, the palm tree symbolized the unified purpose of all the hearts of Israel, which turn (like the leaves of the palm) to God their Father in heaven (Meg. 14a).

Deborah summoned Barak to lead the Israelite tribes in their victorious campaign against Jabin, king of Hazor, who had oppressed Israel for twenty years. In thanksgiving for God's deliverance of her people, Deborah sang a glorious hymn of triumph to the Lord. This "Song of Deborah" (Judg. 5:1–31) is read in synagogues as the *haftarah* of the weekly Torah portion of *Beshalach*, whose central section is the Song at the Sea (Exod. 15:1–19), in which Moses celebrated the deliverance of the Israelites and the drowning of the pursuing Egyptian army at the Sea of Reeds.

Delilah, lover of Samson.

Delilah was a woman of Sorek who was loved by Samson (Judg. 16). A delegation of Philistine nobles each offered her 1,100 shekels of silver as a bribe to discover the source of Samson's great strength, "so we can overpower him, tie him up, and make him helpless." Three times she asked Samson the source of his incredible strength. He first said, "If I were to be tied with seven fresh tendons that had not been dried, I should become as weak as an ordinary man." When these were supplied to Delilah with the Philistines waiting in ambush in an adjacent room, she bound Samson with them and then shouted to her lover, "Samson, the Philistines are upon you!" Immediately Samson "pulled the tendons apart, as a thread comes apart at the touch of fire." This sequence then was repeated after tying him with "new ropes," which Samson tore off his arms like a thread, and "weaving seven locks of my head into a web and pinned with a peg," which proved equally unsuccessful. Finally, Delilah complained, "How can you say you love me, when you do not confide in me." After continual nagging, Samson "was wearied to death and confided everything to her." He admitted that he had been a Nazirite since birth, and "no razor has ever touched my head. If my hair were cut, my strength would leave me, and I should become as weak as an ordinary man."

Sensing that Samson had indeed confided everything to her, Delilah sent a message for the Philistine nobles to again assemble in an adjoining room. "She lulled him [Samson] to sleep on her lap and called in a man to cut off the seven locks of his head; thus she weakened him and made him helpless; his strength slipped away from him." This time when she cried that the Philistines were upon him, Samson's power was gone. After the Philistines seized

Samson, gouged out his eyes and shackled him, he became a mill slave in prison.

According to the Talmud, Delilah was so named because "she weakened (*deldelet*) Samson's strength, his understanding, and his merit" (Sot. 9b).

Dinah, youngest child of Leah and Jacob.

According to the Talmud, Leah "passed judgment" (*dinah din*) on herself out of compassion for her sister, Rachel. She knew that twelve tribes (sons) were destined to issue from Jacob. Leah already had six and the handmaids two each. If the child Leah was carrying would also be a male, Rachel would be fated to have only one son and thus not even be equal to one of the handmaids. When Leah prayed that the child in her womb would be a girl, the embryos were switched. Thus Joseph was moved into the womb of Rachel, and Dinah into that of Leah (Ber. 60a).

When Dinah "went out to visit the daughters of the land," she was raped by the uncircumcised Shechem, the son of Hamor, the prince of the country (Gen. 34:2). Shimon and Levi, sons of Jacob who were Dinah's full brothers, took revenge by slaughtering the male population of Shechem, carrying off the women and children and taking their goods and livestock as spoil. Jacob condemned their actions, initially based on a fear of reprisal by the local population (Gen. 34:30). On his deathbed, he prophesied that their descendants would be scattered throughout the Land of Israel (Gen. 49:5–7). However, Shimon and Levi justified their behavior by retorting, "Should our sister be treated like a whore?" (Gen. 34:31). The only other biblical mention of Dinah was her being listed among those who went down with Jacob to Egypt (Gen. 46:15).

The sages blamed Dinah for the affair with Shechem, based on an interpretation of the phrase "went out," to imply that she was excessively outgoing and provocative, rather than acting with the proper modesty expected of a patriarch's daughter. Some argued that she never should have left the security of her home without an escort to consort with strangers in an alien city. Another view was that Jacob was to blame for concealing Dinah when he took "his eleven sons" to greet his brother Esau (Gen. 32:23). "Where then was Dinah? Jacob had locked her in a chest, after saying to himself: 'That wicked man [Esau] has lascivious eyes; perhaps he will see her and want to take her away from me [i.e., marry her].' God said, 'Since you have withheld kindness from your brother and were unwilling to give her in a legitimate marriage, she will be married in a forbidden way'" (Gen. R. 76:9). Others maintained that her brothers had to drag Dinah away from Shechem by force. She pleaded, "Where will I take my shame?" and refused to accompany them until Shimon vowed to marry her (Gen. R. 80:11).

According to one view, Job lived during the time of Jacob and married Dinah (BB 15b). Another declared that Dinah's daughter was Asenath, the wife of Joseph (Gen. 41:45). Sent away by Jacob to save her from being killed by his sons, Asenath was found and adopted by Potiphar (Poti-Phera) in Egypt (PdRE 38). *See also* Asenath.

Doeg, the Edomite, a trusted adviser of King Saul.

According to the *aggadah*, among the reasons he was called the Edomite (the red) were: his superior Torah learning enabled him to redden the faces of those shamed at their ignorance; his jealousy and hatred of David (because David, rather than he, was permitted to choose the site for the Temple; Zev. 54b); his permitting the bloodbath at the priestly city of Nob in revenge for its sheltering David when he fled from Saul; his attempt to refute the legitimacy of David as a descendant of Ruth the Moabite; and his causing Saul to sin by failing to shed the blood of Agag in direct disobedience of a Divine command (Mid. Ps. 52:4).

Doeg had a passion for evil speech (JT Pe'ah 1:1). Consequently, he effusively praised David in Saul's presence (1 Sam. 16:18), merely to stoke Saul's anger toward him (Sanh. 93b). Although a Torah scholar (Mid. Ps. 3:5), "Doeg's learning was only from the lips without [i.e., it did not penetrate into his heart and mold his character]" (Sanh. 106b). According to legend, "Three destroying angels appeared before Doeg: one caused him to forget his learning, one burned his soul, and the third scattered his ashes in the synagogues and schoolhouses (Sanh. 106b). Another tradition maintained that he was killed by his students when they saw that he was declaring the *tahor* (ritually clean) as *tamei* (ritually unclean), and vice versa (Yalkut Shimoni, Samuel 131). Like Ahithophel, Doeg was one of those "who set their eyes upon that which was not proper for them; what they sought was not granted to them, and what they possessed was taken from them" (Sot. 9b). He also was described as one of "four commoners who have no share in the World to Come" (Sanh. 10:2).

E

Eber, great-grandson of Shem, and the eponymous ancestor of the Hebrews (children of Eber).

According to the *aggadah*, Eber joined Shem in the *bet midrash* (school for Torah study) where Jacob studied for fourteen years (Meg. 17a).

Ecclesiastes, title figure of the biblical book bearing his name.

The Book of Ecclesiastes is one of the five *megillot* (scrolls) in the Writings section of the Bible and is read in the synagogue on the Festival of Sukkot. The name "Ecclesiastes," which is derived from the Septuagint (Greek translation of the Bible), means "Assembler" or "Convoker"—a reasonably accurate rendering of *Kohelet*, the Hebrew name for the book. Although its composition is traditionally ascribed to the aging and despondent King Solomon, linguistic analysis and content suggest the third century B.C.E. as its likely date.

The author observes that although human beings cannot predict the phenomena of nature nor their personal fate, they are determined in advance by God: "For everything there is a season, a time for every activity under heaven. A time to be born and a time to die, a time to plant and a time to uproot . . . a time to love and a time to hate, a time for war and a time for peace" (Eccles. 3:1–8). Looking back at the end of his life on his many accomplishments and his amassing of numerous possessions, the author grimly concludes that "vanity of vanities . . . all is vanity" (Eccles. 1:2) and "everything was emptiness and chasing after wind, of no profit under the sun" (Eccles. 2:11). Nevertheless, the book ends with the affirmation of an ultimate purpose to life—"Fear God and obey His commandments, for this is the whole of man" (Eccles. 12:13).

The Talmud relates that the sages wished to hide the Book of Ecclesiastes (eliminate it from the biblical canon) "because its words are self-contradictory," but they did not do so because its beginning and end "is religious teaching [lit., 'words of Torah']" (Shab. 30b).

Ehud, son of Gera the Benjamite, and the second judge of Israel (Judg. 3:15–29).

Ehud headed a tribute-bearing delegation to Eglon, king of the Moabites, to whom the Israelites had been subjected for eighteen years. Being left-handed, Ehud wore a sword under his garments on his right thigh, escaping the detection of the guards who were not used to looking there for a suspicious bulge. Ehud gained admittance to the king's private chamber by pretending to be the bearer of a secret message. As Eglon rose as a mark of respect when the Israelite announced that his message came from God, Ehud thrust the dagger into the belly of the corpulent king. Making his escape before the deed was discovered, Ehud sounded the ram's horn for the armies of Israel to gather and led them to victory over the Moabites.

Eldad, one of the two elders (the other was Medad) who "prophesied" in the wilderness encampment of the Israelites.

When the Israelites complained about the lack of meat (Num. 11:4–10), God raged that He would send quails that would be their diet for a month, "until it comes out of your nostrils and becomes loathsome to you" (Num. 11:20). He ordered Moses to gather seventy elders of Israel, to whom God would speak at the Tent of Meeting so they could share the administrative burden of dealing with the people (Num. 11:16–17). Then God increased the Divine spirit that was on Moses and distributed some of it to the seventy elders. "And when the spirit rested upon them, they spoke in ecstasy, but did not continue" (Num. 11:24–25).

According to the *aggadah*, Eldad and Medad were so humble that they thought themselves "not worthy of that dignity" and thus remained in the camp rather than going out with the other elders to the Tent of Meeting. Consequently, God replied that He would "add to your greatness yet more greatness" by allowing them to continue to prophesy after all the others had ceased from this activity (Sanh. 17a). When a young man reported to Moses that "Eldad and Medad are acting the prophet in the camp!" (Num. 11:27), Joshua was furious and sought to incarcerate them, either because of their disrespect in daring to prophesy in the presence of Moses or because of what they said: "Moses shall die and Joshua shall bring Israel into the land" (Sanh. 17a). However, Moses calmed his young lieutenant. "Are you jealous on my account? Would that all the Lord's people were prophets, that the Lord put His spirit upon them!" (Num. 11:29–30).

Eleazar, third son of Aaron and Elisheba.

After the sudden death of his two elder brothers, Nadab and Abihu, who had offered "strange fire" before the Lord (Lev. 10:1–2), Eleazar became the "head chieftain of the Levites" and the principal assistant of his father (Num.

3:32). In his role of being "in charge of those attending to the duties of the Sanctuary," Eleazar supervised "the oil for lighting [the seven-branched menorah], the aromatic incense, the regular grain offering, and the anointing oil." He also had "responsibility for the whole Tabernacle and for everything consecrated that is in it or in its vessels" (Num. 4:16).

When Aaron died, Eleazar succeeded him as high priest (Num. 20:28) and assisted Moses in taking the first census of the Israelites (Num. 26:1–3). Constituting the new leadership following Moses and Aaron, Eleazar and Joshua were responsible for apportioning territory among the tribes after the Israelites conquered the Promised Land (Num. 34:17; Josh. 14:1). As the Talmud relates, "Eleazar was wearing the *Urim and Thumim*, while Joshua and all Israel stood before him. One lottery urn containing the names of the twelve tribes and another with the names of the districts of the Land of Israel were placed before him. Focusing his thoughts through Divine inspiration, Eleazar said: 'Zebulun is coming up and the district Acre is coming up with it.' Then he shook well the urn of the tribes and Zebulun came into his hand. Similarly, he shook well the urn of the districts and picked out the district of Acre." This same procedure was repeated until each territory was apportioned to its appropriate tribe (BB 122a).

The father of the zealous Pinchas (Num. 25:10–13), who was promised "a pact of priesthood for all time" (Num. 25:13), Eleazar was the ancestor of most of the priestly families (1 Chron. 30–40). *See also* Aaron.

Eli, high priest of the line of Ithamar at the central sanctuary at Shiloh and judge over Israel for forty years.

He is best known for wrongly accusing the barren Hannah of being drunk as she fervently prayed for a child (1 Sam. 14). Although the Rabbis considered this an indication that the Holy Spirit (Divine Inspiration) did not rest upon him (Ber. 31b), Eli was the priest into whose care Hannah entrusted her son, Samuel (1 Sam. 1:25).

Although a pious man, Eli was incapable of controlling his "worthless" sons, Hophni and Pinchas, whose wickedness was a disgrace to the family (1 Sam. 2:12–17). When the aged Eli learned that his evil sons were killed accompanying the Ark of the Covenant into battle against the Philistines, confirming the Divine prediction that they would die on the same day, "he fell from off the seat backwards by the side of the gate, and his neck was broken, and he died; for he was an old man, and heavy" (1 Sam. 4:10–18). The descendants of Eli continued as high priests until the time of Solomon, when Abiathar, who had supported the failed bid of Adonijah to become king, was replaced as high priest by Zadok (1 Kings 2:22, 35).

In deducing that a decree accompanied by an oath was never annulled, the Talmud cited the verse: "Therefore I have sworn unto the house of Eli, that the iniquity of Eli's house shall not be expiated with sacrifice nor offering

forever" (1 Sam. 3:14). When faced with the fact that two of the most prominent Rabbis (Rabbah and Abbaye) were both descendants of the house of Eli,
the Talmud explained that the curse may be expiated "with words of Torah"
or "with the practice of lovingkindness" (Yev. 105a).

Eliab, son of Helon and chieftain of the tribe of Zebulun.
Eliab made the third of the twelve identical offerings for the dedication of
the Tabernacle in the wilderness (Num. 7:24–29).

Eliasaph, son of Deuel and chieftain of the tribe of Gad.
Eliasaph made the sixth of the twelve identical offerings for the dedication
of the Tabernacle in the wilderness (Num. 7:42–47).

Eliezer, younger son of Moses and Zipporah.
According to the text, the name meant "the God of my father was my help"
and related to the Divine deliverance of Moses "from the sword of Pharaoh"
(after killing the Egyptian overseer) (Exod. 2:12–15).

Eliezer, chief servant of Abraham.
After the death of Sarah, Abraham sent Eliezer to his ancestral homeland
to find a wife for his son, rather than have Isaac marry one of the "daughters
of the Canaanites among whom I dwell" (Gen. 24:3). Arriving in "Aram-
Naharaim, the city of Nahor," Eliezer stopped with his camels by the well
outside the city and spoke the first prayer recorded in the Bible. He asked
God to bring a kind and generous maiden, who would offer to draw water not
only for this stranger but also for his camels and thus be a suitable wife for
his master's son (Gen. 24:12–14). "He had scarcely finished speaking" when
Rebecca came to the well and Eliezer's prayer was answered. After Rebecca
successfully passed the test of compassion, Eliezer's first question to Isaac's
future wife was, "Whose daughter are you?" (Gen. 24:23). The Rabbis interpreted this verse as stressing the importance of a bride's lineage, observing
that before marriage "one should pay close attention to the wife's brothers,
because her children will probably be like them." Although in biblical times
parents usually arranged marriages, Eliezer asked Rebecca if she would agree
to travel to Canaan to marry Isaac (Gen. 24:58).
The biblical text describes Eliezer as the one "who *controlled* all that was
his [Abraham's]" (Gen. 24:2). One *aggadic* interpretation was that this meant
that Eliezer had "controlled" (i.e., mastered) the teachings of Abraham. As
wordplay on his full name, Eliezer of Damascus (*damshek*), the Talmud suggests that Eliezer would draw (*doleh*) from his master's teachings and give
drink (*mashkeh*) to others from them (Yoma 28b). In another play on words,

as the elder (*zakein*) of the household, who had acquired wisdom through study, Eliezer's countenance (*ziv ikunin*) resembled that of Abraham and thus he could "control" his evil inclinations like his master (Gen. R. 59:8).

When Eliezer once was in Sodom, he was attacked and wounded by an inhabitant of the city. Eliezer appeared before the judge, who declared that Eliezer must pay his attacker a fee for bloodletting. Immediately, Eliezer took a stone and struck the judge, saying: "The fee that you now owe me, pay to the man who attacked me, while my money will remain with me." The men of Sodom had a special bed for travelers. If the guest was too long for the bed, they shortened him by cutting off his feet; if too short, they stretched him out. When Eliezer chanced to visit Sodom, they invited him to sleep on that bed. Eliezer replied, "Since the day my mother died, I vowed never to sleep in a bed." The people of Sodom agreed that if a poor man came to their city, every resident gave him a dinar, upon which he wrote his name, but no bread was given him. When the poor visitor died, each came and took back his money. Another mutual agreement was that anyone who invited a stranger to a feast would be stripped of his clothes. When Eliezer came to Sodom, they would not sell him bread. Seeing that a banquet was in progress, the hungry Eliezer sat down at the end of the table. When they asked who had invited him, Eliezer replied: "The person sitting next to me." Fearing that his clothes would be taken away, that person promptly left. So it went with each in turn, until the place was empty and Eliezer ate the entire feast (Sanh. 109b).

Elijah, Tishbite from Gilead, east of the Jordan, and the foremost prophet of the Northern Kingdom.

Elijah was active during the reign of Ahab (874–853 B.C.E.), who "did what is evil in the eyes of the Lord." Ahab had married the wicked Phoenician princess Jezebel and permitted her to build a pagan altar and sanctuary to Baal. A gaunt figure clothed in goatskin, Elijah prophesied drought as a punishment for this idolatry. Forced to flee for his life, Elijah disappeared into the desert, where he was fed by ravens that brought food to the righteous from the table of Jehosaphat rather than that from the house of the wicked Ahab (Num. R. 23:9). When the people cried out for rain, Ahab still refused to forbid idol worship. In a dramatic confrontation on Mount Carmel (1 Kings 18), Elijah issued a challenge to the 450 priests of Baal—both he and they would each build an altar and lay a burnt offering upon it. The deity who sent down fire from heaven to consume the sacrifice would be accepted as the true God. For hours the priests vainly beseeched Baal, but received no response. Then Elijah mocked them: "'Shout louder, for he is a god; he may be talking, or he may be detained, or he has gone on a journey, or perhaps he is asleep and must be awakened.' And they shouted louder, and cut themselves with knives and spears as was their custom, until the blood streamed over them" (1 Kings 18:27–28). When it was almost time for the evening sacrifice, Elijah had a trench dug around the altar and ordered the people to pour water over the burnt offering until it filled the space. Elijah called on God to send down a heavenly fire so that "this people may know that you are the Lord God." Then the "fire of the Lord fell and consumed the burnt sacrifice, the woodpile, the stones, and the earth" (1 Kings 18:38). Witnessing this awesome sight, all the people fell on their faces chanting, "The Lord, He [alone] is God; the Lord, He [alone] is God." A heavy rain then fell and the drought ended.

Despite this triumph, Elijah was forced to flee the wrath of Jezebel and came to Horeb, the mountain of God. While hiding in a cave, "the word of the Lord" came to Elijah and ordered him to go out onto the mountain. "And, behold, the Lord passed by"—but God was not manifest in the great and mighty wind that split the mountains and shattered the rocks, nor in the subsequent earthquake or fire, but only in the "still small voice." When asked why he had come to this sacred place, Elijah replied: "I have been very zealous for the Lord, God of Hosts; because the Israelites have forsaken Your covenant, torn down Your altars, and killed Your prophets with the sword. I alone am left; and they are out to take my life" (1 Kings 19:11–14). God commanded Elijah to anoint a foreign enemy of Israel (Hazael) as king of Aram, a new Israelite king (Jehu) to rival Ahab, and a successor as prophet (Elisha). "And it shall come to pass, that he [the idolater] who escapes the sword of Hazael shall Jehu slay; and he who escapes from the sword of Jehu shall Elisha slay" (1 Kings 19:15–17). Having passed the mantle to Elisha, Elijah departed the scene (2 Kings 2:2).

Elijah appears in numerous Talmudic legends. Rabbah bar Abbuha met the prophet and complained that his poverty forced him to work so hard to eke out a living that he could not concentrate properly on his studies. "Elijah took him into the Garden of Eden and ordered him to fill the pocket of his cloak with leaves. As he was leaving, the sage heard a voice say: 'Who is consuming [his reward in the World to Come] like Rabbah bar Abbuha has done [i.e., miraculous assistance in this world is deducted from the reward in the future world]?' Immediately, he shook the leaves out of his pocket and threw them away. However, since he had carried the leaves in his cloak, the garment had absorbed their fragrance from the Garden of Eden. So he sold the cloak for 12,000 dinars and distributed [the money] among his sons-in-law" (BM 114b). He did not give the money to his own sons, because that still would be considered of benefit to him since they were his heirs.

As is the message of the biblical Book of Job, the Rabbis stressed that human beings can have only an extremely limited comprehension of God's ways. In a famous story, R. Joshua ben Levi asked to accompany Elijah on his wanderings and gain wisdom by observing his deeds. The prophet warned that Joshua ben Levi would be shocked by what he saw and would want to barrage him with questions, but if the sage asked even one question about the miracles Elijah would perform, he would have to return to his home. The two soon arrived at the hut of a poor couple, who invited them in, gave them food and drink, and asked them to stay the night. In the morning, Elijah prayed to God that the poor man's cow die, and this promptly occurred. When the heartbroken Joshua ben Levi began to ask why this was the reward for the poor couple's gracious hospitality, Elijah warned his companion of his agreement to ask no questions. The next night they stayed at the home of a wealthy man, who refused to feed or treat them in a respectful manner. When they departed in the morning, Elijah prayed that a crumbling wall of the house be rebuilt immediately, and it was so. Joshua ben Levi was angry at this injustice, but held his peace. The next evening they lodged in the synagogue of a wealthy town, whose most important members had arranged to sit on silver benches. However, when one asked the other who would provide for the poor visitors that night, the latter contemptuously retorted that Joshua and Elijah should be content with their bread, water, and salt. Yet the next morning Elijah blessed the rich members of the synagogue that they all become leaders. That night, they were cordially welcomed in a different community, given the best food, and treated with the utmost respect. The next morning Elijah blessed them, praying that God set only one leader over them. Joshua ben Levi could no longer keep quiet and demanded an explanation for Elijah's seemingly senseless actions. The prophet explained that, learning that heaven had decreed that the wife of the poor man whose cow died would die that same day, he had prayed that God would accept the cow as a redemption for the wife's life. Had he not prayed that the miser's wall be rebuilt before it collapsed, the miser would have dug down to the foundation and discovered there a treasure of gold and silver. Elijah prayed that the hard-hearted wealthy members of the first synagogue all become leaders, since this would inevitably result in dissension and strife, leading to the breakup of the community. Conversely, his prayer that the other community have only one head was for their benefit, since all would follow him and prosper. Elijah concluded that human beings should never wonder about Divine justice when a wicked man appears to thrive or a righteous one to suffer, for God alone is omniscient and supervises all the deeds of men.

When the Talmudic sages had a difference of opinion and could not arrive at a decision, they tabled the discussion by deferring it "until the appearance of Elijah the prophet." Elijah was described as the comforter of the poor and the suffering, appearing miraculously when the need was greatest. To this day, a special cup for Elijah is filled with wine at the Passover seder. Because

Elijah is said to appear at every circumcision to determine whether this child will be the long-awaited Messiah, a special chair is left for the prophet. In the Grace after Meals, Elijah is described as the bearer of good tidings for the Jewish people.

According to tradition, Elijah did not die but was carried to heaven in a fiery chariot pulled by horses of fire (2 Kings 2:11). The prophet was portrayed as eventually descending from heaven to usher in the Messianic age. In the words of Malachi, the final prophet: "Lo, I will send the prophet to you before the coming of the great and awesome day of the Lord. He shall reconcile parents with their children, and children with their parents" (Mal. 3:23). However, the Messiah will only come when we are ready. The Talmud relates that R. Joshua ben Levi asked Elijah when the Messiah would come. The prophet replied, "Go and ask him." When the sage asked how he would recognize the Messiah, Elijah answered: "He is disguised as a filthy beggar, sitting among the lepers, untying and retying his bandages." He then asked Elijah, "When will you come and proclaim the Messiah?" Elijah replied, "Today, if you will only hear His voice [and obey the will of God]" (Sanh. 98a). *See also* Jezebel.

Elimelech, husband of Naomi and father of Mahlon and Hilion.

"A man of Bethlehem in Judah in the days of the judges," Elimelech moved with his family to reside in Moab during a time of famine (Ruth 1:2). There he died, and his elder son Mahlon married Ruth (Ruth 1:4). According to some Rabbis, Elimelech was one of the leaders of his generation, and his premature death was a punishment for leaving the Land of Israel to settle on foreign soil. Even if the economic conditions are bad or there is a famine, "One is not permitted to move away from the Land of Israel unless produce cannot be purchased even at inflated prices." If produce is available but only more expensive, one should not leave the Land since there are many *mitzvot* that can be fulfilled only there (BB 91a). Other Rabbis disagreed, saying that Elimelech and his sons were punished because they should have offered special prayers that the famine would cease for the entire generation. Had they done so, God would have saved them together with the community (BB 91b). An *aggadah* describes Elimelech as one of the great men and providers of the generation. However, when the famine began, he thought, "Now all Israel will come to my door, each asking for a donation," and consequently he fled from them (Ruth R. 1:4).

Eliphaz, name of two possibly identical biblical figures.

The first was the oldest son of Esau and his wife Adah, who was the ancestor of several Edomite clans. The most important of these were Teman, which was used poetically as a synonym for "Edom" (Jer. 49:7; Obad. 9) and Amalek (Gen. 36:2, 10–12, 15–16). The other, known as Eliphaz the Yemenite (Temanite), was the oldest of the three friends who comforted Job. The *aggadah* relates that Eliphaz spent little time with his father Esau, becoming a righteous man deserving of Divine inspiration because he had been a disciple of Isaac. Ordered by Esau to attack the sons of Jacob, Eliphaz refused to fight them because he had grown up with the righteous Job.

Timna, a royal daughter who wished to convert, came to Abraham, Isaac, and Jacob but they did not accept her. So she became a concubine of Eliphaz, the son of Esau, and gave birth to Amalek, the archenemy of the Jewish people (Sanh. 99b). Amalek once asked his father, Eliphaz the Yemenite, "Who will inherit this world and the World to Come?" Eliphaz replied, "The Children of Israel. Go out and dig wells and fix roads for them. If you do so, your share will be with the lowly among them, and you will enter the World to Come" (Yalkut Shimoni, Exodus 268).

At the end of days, Eliphaz will be one of those who "testify that Israel has observed the whole Torah" (Av. Zar. 3a).

Elisha, Israelite prophet (ninth century B.C.E.), who was the devoted servant and outstanding disciple of Elijah.

Continuing his master's efforts to rid Israel of Baal worship, Elisha instigated a revolt against King Jehoram, the son of Ahab. This succeeded in destroying Jehoram, his mother (Jezebel, the idolatrous queen), and the priests of Baal.

A peerless miracle worker, Elisha was said to have purified the waters of Jericho (2 Kings 2:19), multiplied the oil so that a poor widow could pay her debts and keep her children from being sold into slavery (2 Kings 4:1–7), resurrected the son of a Shunammite woman whose birth he had predicted as a reward for her hospitality (2 Kings 4:8–37), and healed a Syrian captain (Naaman) of leprosy (2 Kings 5:1–19). On one occasion, however, Elisha called down two she-bears to attack the forty-two children who had mocked his baldness (2 Kings 2:24). The Talmud offers several rationales for this action. Elisha saw that neither they nor their descendants had any trace of good deeds within them; their mothers had all conceived on Yom Kippur (when marital relations are strictly prohibited); and their hair was plaited like idolaters (Sot. 46b).

The many stories of Elisha's miracle working reflected the people's love for this prophet, who healed the sick and helped the poor. *See also* Gehazi.

Elishama, son of Ammihud and chieftain of the tribe of Ephraim.

Elishama made the seventh of the twelve identical offerings for the dedication of the Tabernacle in the wilderness (Num. 7:48–53).

Elisheba, wife of Aaron, and the mother of his four sons—Nadab, Abihu, Eleazar, and Ithamar.

The biblical text describes Elisheba as the daughter of Amminadab and the sister of Nachshon (Exod. 6:23). Because the second relationship would seem to be obvious from the first, Rava inferred an underlying teaching: "A man who [wishes] to take a wife should inquire about [the character of] her brothers" (BB 110a), because "most children resemble the brothers of the mother" (Soph. 15:20). According to a minority *aggadic* tradition (Sot. 11b), Elisheba and her mother-in-law Jochebed were the Hebrew midwives, Shiphrah and Puah, who bravely refused to obey Pharaoh's order to kill all the newborn Israelite boys (Exod. 1:15).

The Talmud notes that "Elisheba had five joys more than the other daughters of Israel" on the day the Tabernacle was dedicated. "Her brother-in-law [Moses] was a king, her husband [Aaron] was a high priest, her son [Eleazar] was *segan* [deputy high priest], her grandson [Pinchas] was anointed [as deputy high priest to lead the army for battle], and her brother [Nachshon] was the prince of his tribe; yet she mourned her two sons [Nadab and Abihu]" (Zev. 102a).

Elizur, son of Shedeur and chieftain of the tribe of Reuben.

Elizur made the fourth of the twelve identical offerings for the dedication of the Tabernacle in the wilderness (Num. 7:30–35).

Elkanah, father of Samuel.

Elkanah lived in Ramah at the southern end of Mount Ephraim, and the Bible traces his lineage back to Kohath, the son of Levi (1 Chron. 6:7–8). Elkanah had two wives, Hannah and Peninah. The former, who was childless for many years, made a vow to the Lord at Shiloh and then bore Elkanah a son, Samuel, whom she dedicated to the service of God.

According to the *aggadah*, Elkanah was the outstanding righteous man of his generation. He did not marry Peninah until he had lived with Hannah for ten years without having any children (Yalkut Shimoni, Samuel 89). Elkanah made a pilgrimage to Shiloh four times a year—three times on the pilgrimage festivals (Passover, Shavuot, and Sukkot), and once for his personal thanksgiving to God. En route, he and his extended family would stay overnight in the city square. When passersby asked where they were going, Elkanah and his relatives would answer that their destination was the House of God in Shiloh, from which the Torah and the commandments come, and invite them to go with them. Each year, more and more families joined them in the pilgrimage to Shiloh. Moreover, on each of their four yearly visits Elkanah and his family would take a different route, so that progressively more Israelites would go with them. Because his efforts led many people to earn merit through observance of the commandments, God promised that the balance of the scales would also tip in Israel's favor through the actions of Elkanah's son.

En Dor (Witch of), necromancer consulted by King Saul.

En Dor was a city in Lower Galilee, south of Nazareth. After the death of Samuel, "when Saul saw the camp of the Philistines, he was afraid, and his heart greatly trembled. But when Saul inquired of the Lord, the Lord did not answer him, neither by dreams, nor by *Urim*, nor by prophets [the ordinary oracles to discover the Divine will]" (1 Sam. 28:3–6). In desperate straits, Saul learned that there was a woman who possessed a talisman by which she could invoke the dead. When the disguised king came to her at night, she was reluctant to ply her trade for him: "Behold, you know what Saul has done, how he has expelled mediums and wizards, from the land; why then do you lay a snare for my life, to cause me to die?" Assured by Saul that she would not be punished, the woman agreed to summon the spirit of Samuel—who appeared to her as "an old man covered with a mantle." After the surly Samuel voiced a complaint at being disturbed, Saul pleaded that he was in mortal danger and had been abandoned by God. In response, Samuel offered Saul no comfort: "Why do you ask me, seeing that the Lord has departed from you, and has become your adversary? . . . For the Lord has torn the kingdom from your hands, and given it to your fellow, to David, because you did not obey the Lord, and did not execute his wrath upon the Amalekites. That is why the Lord has done this to you today. Moreover, the Lord will deliver the Israelites who are with you into the hands of the Philistines. Tomorrow you and your sons will be with me [i.e., dead]." Stunned by this disastrous prediction, Saul collapsed in a faint. After he revived, Saul left the Witch of En Dor—and as predicted he and three of his sons died in the battle of Gilboa.

Although the Witch of En Dor was not named in the text, the *aggadah* identifies her as Zephaniah, the mother of Abner. According to the Rabbis, when a person dies, the soul leaves the body. However, for the first twelve months the soul retains a temporary relationship to the body, coming and going until the body has disintegrated. Thus the Witch of En Dor was able to raise the prophet Samuel from the dead within the first year of his demise.

Enoch, son of Jared, and the father of Methusaleh.

Enoch was the seventh in the list of the ten generations from Adam to Noah. Unlike Lamech, the seventh in the line of Cain, who was associated with bloodshed, Enoch was described as a pious figure. Enoch lived for 365 years, corresponding to the number of days in the solar year. He was said to have "walked with God; then he was no more, for God took him" (Gen. 5:24), suggesting that Enoch did not die, but rather ascended alive to heaven, like the prophet Elijah. This mystical and esoteric interpretation led to Enoch being the reputed author of several apocalyptic works dating from the Second Temple period. Indeed, Enoch became a significant figure in the Jewish spiritual movement that gave rise to the Dead Sea sect.

According to the *aggadah*, Enoch was one of nine righteous men who entered paradise without suffering the pangs of death. The Sefer ha-Yashar related that, while living in a secret place, angels called Enoch to teach the Divine ways to human beings. They were so profoundly moved by his teachings that they made him their ruler and enjoyed more than two centuries of peace and prosperity. As a reward, God determined to also place Enoch as king over the angels, ordering that he ascend to heaven in a fiery chariot. Rejecting the complaint of the angels that a mortal rule over them, God urged them not to be offended. He explained that when human beings had denied Him and worshiped idols, God withdrew His Presence (*Shechinah*) from earth to heaven, with Enoch being "the elect of men." God clad Enoch in a magnificent garment and glowing crown, gave him entry to all the gates of wisdom, and made him the head of the heavenly hosts. Renaming him "Metatron," God transformed his body into a flame and surrounded him with storm, whirlwind, and thunder.

Some more rationalistic Jewish sages opposed this mystical view, portraying Enoch as a generally righteous man who was liable to lapses in his piety. To prevent him from going astray, God cut Enoch's life short, removing him from the world before sin could overcome him—as evidenced by the biblical description that "he was no more," rather than the usual "he died" (Gen. R. 25:1). This more critical assessment of Enoch may have been a polemic against the Christian use of the legend of Enoch's miraculous ascent to heaven.

Enosh, eldest son of Seth, and the grandson of Adam.

Born when Seth was 105 years old, Enosh ("man or mankind" in Hebrew) lived to the age of 905 (Gen. 5:11). The single ambiguous biblical verse (Gen. 4:26) describing the generation of Enosh can be translated, "It was then that men began to invoke the Lord by name," an expression referring to the worship of God. However, most read it as, "Then to call in the name of God became profaned," meaning that it was this generation that introduced idolatry to the world. Supporting this latter view, the *aggadah* indicated that four dramatic changes occurred during the days of Enosh: "The slopes of the mountains turned rocky and barren, unfit for plowing; corpses putrefied and generated worms; the faces of human beings became apelike, rather than

God-like; and because the Divine image had departed from men, demons lost their fear of human beings and were able to attack them" (Gen. R. 23:6).

Ephraim, younger son of Joseph.

According to the Bible, Ephraim was given his name by Joseph because "God has made me fertile in the land of my affliction [i.e., in Egypt, where he spent thirteen years in captivity]" (Gen. 41:52). It was also an indication of the future territory of the tribe of Ephraim in the Land of Israel, which was located in the central hill country and blessed with a fertile soil and good rainfall. The bull on the flag of Ephraim was based on the verse, "Like a firstling bull in his majesty" (Deut. 33:17), which the *aggadah* said was a reference to Joshua, who came from this tribe (Num. R. 2:8).

Before his death, Jacob adopted both Ephraim and his older brother Manasseh as his sons, declaring that they "shall be mine no less than Reuben and Shimon," the first two sons of Jacob, thereby making certain that each would become the ancestor of an entire Israelite tribe (Gen. 48:5). Jacob gave Ephraim a greater blessing than his older brother, thus according greater prominence and importance to his tribe. One of the descendants of Ephraim was Jeroboam, the first king of the breakaway Northern Kingdom after the death of Solomon (1 Kings 11:26). Consequently, this name later became a popular alternative to Israel in designating the land of these ten northern tribes.

On Sabbath eve, fathers traditionally invoke a blessing over their sons that God make them "like Ephraim and Manasseh." These two sons of Joseph had the courage and commitment to maintain their Jewish heritage, despite both the antagonism and allure of Egyptian culture and society—a valuable trait during the millennia of dispersion when Jewish parents prayed that their sons would show a similar dedication to the tradition.

Ephron, son of Zohar the Hittite.

After the death of Sarah, Abraham wanted to purchase a burial place for his wife in Hebron (Gen. 23). As a resident alien, he first asked for permission from "the people of the land" (community leaders or a general assembly of citizens of the city) to directly approach the owner of the plot he wished to purchase. They approved his request to bargain with Ephron the Hittite to buy the Cave of Machpelah. In the initial stage of the negotiations, Ephron offered the cave and the surrounding field as a gift, but Abraham insisted on purchasing it to ensure a permanent gravesite for himself and his family. Ephron then indirectly indicated the sale price: "My lord, do hear me! A piece of land worth 400 shekels of silver—what is that between you and me? Go and bury your dead." Abraham accepted Ephron's terms and paid in full. "So

Ephron's cave in Machpelah, near Mamre—the field with its cave and all the trees anywhere within the confines of that field—passed to Abraham as his possession."

An understanding of Hittite law gives additional perspective to this narrative. Rather than the emphasis being on the purchase price, the negotiations actually focused on the quantity of land to be bought. The duty of the owner of land to perform feudal obligations to the ruler passed to the purchaser only if the entire property was bought from the current owner. Therefore, Abraham wanted to purchase solely the Cave of Machpelah as a burial plot so as not to incur any feudal obligations. Conversely, Ephron wanted to sell the entire field for the same reason, effectively insisting that Abraham buy all or nothing. "Since Abraham had on his hands a corpse requiring burial, he had no time for protracted negotiations; instead he yielded and bought the land on Ephron's terms." The specification of the trees in the agreement also was consistent with land sale contracts among the Hittites and elsewhere in the ancient Near East.

Er, firstborn son of Judah, brother of Onan, and husband of Tamar.

Although no specific sin was noted, Er "was displeasing to the Lord, and the Lord took his life" (Gen. 38:7) before he was able to sire a child. *See also* Onan.

Esau, son of Isaac and Rebecca, and the elder twin of Jacob.

Described as having "emerged red, like a hairy mantle all over" (Gen. 25:25), the name Esau may be related to the Hebrew word *se'ir* (hairy). It also was a word play on the land of Seir, known as Edom, and an alternate name for Esau that derived from the Hebrew word *adom* (red). Even while in the womb, Esau and Jacob struggled with each other, and God predicted to Rebecca that "the older shall serve the younger" (Gen. 25:22–23). Although he lived among two righteous people, Isaac and Rebecca, Esau failed to learn from their good deeds (Yoma 38b).

Esau grew up to be "a skillful hunter, a man of the outdoors" (Gen. 25:27) and the favorite of his father, Isaac. One day when he was returning from the fields, the famished Esau begged Jacob to give him some of the "red stuff" he was cooking (Gen. 25:29), which, according to the Bible, "was why he was named Edom [red]." A *midrash* relates that this day was the funeral of Abraham, and Jacob was preparing for Isaac a dish of lentil stew, the usual meal offered to mourners. Jacob agreed to give some to the tired and ravenous Esau, as long as the firstborn Esau would sell him his birthright. The Rabbis stated that the wicked Esau was exhausted because he had committed five crimes the day of Abraham's funeral: "He violated a betrothed maiden, committed murder, and denied God and the resurrection of the dead." Finally, dramatically claiming "I am at the point of death, so of what use is my birthright to me?" Esau "spurned his birthright" (BB 16b). Later Esau married two Hittite women, which angered his parents and clearly indicated that he was not a worthy heir to the patriarchal tradition (Gen. 26:34–35).

When the blind Isaac lay on his deathbed and wanted to give his major blessing to his elder son, he asked Esau to hunt some game and prepare a delicious dish of venison (Gen. 27:1). Overhearing their conversation, Rebecca devised a scheme to substitute Jacob for Esau, so that Isaac's blessing would be given to her favorite son. When Esau returned to his father and learned of the deception, "he burst into wild and bitter sobbing" and begged for Isaac to bless him as well. Although his father answered, "See, your abode shall enjoy the fat of the earth and the dew of the heaven above," he added, "Yet by your sword you shall live, and you shall serve your brother; but when you grow restive, you shall break his yoke from your neck" (Gen. 27:39–40).

Filled with venomous hatred for his brother, Esau plotted to kill Jacob at the end of the period of mourning for their father (Gen. 27:41). Learning of this plan, Rebecca urged Jacob to flee to her family in Haran, using as an excuse her fear that otherwise Jacob would also marry out of the clan. Twenty years later, Jacob returned and the brothers reconciled: "Esau ran to greet him. He embraced him and, falling on his neck, he kissed him; and they wept" (Gen. 33:4). The Hebrew word for "and he kissed him" is dotted in the Masoretic text, which led some commentators to argue that Esau (whom the Rabbis viewed as the unrepentant epitome of evil) actually tried to bite his brother and kill him by sucking his blood. However, Jacob's neck miraculously turned to marble, and Esau wept because he injured his teeth (Gen. R. 78).

Esau's death is not mentioned in the Bible. According to one legend, it occurred when Esau quarreled with Jacob's sons over their right to bury their father in the last remaining gravesite in the Cave of Machpelah. Joseph invoked the "bill of sale" witnessed between Jacob and Esau after Isaac's death, and he sent Naphtali racing to Egypt to fetch the document. Before he returned, Esau unsuccessfully took up arms to prevent his brother from receiving this honor, but was killed by a son of Dan (Sot. 13a).

"Why did Esau come out of the womb first? So that he might take all the blood and other offensive matter with him. Like the bath attendant who first scours the bath and then washes the king's son, so also did Esau issue first so that he might come out together with the unpleasant material. A matron asked this question to R. Jose ben Halafta, who answered: 'Because the first drop [of semen] was Jacob's. If you place two diamonds in a tube, does not the one put in first come out last? So also the first drop was that which formed Jacob'" (Gen. R. 63:8).

Interpreting the biblical verse, "And the boys grew" (Gen. 25:27), R. Pinchas said in the name of R. Levi: "They were like a myrtle and a wild rose bush growing side by side. When they became mature, one yielded fragrance and the other its thorns. So for thirteen years both went to school and came home from school. After this age, one went to the house of study and the other to idolatrous shrines." R. Eliezer ben Shimon said, "A man is responsible for his son until the age of thirteen (to have him educated in Torah); thereafter, he must say, 'Blessed is He who has now freed me from the responsibility of this boy'" (Gen. R. 63:10).

As Isaac lay dying, Esau acted with deliberation: "Why should I grieve my father? After the mourning period, then will I slay Jacob." According to the Rabbis, Esau reasoned that if he himself killed his brother, "Shem and Eber will sit in judgment upon me. Therefore, it will be better for me to marry Ishmael's daughter so that he [Ishmael] will come and dispute the birthright [on behalf of his daughter] and kill him [Isaac]. Then I will then kill Ishmael as a blood avenger and thus become the heir of two families" (Gen. R. 67:8). *See also* Nimrod.

Esther, heroine of the Purim story.

After banishing Queen Vashti for refusing to obey his command to appear before him and his guests at the royal banquet, King Ahasuerus ordered the most beautiful maidens in the kingdom to be brought before him in the ancient Persian equivalent of a beauty pageant. After Esther was selected to be the new queen, her cousin Mordechai told her not to reveal her Jewish origins. When Mordechai offended Haman by refusing to bow down to him, the grand vizier of the land plotted to kill him and all his people. Hearing of the plot, Mordechai tore his clothes and sat in sackcloth and ashes at the entrance to the palace. When Esther learned of the situation, she was "greatly agitated" and sent a servant to investigate. The servant returned with a copy of the royal edict and instructions from Mordechai that she should beg the king for mercy on behalf of her people. Esther sent a message to Mordechai explaining that anyone appearing before the king without being summoned was punishable by death, and Ahasuerus had not called her for thirty days. Mordechai replied, "Do not imagine that you, of all the Jews, will escape with your life by being in the king's palace. On the contrary, if you keep silent in this crisis, relief and deliverance will come to the Jews from another quarter, while you and your father's house will perish. And who knows, perhaps you have attained a royal position for just such a crisis" (Esth. 4:12–14). Chastened by his words, Esther sent back an answer to Mordechai, asking him to assemble all the Jews in Shushan, the Persian capital, and have them fast on her behalf for three days and nights, as would Esther and her maidens. "Then

I shall go to the king, even if contrary to the law; and if I am to perish, I shall perish!" (Esth. 4:16).

When Esther appeared before the king, Ahasuerus was delighted to see her and asked what she might request of him. "Even to half the kingdom, it shall be granted to you" (Esth. 5:3). Esther invited the king and Haman to dine with her that evening and the following one as well. When at the second banquet Ahasuerus again asked what he could do for his beautiful queen, Esther revealed her Jewish origins and requested that the king grant that her life and that of her people be spared. "We have been sold, my people and I, to be destroyed, massacred, and exterminated." Shocked by Esther's words, Ahasuerus asked who would dare to do this. "The adversary and enemy," replied Esther, "is the evil Haman!" (Esth. 7:5–6). The outraged Ahasuerus ordered Haman and his ten sons to be hung on gallows that had been prepared for Mordechai and granted the Jews the right to defend themselves against their enemies. According to the Book of Esther, on the thirteenth day of Adar, the Jews battled successfully against those who attempted to destroy them. "And they rested on the fourteenth day and made it a day of feasting and merrymaking" (Esth. 9:17). This celebration became the yearly festival of Purim, so named because Haman had cast the lot (*pur*) to determine the date for the destruction of the Jews, yet he failed to destroy them. As the Talmud notes, the miracle of Esther was the last miracle recorded in the Bible (Yoma 29a).

According to the Talmud, Esther was one of the four most beautiful women in the world (Meg. 15a), one of the seven prophetesses (Meg. 14a), and a symbol of female modesty. Although her Hebrew name was Hadassah (myrtle), non-Jews called her Esther, a name derived from Ishtar ("beautiful as the moon"), the Persian equivalent of Venus, the Goddess of Beauty. Another explanation was that the name Esther derived from the Hebrew word *seter* (hidden), a foreshadowing of her ability to disguise her Jewish identity until she had won the heart of King Ahasuerus and thus was in a position to save her people from destruction.

The Rabbis said that her father died when Esther was conceived, and her mother died when Esther was born (Meg. 13a). Brought up by her cousin Mordechai, Esther was described as "his [Mordechai's] uncle's daughter" (Esth. 2:7). In the royal palace, Esther did not dine from the king's table, rather eating her own food in order to observe the Jewish dietary laws (Yalkut Shimoni, Esther 1053).

R. Akiva once was lecturing and the congregation became drowsy. Wishing to arouse them, he remarked: "Why did Esther deserve to reign over 127 provinces [as the queen of Ahasuerus]? . . . Because she was a descendant of Sarah, who lived 127 years" (Gen. R. 58:3). *See also* Ahasuerus; Haman; Mordechai.

Eve, first woman, wife of Adam, and the mother of Cain, Abel, and Seth.

According to the text, Adam gave her the Hebrew name *havah* (life/living), because she was the mother of all the living" (Gen. 3:20). Others have suggested that Eve's name comes from Aramaic and Arabic words for "snake," a foreshadowing of the source of her future downfall.

Because "it is not good for man to be alone," God decided to "make a fitting helper for him" (Gen. 2:18). When Adam could find no one appropriate from the beasts of the field and the fowl of the air, God caused a deep sleep to fall upon the man and fashioned her from his *tzela* (Gen. 2:20–22). Although traditionally translated as "rib," many modern commentators prefer "side." Rav argued that the Hebrew word *tzela* means a "face," with the first human being originally created with male and female halves (hermaphrodite). Samuel disagreed, saying that it was a "tail" (i.e., a superfluous part) (Ber. 61a). Seeing Eve for the first time, Adam welcomed her as "bone of my bones, flesh of my flesh" and "called [her] Woman [*ishah*], for from Man [*ish*] she was taken" (Gen. 2:23). In Hebrew, the difference in spelling between *ish* and *ishah* is the addition of the letter *yud* to the former and the letter *hei* to the latter. The Rabbis interpreted this as meaning that as long as a marriage is happy and the spouses respect each other's needs, the Divine Name (*Yud-Hei*) protects them against all harm. If not, the Divine Name will be withdrawn, leaving only the letters *aleph-shin* (fire), which will utterly consume them (Sot. 17a; PdRE 12).

The Talmud relates that God fashioned Eve like a storehouse, narrow on top and broad at the bottom, so that it could best contain its produce (i.e., a fetus) (Ber. 61a). A *midrash* reports that ten brilliant, jewel-covered bridal canopies were fashioned for Eve by God, who gave her away in marriage, served as the best man, and pronounced the blessings, while angels danced, played music instruments, and stood guard over the bridal chamber (PdRE 12). Stressing the importance of marriage, the Bible adds: "Therefore, a man leaves his father and mother and clings to his wife, so that they become one flesh" (Gen. 2:24).

Why did God form woman from the rib/side of man (Gen. 2:21–22)? According to a *midrash*, God determined not to create her from the head, lest she hold up her head too proudly; nor from the eye, lest she be too curious; nor from the ear, lest she be an eavesdropper; nor from the mouth, lest she be a gossip; nor from the heart, lest she be prone to jealousy; nor from the hand, lest she be too acquisitive; nor from the foot, lest she be a gadabout; but from a part of the body that is hidden (bone is covered even when she stands naked), so that she should be modest. However, the Rabbis did not believe that the Divine goal was achieved, since they accused women of having the precise faults that God wanted to avoid: "Four qualities are ascribed to women: they are gluttonous, eavesdroppers, lazy, and jealous. They also are querulous and garrulous" (Gen. R. 18:2). The Talmud adds, "Ten measures of gossip descended to the world; nine were taken by women" (Kid. 49b).

A *midrash* asks, "Why must a woman wear perfume, while a man does not need it? Man was created from dust, which never putrifies and smells, but woman was created from bone [and meat rots if left unsalted for three days]. Why does a woman have a shrill voice, but not a man? If you fill a pot with meat it does not make any sound; but when you put a bone into it, the sound of sizzling spreads immediately. Why is a man easily appeased, but not a woman? Man was created from the earth, and it immediately absorbs a drop of water poured on it. But Eve was created from a bone, which even if you soak it many days in water does not become saturated" (Gen. R. 17:8).

While living in the idyllic Garden of Eden, Eve was tempted by the snake to eat of the forbidden fruit from the Tree of Knowledge of Good and Evil (Gen. 3:1–6). According to the *aggadah*, the snake (which then had almost the shape of a man; Gen. R. 19:1) led Eve to disobey this Divine command either because of his lustful desire to possess her (Sot. 9), or because he was jealous of the special status granted to human beings. Seduced by his persuasive arguments, Eve tasted the forbidden fruit and gave some to Adam to eat. According to the Rabbis, Eve initially hesitated to eat the fruit itself, only doing so after touching the tree and discovering that no harm befell her. She immediately saw the Angel of Death and, fearing that she would soon die, decided to convince Adam to eat the forbidden fruit lest he take another wife after her death (PdRE 13). "Then the eyes of both of them were opened and they perceived that they were naked; and they sewed together fig leaves and made themselves loincloths." When God questioned them, neither Adam nor Eve was willing to accept responsibility and both received punishment. Women, as represented by Eve, were to suffer in childbirth and be subservient to their husbands. Eve had previously conceived and given birth immediately and painlessly (Sforno). However, from this time on conception would not be automatic—witness the difficulties experienced by Sarah and Rachel—and there would be an extended period of pregnancy and labor. However, according the Talmud, "Righteous women were not included in the decree against Eve and thus experience painless childbirth" (Sot. 12a). Just as Eve had influenced her husband to eat at her command, so now she would become subservient to his demands (Nachmanides). As for Adam, he would be forced to work hard to sustain himself: "By the sweat of your brow shall you eat bread." The ultimate punishment for Adam and Eve was their expulsion from the Garden of Eden (Gen. 3:23–24).

As the Talmud states, "When the snake consorted with Eve, he injected lust into her [and by extension to all her descendants, the human race]," an impure passion that can only be overcome by those who accept the moral teachings of the Torah (Shab. 146a). The Zohar argues that from the impurity injected by the snake arose Cain, who killed his brother Abel (1:28b). Only with the birth of her third child, Seth, was the impurity removed (1:36b).

According to a *midrash*, Adam and Eve lived apart for 130 years after the expulsion from the Garden of Eden, before they reunited and she gave birth to Seth (Er. 18b). When Eve died, she was buried beside Adam in the Cave of Machpelah in Hebron (Er. 53a; PdRE 20). *See also* Seth.

Ezekiel, third of the major prophets.

Son of Buzi, a member of the priestly family of Zadok, Ezekiel was carried off to Babylon by Nebuchadnezzar along with King Jehoiachin and the Judean aristocracy in 597 B.C.E. after the first capture of Jerusalem (2 Kings 24:12). In the first half of his book, Ezekiel denounced Judah and Jerusalem and prophesied their inevitable destruction. Ezekiel believed in each person's individual responsibility to God and called for personal repentance to avert the otherwise inevitable catastrophe. In the final part of the book, Ezekiel provided visions of the New Jerusalem and its restored sanctuary, to which the glory of God will return. Ezekiel's prophecies have great poetic beauty and are often steeped in mystical images. His vision of the Divine Chariot (*Merkava*), which is the *haftarah* for the first day of Shavuot (1:1–28), formed the basis of early mystical speculation. In his symbolic vision of a valley of dry bones that were resurrected and rise again (Ch. 37), Ezekiel envisioned a mighty army that will herald the rebirth of Israel.

According to the *aggadah*, Ezekiel (like Jeremiah) was a descendant of Joshua by his marriage with the proselyte Rahab (Meg. 14b). His teaching, "The soul that sins, it [alone] shall die" (Ezek. 18:4), was strikingly different from the Mosaic concept that God would "visit the iniquity of the fathers upon the children" (Exod. 34:7).

The Talmudic observation, "All that Ezekiel saw [in his *Merkava* vision], Isaiah saw," was interpreted as meaning that both prophets had an identical view of God's glory, despite their dramatically different descriptions. The Rabbis compared Ezekiel to a villager who viewed the king, was awed by every detail, and consequently felt compelled to give a minute description of royal splendor to convince his listeners that he actually saw the ruler. In contrast, Isaiah was like a city dweller to whom the king was a familiar sight, so that there was no need to indulge in any lengthy description or to convince his listeners of the truth of his statement (Hag. [Talmud] 13b).

Ezra, religious leader of the exiles returning from Babylonia to the Land of Israel.

Known as Ezra the Scribe, he was a descendant of Seraiah, the high priest. In 458 B.C.E., Ezra received permission from King Artaxerxes of Persia to lead about 5,000 Jews from Babylonia up to the Land of Israel. As a devoted disciple of Baruch ben Neriah, a disciple of Jeremiah, Ezra would not leave Babylonia as long as his teacher was alive, and thus he did not join the first exiles returning to Jerusalem during the reign of Cyrus. The Rabbis interpreted this as meaning that "the study of the Torah was superior to the reconstruction of the Temple" (Meg. 16b).

Soon after his arrival, Ezra took strenuous measures against intermarriage with non-Jewish women, which had become common even among men of high standing. Despite strong opposition, he dramatically insisted on the dismissal of these wives to prevent assimilation. Ezra established the Great Assembly, a collection of scholars who served as the religious and administrative leaders of the nation.

According to the Rabbis, had Moses not preceded him, Ezra would have been worthy of receiving the Torah for Israel (Sanh. 21b). Ezra restored knowledge of the Torah at a time when Israel had largely forgotten it (Suk. 20a). He reestablished the text of the Five Books of Moses, introducing a script of square characters that apparently was a polemical measure against the Samaritans (Sanh. 21b). The Talmud states that Ezra wrote the first part of the Book of Chronicles, which was finished by Nehemiah, and the book bearing his name (BB 16a).

Major enactments made by Ezra included: reading the Torah in public on Monday and Thursday mornings and during the *minchah* (afternoon) service on the Sabbath, with three men reading ten verses; having courts in session on Mondays and Thursdays, which were also the market days and when the people gathered to hear the Torah readings; having clothes washed on Thursdays to prepare for the Sabbath; eating garlic on Friday evening, the eve of the Sabbath, to increase fertility; having women rise early and bake bread in the morning, so that it would be available for the poor who came to the door; having women wear undergarments and having them wash their hair prior to immersion in the *mikveh* (ritual bath); allowing peddlers to sell goods, such as spices and cosmetics, throughout the town, even against the wishes of those living there; and requiring men who experienced a nocturnal emission to immerse themselves in a *mikveh* (BK 82a). Ezra enacted a regulation that the "curses" in Leviticus (26:14–39) should be read before Shavuot and those in Deuteronomy (28:15–68) before Rosh Hashanah (Meg. 31b), and he was said to have pronounced the Divine Name according to its proper sounds (Yoma 69b).

What are now the Books of Ezra and Nehemiah were originally on a single scroll. Later divided into First and Second Ezra, they finally returned to their former names. The majority of the Book of Ezra was written in Hebrew, but some was in Aramaic.

G

Gad, seventh son of Jacob, borne to him by Zilpah, the maidservant of Leah.

Leah said, "What luck [*gad*]!"—a term that was also the name of fortune and good luck in several ancient Near Eastern cultures. The flag of the tribe of Gad was black and white, on which was embroidered a camp or tent. This was based on the verse, "Gad will recruit a regiment" (Gen. 49:19), in which the name of the tribe is associated with *g'dud* (battalion). Gad was a tribe of fighting warriors, whose territory lay in the mountains of Gilead, east of the Jordan. When the Israelites conquered Transjordan in the time of Moses, the Gadites (together with the Reubenites and half the tribe of Menassah) requested permission to settle in the pasture lands east of the Jordan because of their abundant cattle. Moses agreed, but demanded that they first cross the Jordan and aid the other tribes in the conquest of Canaan (Num. 32:1–33). During the monarchy, the Gadites were described as "expert in war," with countenances "like the faces of lions," and "as swift as gazelles upon the mountains" (1 Chron. 5:18; 12:9).

According to the *aggadah* (Exod. R. 1:5), the name "Gad" presaged the *manna*, which was "like coriander seed" (*gad* in Hebrew; Exod. 16:31).

Gad, prophet at the time of King David (JT Sot. 9:13).

Known as "the seer," Gad and fellow-prophet Nathan were said to have completed the Book of Samuel (BB 15a). Gad urged David to purchase the threshing floor of Araunah the Jebusite and erect there an altar to the Lord (2 Sam. 24:18). This later became the site of the Temple of Solomon (1 Chron. 22:1).

Gamaliel, son of Pedahzur and chieftain of the tribe of Manasseh.

Gamaliel made the eighth of the twelve identical offerings for the dedication of the Tabernacle in the wilderness (Num. 7:54–59).

Gedaliah, governor of Judah.

Gedaliah was appointed to this position by Nebuchadnezzar after Jerusalem fell in 586 B.C.E., when the upper classes of the Jewish people were carried off into captivity in Babylonia. Gedaliah established his residence in nearby Mitzpeh, where he presided over an administration that revitalized the economy and attracted many Jews who had fled to places of safety in neighboring lands during the war of destruction. Although Gedaliah urged the Jews to remain loyal to the king of Babylonia and reap the benefits of peace and security, his wise counsel fell victim to the unquenchable ambition of Ishmael, a descendant of the royal house of Zedekiah, the last king of Judah, who plotted against him. Although aware of the conspiracy, Gedaliah refused to allow his forces to kill Ishmael before he could carry out his nefarious plans. At a New Year's feast to which he was invited, Ishmael and his co-conspirators murdered Gedaliah. Rather than leading to the overthrow of Babylonian rule, the death of Gedaliah was the final blow to any immediate hope of restoring Jewish sovereignty and independence and led to the further dispersal of the Jewish people. Today, this dark day is commemorated by the Fast of Gedaliah, which is held on the day after Rosh Hashanah (third of Tishrei) (RH 18b).

Interpreting the verse, "the dead bodies of the men whom he had slain by the hand of Gedaliah" (Jer. 41:9), the Talmud asks, "Did Gedaliah kill them? Was it not Ishmael who slew them?" The text explains that Gedaliah should have heeded the warning of the conspiracy against him. By his failure to do so, the Torah ascribes their deaths to him (Nid. 61a).

Gehazi, servant of the prophet Elisha.

Gehazi explained to his master the desire of the wealthy Shunammite woman for a son (2 Kings 4:14), but later harshly thrust her away when she beseeched Elisha's aid on behalf of her dead child. Elisha commanded Gehazi to hasten to Shunem, greeting none on the way, and lay the prophet's staff on the child's face, but this failed to revive him (2 Kings 25–31). According to the *aggadah*, Gehazi was one of those who denied the resurrection of the dead and thus have no portion in the World to Come (Sanh. 10:2). Convinced that the staff of the prophet had no power to revive the dead child, Gehazi was unsuccessful (PdRE 33), whereas Elisha succeeded.

In the story of Naaman, the Syrian general, Elisha cursed the greedy Gehazi for running to accept the gifts that the prophet had rejected, making his servant "a leper as white as snow" (2 Kings 5:25–27). In his final appearance, Gehazi was informing Jehoram, king of Israel, of "all the great things that Elisha has done" (2 Kings 8:1–6). His recital was interrupted by the appearance of the Shunammite woman, who had come to petition the king to recover the house and land she had abandoned during the recent famine. The Rabbis interpreted this as indicating that the praise of a holy man should not be sung by a sinner (Lev. R. 16:4), and that Gehazi had been disrespectful to his teacher in calling him by name (Sanh. 100a). The Rabbis also accused

Gehazi of having driven away Elisha's disciples; using a magnet to "suspend between heaven and earth" the golden calf idols of Jeroboam, so that many were convinced to believe in their divinity; and engraving in their mouths the Divine Name so that they continually pronounced the first two Commandments ("I am the Lord your God" and "You shall have no other gods besides Me") (Sot. 47a).

The *aggadah* describes Gehazi as one of those "who set their eyes upon that which was not proper for them; what they sought was not granted to them and what they possessed was taken from them" (Sot. 9b). Elisha went to Damascus to persuade Gehazi to repent. However, Gehazi refused: "This I have learned from you. He who sins and causes others to sin is not given the opportunity to repent." However, the Rabbis criticized Elisha for "thrusting Gehazi away with both hands," instead of using only one for this purpose and simultaneously drawing him in with the other (Sot. 47a).

Gershom, elder son of Moses and Zipporah.

His name, meaning "stranger in a strange land," related to his being born in Midian, the land to which Moses fled after killing the Egyptian overseer (Exod. 2:12–15). *See also* Zipporah.

Gershon, firstborn son of Levi.

Under the direction of Ithamar, the youngest son of Aaron, his clan (Gershonites) was in charge of the external aspects of the Tabernacle—"the tent, its covering, and the screen for the entrance of the Tent of Meeting; the hangings of the enclosure, the screen for the entrance of the enclosure that surrounds the Tabernacle, the cords thereof, and the altar, and all their service equipment and all their accessories [curtains and work tools needed to repair them]" (Num. 4:25–26).

After the Israelites entered into the Promised Land, the Gershonites received "thirteen cities with their pasture lands" from the tribes of Issachar, Asher, Napthali, and the half-tribe of Manasseh (Josh. 21:27–32). Though listed among those who cleansed the Temple during the reign of Hezekiah (2 Chron. 29:12), the Gershonites were not named among the Levites who served in the Temple during the time of Josiah (2 Chron. 34:12).

Gideon, judge of Israel who decisively defeated the Midianites.

After a Divine vision ordering him to destroy an altar to Baal belonging to his father Joash, the Abiezrite, Gideon erected an altar to God and offered a sacrifice there, thus earning the name Jerubaal (let Baal contend [against him]) (Judg. 6:25–32). As Gideon prepared to lead the Israelite troops against the Midianite invaders, he asked for a sign that God would make them victorious over their enemy. "Behold, I will put a fleece of wool on the threshing floor; and if the dew is on the fleece only, and it is dry on all the ground elsewhere, then shall I know that you will save Israel by my hand." When this occurred, Gideon begged God to forgive him for asking that the test be repeated with reverse conditions as a confirming sign (Judg. 6:33–40).

Finally convinced of Divine support, Gideon assembled a force of only 300 fighters to do battle with the thousands of enemy soldiers. In a surprise night attack, his men quietly surrounded the enemy camp, each carrying a shofar and an empty jar with a torch inside it. At Gideon's signal, all the men blew their shofars, smashed their jars on the ground, and waved their torches wildly, while shouting: "The sword of the Lord, and of Gideon." The blare of the trumpets, the clatter of the broken pottery, and the flashing of the torch lights startled the enemy. Terrified and still half asleep, they ran off in all directions, brandishing their weapons and attacking and killing one another in the mass confusion (Judg. 7:16–22). In gratitude, the people offered to make Gideon king, but he immediately refused, saying: "I will not rule over you, neither shall my son. The Lord shall rule over you" (Judg. 8:22–23).

According to the text, Gideon fathered seventy sons and "died in a good old age" (Judg. 8:30–32).

Goliath, giant from Gath who was the champion of the Philistines.

As the Philistines and Israelites prepared for war, with their armies massed on two mountains on either side of a valley, Goliath came down into the valley and stood before the Israelites (1 Sam. 17). An imposing man standing almost ten feet tall, wearing a bronze helmet and covered with a heavy coat of armor, he carried an iron-tipped spear that looked like the trunk of a tree. For forty days Goliath challenged the Israelites to choose their best warrior to fight him, with the people of the loser becoming the slaves of the winner. The poorly armed Israelite warriors were terrified. However, when David, who had been sent by his father to bring food to his brothers in the army, heard Goliath's challenge, he asked: "What shall be done to the man who kills this Philistine and removes reproach from Israel? For who is this uncircumcised Philistine, that he should defy the armies of the living God?"

When Saul heard of this brash young man who was volunteering to fight the giant, he summoned David, who related his experiences of killing a lion and a bear with his bare hands to protect the sheep under his care. Saul dressed David in his own armor and a helmet of bronze, but they were so heavy that David could barely move. So David took off the armor and went out to meet Goliath armed with only five smooth stones and a slingshot. Goliath treated David with disdain, asking whether the Israelites thought him "a dog that you come against me with sticks?" But David refused to be cowed by the mighty Goliath. "You come against me with sword, spear, and javelin; but I come to you in the name of the Lord of Hosts, the God of the armies of Israel, whom you have defied. This day the Lord will deliver you into my hands. I will kill you and cut off your head. I will give the carcasses of the Philistine camp to the birds of the air and to the wild beasts of the earth. And the earth [and all this assembly] shall know that there is a God in Israel." As the enraged Goliath moved forward to attack, David slung a stone that struck the Philistine giant in the forehead, and Goliath fell face down on the ground. David ran to Goliath, took the fallen warrior's sword, and chopped off his head. When the Philistines saw that their champion was dead, they fled in terror. With a great shout, the Israelites pursued the fleeing Philistines and destroyed the enemy camp.

Gomer, daughter of Diblaim, and the wife of the prophet Hosea.

God had commanded Hosea to find a wife he suspected would be unfaithful. In this way, the adulterous acts of Gomer would symbolize Israel's violation of the Divine covenant. She was called Gomer (finished) because everyone "satisfied their lust" on her, and as the daughter of Diblaim (lit., "two evil speeches") because of the evil reputations of both her and her mother (Pes. 87a).

Gomer bore the prophet Hosea three children, all of whom were given names symbolic of God's temporary rejection of Israel. The first was a son named "Jezreel," because God declared that Israel would be destroyed in the Jezreel Valley. Her second child, a daughter, was named "Unloved," because God had decided that Israel was not worthy of Divine love and compassion since it had turned away from God and worshiped idols. Gomer's final son was named "Not My People," symbolizing the Divine decision to reject Israel. Eventually, Hosea purchased Gomer from a slave owner and returned her to his home, a symbol of God's ultimate redemption of the Jewish people. *See also* Hosea.

Habakkuk, eighth of the minor prophets (seventh century B.C.E.).

In the first chapter of his fifty-six-line book, Habakkuk foresaw the Chaldean invasion of Judea. In the second chapter, the prophet cried out against injustice, while in the third chapter he presented a terrifying vision of God on a storm chariot and dramatic imagery of the Divine power to devastate the natural world. The final chapter of the book was selected as the *haftarah* for the second day of Shavuot, the traditional date of the giving of the Ten Commandments. Rashi related this to the verse, "God is coming from Teman" (3:3), explaining that Teman was a reference to the Sinai wilderness and the *midrash* that when God evaluated the various mountains on earth, only Sinai was deemed "worthy" for the Revelation (Gen. R. 99:1).

According to the Zohar (1:7b), Habakkuk was the son of the Shunammite woman who was told, "At this season, when the time comes round, you will embrace (*hoveket*) a son" (2 Kings 4:16). The prophet once drew a circle and stood within it, declaring to God: "I will not budge from here until You tell me why You show patience toward the wicked in the world." God replied, "I do this to give them a chance to repent, so that their willful transgressions may be considered as errors" (Mid. Ps. 77:1).

R. Simlai said, "613 commandments were addressed to Moses at Sinai . . . the prophet Habakkuk [2:4] reduced them to a single principle: 'The righteous person shall live by his faith'" (Mak. 24a).

Hagar, Egyptian handmaid of Sarah, and the mother of Ishmael.

Bearing no children after ten years of marriage, Sarah urged Abraham to take Hagar as a concubine, "so that I shall have a son through her" (Gen. 16:2). In this way, the infertile Sarah could adopt Hagar's child as her own. When Hagar became pregnant, she treated her mistress with brazen contempt. In turn, Sarah "treated her harshly and she [Hagar] ran away from her" (Gen. 16:6). As Hagar sat by a spring of water in the wilderness, an angel of the Lord appeared to her, commanding Hagar to "go back to your mistress" and submit to her (Gen. 16:9). The angel promised that Hagar would bear a son who would be called Ishmael ("for the Lord has paid heed to your suffering"), assuring Hagar that he would be "a wild ass of a man [a strong fighter]" (Gen. 16:11–12).

Several years after Sarah finally gave birth to Isaac, she accused Ishmael of "mocking" Isaac (interpreted in a *midrash* as cruelty and possibly even sexual molestation) and demanded that Abraham cast Hagar and her son out into the wilderness (Gen. 21:9–10). When their water was gone and it appeared that Ishmael would die of thirst, Hagar "left the child under one of the bushes and went and sat down at a distance" rather than watch him die (Gen. 21:15–16). However, in response to Ishmael's cry, an angel of God appeared to Hagar and showed her a well, promising that her son would found a great nation (Gen. 21:17–19).

According to a *midrash* (Gen. R. 45:1), Hagar was the daughter of Pharaoh. After seeing the great miracles that God had done for Sarah's sake (the "mighty plagues" that afflicted the Egyptian court when Sarah had been taken from Abraham and brought there) (Gen. 12:17), Pharaoh said: "It is better for Hagar to be a slave in Sarah's house than mistress in her own." Another legend was that, in Abraham's merit, the water that he gave Hagar when sending her off from his house was not consumed from the flask. However, when she reached the desert and began to stray after the idols of her father's house, the water of the flask was consumed (PdRE 30). Later, Hagar repented fully for her lapse into idolatry and dedicated herself to good deeds, for which her name was changed to Keturah. After the death of Sarah, Abraham sent for Hagar/Keturah and remarried her (Zohar 1:133b). *See also* Keturah.

Haggai, tenth of the minor prophets.

Living in the post-Exilic period, Haggai's existing prophecies consist of only thirty-eight verses and date from the second year of the reign of Darius I, king of Persia (520 B.C.E.). They deal mainly with the construction of the Temple and the future momentous events that the nation would experience as a result of it. Urging Zerubbabel, the governor of the Jews after the return from Babylonian Exile, to rebuild the Temple, Haggai prophesied that the Second Temple would be even more beautiful than the first and would eventually be honored by all the world.

As the Talmud notes, "With the deaths of the last prophets—Haggai, Zechariah, and Malachi—Divine Inspiration [Holy Spirit] departed from Israel" (Yoma 9b).

Ham, second son of Noah.

Always described with the epithet "the father of Canaan," Ham mocked his drunken father lying naked in his tent, disrespectfully leering at him and rushing to inform his brothers rather than averting his gaze and covering Noah's nakedness (Gen. 9:22). The Rabbis maintained that Ham either castrated or sexually abused his father (Sanh. 70a). When Noah recovered from the effects of the wine, he wrathfully exclaimed: "Cursed be Canaan, the lowest of slaves shall he be to his brothers" (Gen. 9:25).

The Talmud adds that Ham was one of the three, along with the dog and the raven, who copulated in the ark and were punished—"the dog was doomed to be tied, the raven expectorates [his seed into his mate's mouth], and Ham was smitten in his skin [i.e., he was the ancestor of Cush, who was black-skinned]" (Sanh. 108b).

Haman, son of Hammedatha the Agagite, and the villain of the Purim story.

The prototype of the enemy of the Jews throughout the ages, Haman was traditionally considered a descendant of Amalek (Meg. 13a), the ancient adversary of Israel whose roots reached back to Esau. Second in command to King Ahasuerus of Persia, Haman had set himself up as an "object of worship" to whom all the king's courtiers in the palace gate were required to "kneel and bow low" (Esth. 3:2). When Mordechai refused to comply, "Haman was filled with rage . . . and plotted to destroy all the Jews, the people of Mordechai, throughout the kingdom of Ahasuerus" (Esth. 3:5–6). So Haman approached the king and said, "There is a certain people, scattered and dispersed among the other people in all the provinces of your realm, whose laws are different from those of any other people and who do not obey the king's laws." He suggested that "an edict be drawn for their destruction" and, to sweeten the deal, offered to pay "ten thousand talents of silver" to the royal treasury (Esth. 3:8–9).

Excited when invited to dine with Esther and Ahasuerus at the queen's request, Haman left the party "happy and light-hearted," though his mood soured rapidly when he passed Mordechai in the palace gate and the Jew failed to rise or bow before him. Returning home, his wife Zeresh and friends suggested he solve the problem by erecting high gallows to hang his enemy. When Ahasuerus heard that Haman had returned to the royal court, the king asked him, "What should be done for a man whom the king desires to honor?" (Esth. 6:6). Convinced that this must be referring to him, Haman replied that he should be clad in royal garb and diadem and sit on "a horse on which the king has ridden" and paraded through the city square by a noble courtier proclaiming before him, "This is what is done to the man whom the king desires to honor!" Haman was mortified when told that the person to be honored was Mordechai, in recognition of his having discovered a plot to assassinate the king. Returning home after the humiliation of honoring his enemy, Haman received an ominous warning from his wife and advisers: "If Mordechai, before whom you have begun to fall, is of Jewish stock, you will not overcome him; you will fall before him to your ruin" (Esth. 6:6–13).

Haman was raised from the depths of despair when he received another invitation to attend a banquet with Ahasuerus hosted by the queen. However, his temporary exhilaration was shattered by Esther's accusation that Haman was "the adversary and enemy" planning to kill her and her people. Ahasuerus fled the room in fury, while Haman remained behind pleading with Esther to save his life. "When the king returned from the palace garden to the banquet room, Haman was lying prostrate on the couch on which Esther reclined. 'Does he mean to ravish the queen in my own palace?'" When a servant observed that a stake was already standing nearby, the king ordered that Haman be hung on the gallows that he had prepared for Mordechai.

At the synagogue reading of the Megillah (Book of Esther) on Purim, it is customary for the congregation to make noise each of the fifty-four times that the name of Haman is uttered, in order to fulfill the biblical commandment to "blot out the name of Amalek" (Deut. 25:19), the ancestor of Haman. While any kind of noisemaking device is acceptable, including booing and stamping one's feet on the floor, it is traditional to use a *grager* (rattle) for this purpose. Some even write the name Haman on the soles of their shoes, so as to literally blot out the name as they stomp their feet.

Two of the special foods associated with Purim are related to Haman. The most popular are the Ashkenazic triangular pastries filled with poppy seeds or fruit known as *hamantashen* (lit., "Haman's pockets"), which may represent the bribes filling the pockets of this corrupt villain. *Hamantashen* are sometimes called "Haman's hat," and this Persian villain was often anachronistically portrayed in medieval depictions as wearing a three-cornered hat popular in Europe at that time. Sephardim consume ear-shaped cookies called *oznei Haman* (Haman's ears). This name may have derived from the former practice of cutting off the ears of criminals before hanging them—appropriate since Haman was hanged at the conclusion of the Book of Esther.

Despite the wicked Haman's attempt to destroy the Jews, the Talmud observes that "descendants of Haman learned Torah in B'nai Brak [in the Land of Israel]" (Sanh. 96b). *See also* Esther; Mordechai.

Hamor, Hivite ruler of the city-state of Shechem.

His son Shechem, who was in love with Jacob's daughter Dinah but unable to control his passion, raped her and then begged Hamor to arrange for them to marry. While the men of Shechem were in intense pain three days after undergoing circumcision as a prerequisite to the marriage, Shimon and Levi (two full brothers of Dinah) killed Hamor, Shechem, and all the males of the city (Gen. 34).

Hananiah, Mishael, and Azariah (Shadrach, Mishach, and Abed-Nego in Babylonian), three young men of aristocratic stock from the tribe of Judah.

Together with Daniel, they were carried off to Babylonia and educated in the Babylonian court of Nebuchadnezzar, where they were trained for the king's service (Dan. 1:6–7). Refusing to consume pagan food that did not conform to the Jewish dietary laws, they were given vegetables to eat instead (Dan. 1:8–16). At the end of their training, they quickly rose in rank at court, with Daniel attaining the position in the "King's Gate" and the others made administrators of the province of Babylon. However, when the three refused to bow down to the king's golden image or worship the gods of Babylon, Nebuchadnezzar had them thrown into a "burning fiery furnace," from which they miraculously emerged unharmed (Dan. 3:19–25). According to the *aggadah*, the archangel Gabriel arranged for the interior of the furnace to be cooled, while its exterior glowed so hot that the pagans viewing it were killed (Pes. 118a–b). Marveling at their deliverance from certain death, Nebuchadnezzar praised the greatness of the God of Israel: "Blessed be the God of Shadrach, Meshach, and Abed-Nego, who has sent His angel to save His servants who, trusting in Him, flouted the king's decree at the risk of their lives rather than serve or worship any god but their own God" (Dan. 3:28).

The Bible describes Hananiah, Mishael, and Azariah as "youths without blemish, handsome, knowledgeable and intelligent, and understanding science." They also had the "strength to stand in the king's palace" (Dan. 1:4), which the Rabbis interpreted as meaning that they had the ability to "restrain themselves from smiling, talking, and sleeping and to control their bodily functions [in the presence of the king] out of fear for his royal position" (Sanh. 93b). *See also* Daniel.

Hannah, mother of Samuel.

Though the favored wife of her husband, Elkanah, Hannah was bitterly unhappy because she was childless for many years and taunted by Elkanah's other wife, the fertile Peninah. An *aggadah* relates that Peninah would rise early and ask Hannah, "Are you not going to get up and wash your children's faces so they can go to school?" At midday, she would say: "Are you not preparing to welcome your children home from school?" At the evening meal, she would remind Elkanah to give *her* sons their portions (Pes. Rab. 43).

Observing all the Israelites gathered together at Shiloh on the pilgrimage festivals, Hannah would bitterly cry out to God: "Master of the Universe, You have all these hosts [that you created in Your world], is it so hard for you to give me one son?" (Ber. 31b). She added, "There is a host in heaven and a host on earth, and I do not know to which I belong. If the heavenly, I should not eat, drink, procreate, or die, and I should live forever. And if I am of the earthly host, I should eat, drink, and also give birth to a child!" (Pes. Rab. 43:3). Hannah said before God, "When the life of a woman is in danger, she is examined in three areas to see whether she is worthy of surviving—*niddah* [family purity], *hallah* [separation of a portion from the dough] and kindling the Sabbath candles [Shab. 32a]. Have I transgressed a single one of them?" She added, "Nothing that you created in a woman is without a purpose . . . [including] breasts to nurse. And these breasts that You placed on my heart, are they not to give suck? Give me a son to nurse!" Hannah even went so far as to cry out, "God, if You see [i.e., heed my prayer], it is well; but if not, I will go seclude myself up with another man after being warned [not to do so] by my husband [so that he will become jealous and force me] to drink the water of the suspected wife [*sotah*]. Then You will not make your Torah a fraud [by failing to fulfill the prediction that 'if the woman be guiltless, she shall be cleared and conceive a child'] (Num. 5:28)" (Ber. 31b).

Hannah once stood in the Sanctuary, quietly pouring out her intense anguish so that only her lips moved, vowing that if granted a son she would dedicate him to the service of God. Eli, the high priest at Shiloh, initially rebuked Hannah for her apparently drunken behavior. However, once he learned the true cause, Eli added his blessing and assured Hannah that her pleas would be answered. Hannah gave birth to a son, Samuel, and after weaning him brought him to Shiloh, offered a sacrifice and a song of thanksgiving, and left him with Eli to serve in the Sanctuary.

The story of Hannah's prayer and Samuel's birth is the *haftarah* for the first day of Rosh Hashanah (1 Sam. 1:1–2:10), for according to tradition she was remembered by God on New Year's Day (RH 11a). The Talmud (Ber. 29a) states that the nine blessings in the Musaf Amidah for Rosh Hashanah are equal to the number of times that Hannah mentioned the Divine Name in her prayer (1 Sam. 2:1–10). The *aggadah* lists Hannah as one of the seven prophetesses (Meg. 14a).

Haran, youngest son of Terah, and the brother of Abraham and Nahor.

Haran was born in Ur of the Chaldees, dying there while his father was still alive (Gen. 11:28). According to a *midrash*, when Nimrod threw Abraham into the fiery furnace, Haran was tossed in after him. Lacking his brother's firm belief in God, Haran said to himself: "Should Abraham perish in the furnace, I will side with Nimrod; if he comes out alive, I will be with Abraham"—and thus he was killed in the flames. In a different version, Haran stood by the furnace undecided as to his proper course of action. After Abraham was saved, when Haran was asked whose side he was on, he replied "Abraham's." Immediately, agents of Nimrod seized Haran and threw him into the fire, where he died (Gen. R. 38). Haran had three children: Lot, Milcah, and Iscah. According to the Talmud (Sanh. 69b), Iscah was Sarah, who thus was the niece of her husband, Abraham.

Hezekiah, twelfth king of Judah (719–687 B.C.E.).

He received his name because "God strengthened him (*hizko Yah*), and because he [Hezekiah] strengthened (*hazak*) the Israelites [in their devotion] to their Father in Heaven" (Sanh. 94a). One of the best kings of Judah, Hezekiah was the father of Manasseh and grandfather of Amon, generally considered two of the most evil rulers. Indeed, the *aggadah* (Sanh. 63b) claims that Ahaz, his wicked father, wanted to burn his son before the idol Molech, but his mother covered him with a fireproof shield of the blood of a salamander, a reptile believed to be engendered in fire (Hag. [Talmud] 27a).

Hezekiah renewed the full-scale worship of God following a lengthy period in which idolatry had taken root in Jerusalem. With the encouragement of the prophet Isaiah, Hezekiah repaired and purged the Temple, reorganized the services of the priests and Levites, and reopened it with a huge number of sacrifices (2 Chron. 29:3–36). Hezekiah abolished the pagan shrines, smashed the pillars, and destroyed the copper serpent that Moses had made in the desert (Num. 21:5–9).

Early in his reign, Sennacherib besieged Jerusalem and forced Hezekiah to pay a heavy tribute, which even required him to strip the doors and pillars of the Temple (2 Kings 18:13–16). In anticipation of a later Assyrian siege, which Sennacherib finally laid on Jerusalem in 701 B.C.E., Hezekiah supervised the construction of a tunnel (an extraordinary engineering feat) to provide underground access to the waters of the Gihon Spring. Jerusalem was saved when a plague ("the angel of the Lord") wiped out the Assyrian camp (2 Kings 19:35). During the siege of Jerusalem, the childless Hezekiah became seriously ill and feared that his death would bring an end to the Davidic dynasty. To comfort the ailing monarch, God told Isaiah to inform Hezekiah that his prayer had been heard and that fifteen years had been added to his life (2 Kings 20:1–19).

According to the Talmud, "A childless person is accounted as dead" (Ber. 64b), because his name will perish with him. Intentionally remaining childless was deemed a terrible sin. This was illustrated by the *aggadic* description of the declaration of the prophet Isaiah to the seriously ill King Hezekiah: "Thus says the Lord: 'Set your house in order, for you shall die and not live'" (Isa. 38:1). Why the apparent redundancy? "You shall die" referred to this world; "and not live" related to the World to Come. When Hezekiah asked the reason for such a severe punishment, Isaiah replied, "Because you did not try to have children." Attempting to justify his decision, Hezekiah explained: "The reason was that I saw by the [aid of the] Holy Spirit that the children issuing from me would not be virtuous." However, Isaiah remained unmoved: "What have you to do with the secrets of the All-Merciful? You should have done what you were commanded, and let the Holy One, blessed be He, do what pleases Him" (Ber. 10a).

Interpreting the verse, "And in that day, his burden shall be removed from your shoulders, and his yoke from your neck, and the yoke shall be destroyed because of the oil" (Isa. 10:27), R. Isaac said it meant: "The yoke of Sennacherib shall be destroyed on account of the oil of Hezekiah, which burned in the synagogues and houses of study. He stuck a sword at the entrance of the house of study and proclaimed, 'Whoever does not engage in Torah study will be pierced by this sword.' They searched from Dan to Beersheba [all of Israel], and no ignoramus was found; from Geves to Antiprais, and no boy or girl, man or woman, was found who was not thoroughly versed in the laws of purity and impurity" (Sanh. 94b).

As the Talmud relates, "Hezekiah did six things; of three the sages approved and of three they did not. He hid [Solomon's] Book of Cures, smashed the copper snake [of Moses, so that it would not be worshiped], and dragged his [wicked] father's bones [to the grave] on a bier of ropes [instead of giving him a royal burial], and they approved. [Conversely,] he stopped up the waters of Gihon [so that the attacking Assyrian armies would not find water to drink, though it saved Jerusalem from siege], he cut off [the gold] from the doors of the Temple and sent it to the King of Assyria [to appease him], and he added the extra month of a leap year during the month of Nisan [because he was afraid that he would not finish purifying all Israel of idolatry in time for Passover; Sanh. 12a], and these they did not approve" (Ber. 10b).

When Hezekiah died, 36,000 warriors marched before his body with bare shoulders (as a sign of mourning for a righteous man and scholar).They placed a Torah scroll upon his bier and said, "This man fulfilled all that is written in it" (BK 17a). *See also* Ahaz; Isaiah; Manasseh (king).

Hilkiah, high priest during the reign of Josiah.

Hilkiah discovered the Book of the Law during the renovation of the Temple (2 Kings 22:8). He gave the scroll, which probably contained a large portion of the Book of Deuteronomy, to Shaphan the Scribe, who read it to the king. Realizing that for decades the people of Judah had neglected the commandments, Josiah was alarmed by the calamities predicted for failure to observe them. Fearing Divine punishment, Josiah instituted a sweeping series of religious reforms that included the destruction of the corrupt local sanctuaries ("high places") throughout the land and the centralization of religious worship in Jerusalem (2 Kings 23).

Hiram, king of Tyre (961–936 B.C.E.).

Hiram established political and economic relations with David and Solomon. After David had conquered Jerusalem, Hiram sent him "cedar trees, carpenters, and masons" to build the royal palace (2 Sam. 5:11). When Solomon ascended to the throne, Hiram gave him cedar and cypress trees and expert craftsmen to build the Temple in Jerusalem, in exchange for an annual payment of "20,000 kor [200,000 bushels] of wheat and 20 kor [2,000 gallons] of pure oil. . . . And there was peace between Hiram and Solomon; and they made a treaty together" (1 Kings 5:24–26).

Twenty years later, after Solomon's extravagant building projects had almost bankrupted Israel, Hiram sent Solomon more cedar and cypress trees and "120 talents of gold" in return for "20 cities in the land of Galilee" (1 Kings 9:24–26). Solomon then built a fleet of merchant ships that were guided by Tyrian mariners, presumably reflecting a joint venture by which Solomon could repay the loan from Hiram and regain the Galilean cities pledged as collateral (1 Kings 9:26–28).

Hoham, king of Hebron.

He joined the coalition of five Amorite kings that was defeated by Joshua at Gibeon (Josh. 10:3). *See also* Adoni-Zedek.

Hophni, elder son of Eli, who officiated as a priest in the sanctuary at Shiloh.

Hophni and his younger brother, Pinchas, flagrantly abused their high positions by such wicked deeds as taking portions of meat from a sacrifice before it was dedicated to God and sexual impropriety with women serving at the sanctuary (1 Sam. 2:12–17, 22). Their heinous acts earned Hophni and Pinchas a Divine curse, first spoken by an unknown prophet and later by Samuel, that they would both die on the same day (1 Sam. 2:34). The prediction came true when the Philistines killed both brothers as they were accompanying the Ark of the Covenant into battle (1 Sam. 4:11).

Hosea, first of the minor prophets (c. 784–725 B.C.E.).

Hosea lived in the turbulent days of the idolatrous Northern Kingdom (Ephraim), when it was at the height of its power under the rule of Jeroboam II. His prophesies were oracles of doom, thundering against moral, religious, and political evils as offenses against God. He predicted the devastation of Israel as just punishment for its idol worship and social injustice. Nevertheless, Hosea stressed that God's love for Israel would never cease. Through punishment, God would purify Israel and lead His people to repentance. The surviving remnant of Israel would no longer worship foreign gods or seek foreign help, but would rely solely on God, who would preserve them and eventually restore Israel to its former glory.

The verses from Hosea that open the *haftarah* for the Sabbath of Repentance (*Shabbat Shuvah*), between Rosh Hashanah and Yom Kippur, presaged Maimonides' doctrine that true repentance required an intellectual awareness of sin, confession and appeal for Divine mercy, and the resolve never to engage in such practices again.

The ideal of love was the central theme of Hosea, who compared God to a loving father and faithful husband of the Jewish people. Verses from Hosea, in which the word "betrothal" is used three times in the description of Israel's spiritual engagement to God (2:21–22), are recited each weekday morning by the observant Jew who puts on *tefillin*, while winding the thong of the hand phylactery three times around his middle finger.

In his personal life, Hosea was Divinely ordered in a vision to marry Gomer, "a wife of whoredom," to symbolize Israel's disloyalty of God. Just as the prophet redeemed Gomer, paying the price for her freedom even though she continued to be unfaithful, so God will eventually redeem the people of Israel despite their transgressions. *See also* Gomer.

Huldah, one of the seven prophetesses (Meg. 14a), and the only one mentioned during the period of the monarchy.

An *aggadah* relates that Huldah's husband was one of the great men of his generation. Every day he would fill a pouch with water and go to the entrance of the city, where he would give each traveler a drink. As a reward for this kindness, the Divine Inspiration rested on his wife (Huldah) and she became a prophetess (PdRE 33).

A descendant of Joshua and Rahab (Meg. 14b), she was the wife of Shallum, the "keeper of the wardrobe" who lived in Jerusalem. Huldah, whose name means "weasel," was consulted by Josiah concerning the Scroll of the Law discovered during the restoration of the Temple (622 B.C.E.). She prophesied God's ultimate judgment upon the nation, but this was to be postponed until after Josiah's peaceful death because of the king's acts of repentance (2 Kings 22:14–20).

Hur, faithful attendant of Moses.

According to a later tradition, Hur was the son of Miriam and Caleb, and thus the nephew of Moses. When the Amalekites made a surprise attack on the tired Israelites fleeing Egypt, Hur went with Moses and Aaron to the top of a hill overlooking the field of battle. "Whenever Moses held up his hand, Israel prevailed; but whenever he let down his hand, Amalek prevailed. But Moses' hands grew heavy . . . [and] Aaron and Hur, one on each side, supported his hands [which] remained steady until the sun set . . . [so that] Joshua overwhelmed the people of Amalek with the sword" (Exod. 17:9–14). According to a *midrash*, the Israelite victory was the result not of their military prowess, but of their faith in God as their eyes gazed heavenward toward the outstretched hands of Moses (RH 29a).

When Moses ascended Mount Sinai to receive the Ten Commandments, Hur and Aaron were placed in charge of the Israelite camp (Exod. 24:14). According to the *aggadah*, when the people despaired of Moses returning and clamored for the making of "a god who shall go before us" (Exod. 32:1), Hur was killed by the mob after severely rebuking the Israelites for their idolatrous intentions and their ingratitude in forgetting the miracles God had performed for them (Exod. R. 41:7). Seeing Hur's lifeless body and realizing that the same fate would befall him if he refused, Aaron agreed to comply with the wishes of the people, for the future high priest preferred to commit a sin himself rather than see the Israelites collectively burdened with the crime of a second murder. As a reward for Hur's willingness to sacrifice himself to prevent the Israelites from descending into idolatry, his grandson (Bezalel) was appointed the chief architect of the Tabernacle (Exod. R. 48:3).

Hushai, "king's companion" (1 Chron. 27:33) and "friend of David" (2 Sam. 15:37).

At the time of Absalom's rebellion, the loyal Hushai wanted to join David when he fled Jerusalem. However, David convinced Hushai that he would be far more valuable if he remained behind and pretended to have switched allegiance to Absalom. As a spy in the enemy camp, Hushai could report everything he heard through the sons of the priests Zadok and Abiathar. Of even more value, he could "defeat for me the counsel of Ahithophel" (2 Sam. 15:32–37). When Ahithophel urged Absalom to immediately pursue and completely destroy the forces of David, the wise military course of action, Hushai successfully proposed that the attack be delayed, thus allowing David time to escape (2 Sam. 17:1–16).

According to the *aggadah*, when Absalom rebelled against his father, David "wished to worship idols" (which some interpreted as meaning "to leave the Land of Israel," which is comparable to worshiping idols). Hushai incredulously asked, "Shall people say that such a [pious] king worshiped idols?" David replied, "Should it rather be said that a [pious] king like me was slain by his son?" (i.e., people might whisper that God does not protect the pious, thus desecrating the Divine Name). David continued, "It is better that I worship idols [i.e., by desecrating the Name of Heaven as an individual, the nation would understand that he deserved the punishment of his son killing him], rather than the Divine Name be publicly profaned." Hushai retorted that God does not bring affliction without cause. "Why did you marry a beautiful woman captured in battle [Absalom's mother, Maacah]?" Justifying his action, David replied: "But the Torah permits it." Hushai then pointed out to the king that the biblical verse permitting marrying a woman captured in war was immediately followed by a description of the rebellious son (Deut. 21:18), effectively foretelling David's punishment by teaching that a rebellious son such as Absalom was the natural issue of such a marriage (Sanh. 107a).

I

Isaac, son of Abraham and Sarah, father of Jacob and Esau, and the second patriarch of Israel.

Sarah, who was almost ninety years old, had given up hope of ever bearing a child. When she overheard an angel of the Lord informing Abraham that within a year she would have a son, she laughed with disbelief at the news (Gen. 18:9–14). Therefore, their son was named Isaac (*Yitzhak* in Hebrew, meaning "he will laugh"), for "God has brought me laughter; everyone who hears will laugh with me" (Gen. 21:6). According to one form of numerology, *Yitzhak* has the following meaning: the *yud* has a numerical value of ten, which refers to the ten trials with which Abraham (Isaac's father) was tested according to the Rabbis. The *tzadi* has a numerical value of ninety, the age of Sarah when she gave birth to Isaac. The *chet* is equal to eight, referring to the eighth day on which Isaac was circumcised (Gen. 21:4). Finally, the *kuf* has a numerical value of 100, the age of Abraham when his son Isaac was born (Num. R. 18:21) (Isaacs, *Numbers*, 182–83).

Isaac was the first child circumcised at eight days old (Gen. 21:4), in keeping with the covenant between God and Abraham (Gen. 17:12). God tested Abraham's faith by commanding him to sacrifice Isaac as a burnt offering (Gen. 22). While Isaac lay bound on the altar, Abraham picked up the knife to slay his son, but at the last moment was stopped by an angel of the Lord. Instead of his son, Abraham offered as a sacrifice a ram caught by its horns in a thicket.

The biblical text explicitly states that "Abraham returned to the servants" and they then left for Beersheba. This raises the question of where was Isaac? The standard rabbinic interpretation is that Isaac went to devote himself to Torah study at the *yeshivah* of Shem and Eber. A controversial *midrash* is that the angel of God did *not* stop Abraham in time—so that Isaac was actually killed but resurrected. This *aggadic* tale was popular in Second Temple times, but the Rabbis later suppressed it lest it be used as a Christian polemic as evidence of a foreshadowing of Jesus.

After the death of Sarah, Abraham sent his servant Eliezer to his family in Haran, where he found Rebecca as a suitable wife for Isaac (Gen. 24). However, after twenty years of marriage, the couple remained childless. In response to Isaac's fervent prayer, Rebecca finally gave birth to twins—Esau and Jacob (Gen. 25:19). As the children grew, the gentle Isaac favored Esau, a brash hunter who supplied him with game, but Rebecca preferred Jacob (Gen. 25:27–28). When forced by famine to settle among the Philistines, Isaac resorted for protection to the same stratagem used by his father Abraham, pretending that the beautiful Rebecca was his sister rather than his wife (Gen. 26:6).

As Isaac grew older, "his eyes were too dim to see" (Gen. 27:1). According to a *midrash* (Gen. R. 65:10), this condition had its origin when Isaac lay on his back, bound by Abraham to the altar, and "glimpsed the light of heaven when the angel appeared to save his life. Blinded to lying and deceit on earth, Isaac could no more recognize the transparent lies of Jacob than he could recognize the unworthiness of Esau." When Isaac sent Esau to prepare a venison stew before giving him "my innermost blessing before I die [i.e., making him his heir]" (Gen. 27), Rebecca urged Jacob to present himself in place of his brother and receive the blessing from his blind father. Learning of this duplicity, the infuriated Esau threatened violence, and Jacob was forced to flee for his life. Isaac died in Hebron at the age of 180, shortly after Jacob and his family returned from years in exile in Mesopotamia, and was buried by his two sons (Gen. 5:27–29).

The Talmud (Ber. 26b) attributes the institution of the afternoon (*Mincha*) prayer to Isaac, based on the verse that he "went out walking in the field [to meditate] toward evening" (Gen. 24:63). *See also* Abraham; Esau; Jacob; Rebecca.

Isaiah, first of the major prophets (eighth century B.C.E.).

According to the *aggadah*, Isaiah was a descendant of Judah and Tamar (Sot. 10b). The son of Amoz, Isaiah prophesied in Judah from the death of King Uzziah (c. 742) until the middle of the reign of King Hezekiah. He attacked the moral laxity and injustice of his time. In a passage read as the morning *haftarah* in synagogues on Yom Kippur (Isa. 57:14–58:14), Isaiah railed against those who piously fast and then oppress their neighbors. He argued that God is more interested in social justice for the weak and the poor than in the sacrificial offerings in the Temple. "Is this the fast I desire, a day for men to starve their bodies? Is it bowing the head like a bulrush and lying in sackcloth and ashes? . . . No, this is the fast I desire; to unlock fetters of wickedness and untie the cords of the yoke; to let the oppressed go free, to break off every yoke. It is to share your bread with the hungry, and to take the wretched poor unto your home; when you see the naked clothe him, and do not ignore your own kin" (Isa. 58:5–7).

Isaiah envisioned a Messianic era of world peace at the end of days. "The wolf shall dwell with the lamb, the leopard shall lie down with the kid; the calf and the beast of prey shall feed together, with a little boy to herd them. The cow and the bear shall graze, their young shall lie down together, and the lion, like the ox, shall eat straw" (Isa. 11:6–7). During this idyllic time, "They shall beat their swords into plowshares and their spears into pruning hooks; nation shall not lift up sword against nation; neither shall they learn war any more" (Isa. 2:4). Isaiah also prophesied the end of idolatry: "For the land shall be filled with knowledge of the Lord as water covers the sea" (Isa. 11:9). All of these wondrous events will occur under the rule of an ideal king of the Davidic dynasty ("A shoot shall grow out of the stump of Jesse"), who will be guided by the "spirit of the Lord—a spirit of wisdom and insight, a spirit of counsel and valor, a spirit of devotion and reverence for the Lord"—one who "shall judge the poor with equity and decide with justice for the lowly of the land" (Isa. 11:1–4). All the nations of the world will come to Israel to learn God's ways. "For instruction [Torah] shall come forth from Zion, the word of the Lord from Jerusalem" (Isa. 2:3).

Many scholars consider chapters 40–66 of the Book of Isaiah to be written by a different prophet ("Second Isaiah"), who lived during the time of the Babylonian Exile. This prophet comforted the exiled, suffering, and despairing people, assuring them that God would send a servant to lead Israel from darkness to light, and that Israel would become a "light unto the nations" (Isa. 49:6). This portion of the Book of Isaiah is the source of the seven prophetic sections that are read each week from the Sabbath immediately following Tisha b'Av, the date of the destruction of the First and Second Temples, until Rosh Hashanah, which are collectively known as the "*haftarot* of consolation." Beginning with Shabbat Nachamu (Sabbath of Comfort), a name derived from the first word of the *haftarah* (Isa. 40:1), they prophesize the redemption of Israel, the ingathering of the exiles and the restoration of the Jewish people to their Land, and the coming of the Messianic age of peace and justice.

Although generally considered by the Rabbis to be below Moses in greatness, in some respects Isaiah was deemed to surpass the Lawgiver. For example, Isaiah reduced the commandments from ten to six (Mak. 24a): "[1] He who walks righteously [honesty in dealing] and [2] speaks uprightly [sincere speech]; [3] he who despises the gain of oppression [refuses improper gain] and [4] who waves away a bribe rather than grasping it [absence of corruption]; [5] he who stops his ears against hearing of blood [nonviolence] and [6] shuts his eyes against seeing evil [contempt for any sinful activity]—he shall dwell on high [in lofty security]" (Isa. 33:15–16).

One of Isaiah's most famous phrases is the first of three verses that are the core of the *Kedushah* ("Holiness" or "Sanctification"), the proclamation of God's holiness and glory in the third benediction during the repetition of the *Amidah* (Standing Prayer) when a *minyan* is present. "*Kadosh, Kadosh,*

Kadosh . . . [Holy, holy, holy (is the Lord of Hosts; the whole world is full of His glory)]" (Isa. 6:3) is taken from the prophet's vision of the angels surrounding the Divine throne and proclaiming the holiness of God. The angelic quality of the *Kedushah* is dramatically emphasized during the recitation of *Kadosh, Kadosh, Kadosh*. Worshipers rise up on their toes and lift their heels off the ground to symbolize their desire to escape the fetters of the material world on earth and ascend to heaven to join the angelic choir praising God. The verse "Holy, holy, holy, is the Lord of Hosts" became a source of conflict with the Christians, who realized that the Jews were failing to perceive it as a reference to the Trinity. Instead, the Jews employed the verse to proclaim the absolute Unity of God and as an implied repudiation of core Christian doctrine by using the Aramaic translation of Onkelos, who interpreted it to mean: "God is holy in the heavens above; God is holy on the earth below; and God is holy to all eternity."

A highly controversial passage from Isaiah consists of two verses from chapter 9 (5–6), which Christians have translated in the future tense ("For unto us a child is born and the government shall be upon his shoulders"), interpreting it as a messianic prophecy that foretells the birth and divinity of Jesus. Jews have translated it in the past tense as describing an event that had already taken place in Jewish history—the birth of Hezekiah and a prophecy concerning his future reign as King of Judah, praising God for miraculously sparing the Southern Kingdom from destruction at the hands of Sennacherib and the Assyrians (who had besieged Jerusalem after defeating the Northern Kingdom). *See also* Manasseh (king).

Ishbosheth, son of King Saul.

After the death of his father and three brothers, Ishbosheth was proclaimed king of Israel at Mahanaim by Abner, Saul's chief commander (2 Sam. 2:10). Seven and a half years later, after David's forces under Joab had vanquished Abner, Ishbosheth was killed by two of his officers (2 Sam. 4). Then David united all the Israelite tribes into a single kingdom (2 Sam. 5).

Ishmael, eldest son of Abraham by his Egyptian handmaiden, Hagar.

Born when Abraham was eighty-six years old (Gen. 16:15–16) and circumcised at age thirteen (Gen. 17:23–26), Ishmael was blessed in the Divine promise to the patriarch: "I will make him fertile and exceedingly numerous. He shall be the father of twelve chieftains, and I will make of him a great nation" (Gen. 17:20). However, in the next verse God made clear that the Divine covenant would be made with Isaac, "whom Sarah shall bear to you at this season next year."

When Sarah saw Ishmael "mocking" Isaac (or "making sport with"; lit. "playing with" him and interpreted in a *midrash* as cruelty and possibly even sexual molestation; Gen. R. 53:11), she urged Abraham to "cast out that slave-woman and her son." Sarah feared Ishmael's corrupting influence and was convinced that Ishmael was unworthy to be the heir of her husband ("for the son of that slave shall not share in the inheritance with my son, Isaac"). Although "the matter distressed Abraham greatly," God commanded him to accede to Sarah's wishes, comforting Abraham with the assurance that "I will make a nation of him, too, for he is your seed" (Gen. 11–13). Providing Hagar and Ishmael with bread and water, he sent them away. When the water ran out and it appeared that Ishmael would die of thirst, "God heard the cry of the boy" and showed Hagar a well of water, from which she filled a container to let her son drink (Gen. 21:14–19).

Ishmael continued to dwell in the desert, where he became a skillful archer and followed the nomadic way of life that characterized his descendants. When Abraham died, Ishmael joined Isaac in burying their father in the Cave of Machpelah (Gen. 25:9).

The Rabbis of the Talmud treated Ishmael harshly. At a feast for the righteous in the World to Come, the honor of leading the Grace after Meals will be offered to Abraham, but he will decline saying, "I cannot do so because Ishmael issued from me" (Pes. 119b). Nevertheless, "If one sees Ishmael in a dream, [it is a sign that] his prayer is accepted [as was Ishmael's; Gen. 21:17]" (Ber. 56b). *See also* Abraham; Hagar; Sarah.

Issachar, ninth son of Jacob and the fifth of Leah.

Issachar's name was derived from two Hebrew words meaning "man of [Divine] favor," reflecting that his birth after a long hiatus from childbearing came as a reward to Leah for giving her handmaid, Zilpah, to Jacob (Gen. 30:18). The flag of the tribe of Issachar was black and embroidered with the sun and moon, because of the *aggadic* inference that his descendants were astronomers and experts on intercalating extra months into the calendar (Num. R. 2:7). This was based on the verse describing the children of Issachar as "men with understanding of the times, to know what Israel should do" (1 Chron. 12:33). More than 200 heads of the Sanhedrin came from this tribe, and their *halachic* decisions were accepted as authoritative by all.

Jacob termed Issachar a "strong-boned ass, crouching between the saddlebags" (Gen. 49:14). This may have reflected the topographical fact that the major part of the territory of the tribe was in a plateau that sloped down to the Jordan Valley on one side and the Jezreel Valley on the other. Rashi interpreted this description metaphorically as referring to Issachar bearing the yoke of caring for the spiritual wealth of the people.

The tribe of Issachar was invariably associated with Zebulun—in the order of birth, in the blessings of Jacob (Gen. 49:13–14) and Moses (Deut. 33:18–19), and in their adjoining territories and the close ties between them.

The *aggadah* stresses the symbiotic relationship between the two tribes, with the economic activities of Zebulun the merchant providing for his brother Issachar, so that the latter was free to devote his life to Torah study (Gen. R. 98:12). Based on this, it became an honored tradition in Judaism for wealthy individuals to support Torah scholars and for a rich man to take a brilliant student as a son-in-law, freeing him from the need to earn a living and allowing him to immerse himself completely in acquiring Torah knowledge. According to R. Yochanan, "Whoever puts the profits of business into the purse of a scholar [by contributing to his support] will be rewarded with the privilege of sitting in the Heavenly Academy" (Pes. 53b).

Ithamar, youngest of the four sons of Aaron and Elisheba.

After the sudden death of his two elder brothers, Nadab and Abihu, who had offered "strange fire" before the Lord (Lev. 10:1–2), Ithamar was appointed as supervisor of the Gershonites and Merarites. These levitical clans were responsible for the planks, posts, and covering fabrics of the Tabernacle, as well as the screen for the Tent of Meeting and the Altar (Num. 3:21–26, 33–37).

Although the high priesthood passed to Eleazar and his line following the death of Aaron, Eli and his house of high priests were descendants of Ithamar. The high priesthood remained in their hands until Solomon removed Abiathar from that position (1 Kings 2:27) and the honor reverted back to the descendants of Eleazar.

Ithream, sixth son of King David, born in Hebron to Eglah.

The Targum interpreted the biblical description of Eglah as the "wife of David" (2 Sam. 3:5) to mean that she was actually his favorite wife, Michal. *See also* Michal.

J

Jabal, son of Lamech and descendant of Cain.

As the "ancestor of those who dwell in tents and with the herds" (Gen. 4:20), Jabal was the forebear of all nomads and shepherds.

Jacob, son of Isaac and Rebecca, younger twin of Esau, father of the twelve tribes, and the third patriarch of Israel.

According to the text, he was given the name Jacob (*Ya'akov* in Hebrew) because he emerged from the womb clinging to the heel (*eikev*) of his older twin brother (Gen. 25:26). Elsewhere, the name was said to mean "supplanter" or "deceiver" (Gen. 27:36), relating to Jacob having "stolen" the major blessing from Esau. Modern scholarship suggests that it comes from a Semitic verb meaning "to protect," thus representing a parental plea that God save the newborn from harm.

The favorite of his mother, Jacob was "a mild man who stayed in camp," unlike Esau, who "became a skillful hunter, a man of the outdoors" (Gen. 25:27). One day when Esau returned hungry and "at the point of death" from hunting in the fields, Jacob persuaded his twin to sell him his birthright for a stew of lentils (Gen. 25:29–34). The *aggadah* explains that Jacob's desire to have the birthright was not influenced by any selfish motives, but by his wish to be privileged to offer the sacrifices, which at that time was the prerogative of the firstborn (Gen. R. 63:13; Num. R. 4:8).

Many years later, the dying Isaac sent Esau out to hunt and cook game before conferring the primary blessing on his firstborn (Gen. 27). Rebecca convinced the hesitant Jacob to take Esau's place, after first covering Jacob's hands and neck with goatskins so that the blind Isaac would think it was his "hairy" son. The *aggadah* claims that Jacob agreed to the plot under duress, bent and weeping, for deception ran counter to his character (Gen. R. 65:15). After eating the meal that Jacob had brought, Isaac gave his blessing: "May God give you of the dew of heaven and the fat of the earth, abundance of new grain and wine. Let peoples serve you, and nations bow to you; be master over your brothers, and let your mother's sons bow to you. Cursed be they who curse you, blessed be they who bless you" (Gen. 27:28–30). This confirmed the oracle given to Rebecca before the twins' birth, that "the older

99

shall serve the younger" (Gen. 23:14). When Esau returned and both he and his father learned of Jacob's trick, Esau vowed to kill his twin. However, Isaac not only did not revoke the blessing, but even confirmed it (Gen. 27:37). To escape Esau's wrath, Jacob fled to Haran.

En route, Jacob had a dream of angels ascending and descending a ladder reaching up to heaven and a vision of God promising to give the land of Canaan to his descendants, who would be as numerous as the dust of the earth (Gen. 28:12–15). After awakening and exclaiming "Surely the Lord is present in this place and I did not know it!," Jacob consecrated the site where he had slept by setting up a pillar and anointing it with oil. He named it Bethel (House of God), vowing to dedicate a tenth of all his possessions on his safe return (Gen. 28:16–22).

Arriving in Haran, Jacob met and fell in love with his cousin Rachel, agreeing to work for Laban seven years to obtain her hand (Gen. 29). Deceived at the last moment by the wily Laban, Jacob married Leah by mistake and was forced to work another seven years for Rachel, though he was permitted to marry her after the seven days of Leah's wedding feast. The Rabbis chastised Jacob for his dislike of Leah, arguing that this was the reason that she was far more fertile than the "beloved" Rachel. They also criticized Jacob for his marriage to two sisters as a violation of Torah law. Even though the Torah had not yet been given, the Rabbis considered that the patriarchs observed all of its rules (Pes. 119b). With Leah, the long-barren Rachel, and their respective handmaidens, Zilpah and Bilhah, Jacob sired twelve sons and a daughter.

After the birth of Joseph, Jacob formally requested that Laban permit him to return to his native land with his wife and children. Realizing that he had become prosperous on Jacob's account, Laban convinced his son-in-law to stay. As wages for his unpaid services, Jacob asked to be given "every dark sheep [most in the area were white] and every spotted and speckled goat [usually dark brown or black]." Through a unique stratagem of genetic engineering involving striped shoots and selectively breeding the strongest animals, Jacob became extremely wealthy. He then received a Divine revelation to return to the land of his birth. Hoping that his brother Esau's anger had cooled after twenty years, Jacob gained the consent of his wives for the family to return to the land of Canaan.

The night before meeting his brother, "a man [angel of God] wrestled with him until the break of dawn" (Gen. 32:24ff). During this titanic struggle—which resulted in Jacob's name being changed to Israel, since he had "struggled with beings Divine and human and prevailed"—the attacker injured Jacob's thigh, resulting in a residual limp. Jews still commemorate this event by not eating the sciatic nerve, "the sinew of the thigh muscle on the socket of the hip." Who was this mysterious being? One explanation was the guardian angel protecting Esau (Gen. R. 77:3). Another was the demon of the river, which was determined to weaken Jacob before his confrontation with his older brother. A third explanation is that Jacob was struggling with himself, gaining the courage to squarely face the impending situation rather than his usual response of deceiving others and fleeing from potential conflict.

The Bible states that "Jacob was greatly afraid and was distressed [before meeting Esau]" (Gen. 32:8), which prompted the Rabbis to ask, "Are not fear and distress identical?" They explained that Jacob was "afraid" lest he be slain, but was "distressed" lest he be forced to kill Esau. As Jacob thought to himself: "During all these years he has dwelled in the Land of Israel; then perhaps he will attack me by virtue of his having done so. Again, during all these years he has duly honored his parents; then perhaps he will attack me because of that virtue [i.e., God may assist him because of it]" (Gen. R. 76:2).

The brothers were reconciled through Jacob's extravagant gifts and skillful diplomacy. Nevertheless, the Rabbis believed that Esau's gracious reconciliation with Jacob did not reflect his deepest feelings. Instead, the *aggadah* argued that Esau had tried to bite his brother, but Jacob's neck miraculously became like marble (Gen. R. 78:9). Jacob settled in Shechem, but after the rape of Dinah and her brothers' murderous revenge (Gen. 34), the family moved to Bethel and then to Hebron, the home of his parents. En route, his beloved Rachel died after giving birth to Benjamin (Gen. 35:16–20). Jacob's next tragedy was when his sons brought back the blood-soaked "coat of many colors," which he surmised meant that Joseph, Rachel's firstborn and his favorite, had been devoured by a wild beast (Gen. 37:31–35). In reality, the brothers had sold Joseph to traders heading toward Egypt. Years later, Jacob was reunited with Joseph, now viceroy of Egypt, whose first words upon revealing his identity to his brothers were, "Is my father still alive?" (Gen. 45:3). Jacob journeyed to Egypt, where Pharaoh warmly received him, and his family settled in Goshen (Gen. 46). Jacob adopted the two sons of Joseph, Ephraim and Manasseh, making them equal to his own sons and thus giving an extra portion to his favorite (Gen. 48). After blessing his sons who had assembled before him (Gen. 49), Jacob died at age 147. As the Talmud notes, "until Jacob there was no illness—one lived his allotted years in full health and then died suddenly. Then Jacob came and prayed, and illness came into being, allowing a person to better prepare for death" (BM 87a). Joseph complied with Jacob's final wish not to be buried in Egypt (Gen. 47:29–31). Jacob's body was embalmed according to Egyptian custom, and a great funeral procession, which included senior members of Pharaoh's court, accompanied it to Canaan. There the patriarch was buried in the family grave in the Cave of Machpelah in Hebron (Gen. 50), which was also named Kiryat Arba (City of the Four; Gen. 35:27) for the four couples who are buried there—Adam and Eve, Abraham and Sarah, Isaac and Rebecca, and Jacob and Leah (Er. 53a).

The Talmud (Ber. 26b) attributes the institution of the evening (*Ma'ariv*) prayer to Jacob, based on his having prayed before going to sleep on his stone pillow and dreaming of angels ascending and descending the ladder connecting the earth to heaven (Gen. 28:11). A *midrash* (Deut. R. 2:35) traces the origin of the *Shema*, the basic declaration of faith of the Jewish people in the Unity and Oneness of God and their acceptance of the yoke of the Kingdom of Heaven, to the last moments of the life of Jacob. The patriarch was concerned that his children and grandchildren, living in Egypt, would depart from the traditions of Abraham and serve the local gods. However, they put his mind at ease by assuring him: "Hear, O Israel [i.e., Jacob]: We accept the one God as our God." Thereupon, Jacob replied in a barely perceptible voice, "Praised is the Name of the glory of His kingdom forever" (Pes. 56a). This is one explanation for the tradition, since rabbinic times, that after the first verse of the *Shema* is recited in the synagogue, the Temple response ("Praised is the Name") is said silently (Pes. 56a). The sole exception is on Yom Kippur, when it is said aloud several times—after the first verse of the *Shema* and during the *Avodah* service in response to the three confessions of the high priest and his utterance of the holy Name of God (Tetragrammaton).

The Rabbis condemned Jacob for his favoritism toward Joseph (Shab. 10b). "Never single out one son, for on account of the two *sela*'s weight of silk [the coat of many colors] that Jacob gave Joseph in excess of his other sons, his brothers became jealous of him, and the matter resulted in the exile of our forefathers into Egypt" (Shab. 10b). The Rabbis also criticized Jacob for his prolonged absence from home, during which he failed to honor his parents. They argued that this was a serious offense, for which Jacob was punished by Joseph's disappearance for an equally long period (Meg. 16b). They also criticized Jacob's failure to plead with God against the Egyptian enslavement of his descendants (Shab. 89b). Nevertheless, the general consensus was that Jacob was a holy and virtuous man, one of those who tasted of the Garden of Eden in his lifetime, was not subject to the power of the Angel of Death (BB 17a), and, according to one view, never died at all (Taan. 5b). According to the *aggadah*, Jacob was the greatest (lit., "chosen one") of the patriarchs (Gen. R. 76:1). Unlike Abraham and Isaac, he did not father any unworthy sons (Gen. R. 68:11). Indeed, "Abraham was saved from the fiery furnace [of Nimrod] only for the sake of Jacob" (Gen. R. 63:2). The entire universe had been created only for the sake of Jacob (Lev. R. 36:4), who served as a symbol of the entire people of Israel. *See also* Ephraim; Issachar; Jephthah; Laban; Leah; Rachel; Samson.

Jael, wife of Heber the Kenite.

When the forces of Deborah and Barak routed the army of the Canaanites, Sisera, the enemy general, fled on foot from the battlefield and took refuge in Jael's tent. Lured by her hospitality, Sisera fell asleep. However, Jael took a hammer and drove a tent peg through his head (Judg. 4:21). Thus Deborah's prophecy to Barak (Judg. 4:9) proved true, as Israel was saved by a woman.

Interpreting the biblical verse, "More than women in the tent shall she [Jael] be blessed" (Judg. 5:24), the Talmud says that "women" referred to the matriarchs—Sarah, Rebecca, Rachel, and Leah (Sanh. 105b). Moreover, "Although the matriarchs gave birth to the children [of Israel], but for her [Jael] they would have been destroyed" (Gen. R. 48:15). In view of Jael being a descendant of Jethro, the father-in-law of Moses, the *aggadah* quips: "Jethro's good deed was that he received in his house a redeemer [Moses] who had fled from an enemy [Pharaoh], whereas from his house arose [Jael] who received an enemy [Sisera] who had fled from a redeemer [Barak], and she slew him" (Exod. R. 4:2).

Jael's voice was so seductive that it could arouse desire (Meg. 15a). Noting that the words "he sunk" and "he fell" occur three times each and "he lay" is found once in the relevant biblical verse (Judg. 5:27), the Talmud concludes: "The wicked wretch [Sisera] had sexual relations with Jael seven times after he fled from the battle . . . but she derived no pleasure from these acts" (Naz. 23b). From Jael's willingness to consort with Sisera, solely for the purpose of weakening the enemy so that she would be able to kill him, the Rabbis observed that a transgression done for the sake of Heaven (with good intentions) is greater than a mitzvah that is not done for the sake of Heaven (with no intent) (Hor. 10b). According to the Targum (Judg. 5:26), Jael killed Sisera with a hammer and a tent pin, rather than a spear or sword, so that she would not violate the biblical proscription (Deut. 22:5) against having a woman put on man's apparel, in this case using a typically male weapon.

Jair, Gileadite who judged Israel for twenty-two years after Tola (Judg. 10:3–5).

Japheth, one of the three sons of Noah.

Although generally considered the eldest (Sanh. 69b), Japheth is always mentioned third in the biblical account. Rather than joining Ham in mocking the drunken Noah who lay sleeping naked in his tent, Japheth assisted Shem in covering their father with a garment (Gen. 9:21–23). For this act, he earned Noah's blessing: "May God enlarge Japheth [increase his territory], and let him dwell in the tents of Shem; and let Canaan be a slave to them" (Gen.

8:26–27). The descendants of Japheth are usually identified as settling in island communities in the Mediterranean and Aegean (such as Javan, the Hebrew word for Greece) and adjacent regions northwest of the Land of Israel.

Japhia, king of Lachish.

He joined the coalition of five Amorite kings that was defeated by Joshua at Gibeon (Josh. 10:3). *See also* Adoni-Zedek.

Jehoahaz, sixteenth king of Judah (609 B.C.E.).

The fourth son of Josiah and also known as Shallum, Jehoahaz was named king "by the people of the land" after Josiah's death, even though not the first in line of succession, presumably because he favored the reformist policies of his father. However, after reigning only three months, Jehoahaz was removed from the throne by Necho, the Pharaoh whose forces had slain Josiah at Megiddo. Imprisoned in Egypt, Jehoahaz was the subject of a moving dirge composed by Jeremiah: "Weep bitterly for him who goes away; for he shall return no more, nor see the land of his birth" (Jer. 22:10).

Jehoash, seventh king of Judah (835–800 B.C.E.).

Hidden from the murderous rampage of his mother, Athaliah, who had killed all the other descendants of the House of David living at the time of his father Ahaziah's death, Jehoash was placed on the throne at age seven by Jehoiada, the high priest (2 Kings 11:4–19). Heavily influenced by Jehoiada, Jehoash repaired the Temple and destroyed the cult of Baal (2 Kings 12:7–16). After Jehoiada's death, however, Jehoash reinstituted the cult of Baal and even killed the high priest's son, Zechariah, when he opposed this return to pagan practices (2 Chron. 24:20–22). The treachery of Jehoash was avenged when he was assassinated by two of his own servants (2 Kings 12:20–21).

Jehoiachin, eighteenth king of Judah (598–597 B.C.E.).

According to the Book of 2 Kings (24:8–15), this son of Jehoiakim, also known as Jeconiah, ruled for less than four months after the peaceful death of his father. Jehoiachin was crowned by Nebuchadnezzar after he executed Jehoiakim. However, when reminded of the proverb, "Do not rear a gentle puppy born to a vicious dog, much less a vicious puppy of a vicious dog," Nebuchadnezzar realized the folly of keeping Jehoiachin as king (Lev. R. 19:6). The Babylonian ruler sent a request to the Sanhedrin to hand over Jehoiachin in exchange for not destroying the Temple. When informed of this, Jehoiachin took the keys to the Temple and went up to the roof and called out to God: "Now that we have not proved worthy stewards, faithful custodians for You, from now on the keys are [returned] to You." Jehoiachin threw the keys up in the air and they did not come down. Some say that a kind of fiery hand descended and took them, or that they remained suspended between heaven and earth (Lev. R. 19:6).

Nebuchadnezzar conquered Jerusalem and Jehoiachin was taken captive to Babylonia, where he was kept in solitary confinement. Realizing that the king was childless and the last survivor of the House of David, the Sanhedrin gained permission for his wife to be sent to him. When she informed Jehoiachin that she was menstrually unclean, he immediately separated from her. She counted the required number of days, purified herself, and immersed in the *mikveh*. God said to Jehoiachin: "In Jerusalem you did not keep the laws of family purity, but now you keep them?" Immediately God forgave Jehoiachin of all his sins (Lev. R. 19:6).

The Talmud notes that God acted charitably toward Israel by having Zedekiah and the bulk of the Jewish people exiled to Babylon in 586 B.C.E., at a time when the sages exiled earlier with Jehoiachin were still alive, so that they could teach Torah to the newcomers (Git. 88a). Jehoiachin remained in prison for thirty-six years. Following Nebuchadnezzar's death, his successor Evil-Merodach freed Jehoiachin and brought him into the royal palace, where he "set his throne above the throne of the kings who were with him in Babylonia" (2 Kings 25:27–30).

Jehoiakim, seventeenth king of Judah (609–598 B.C.E.).

The eldest son of Josiah, he succeeded his younger brother Jehoahaz, who had been deposed by Necho, the Egyptian Pharaoh. Originally known as "Eliakim," his name was changed to Jehoiakim by Necho, who demanded a huge tribute from Judah that required the imposition of crushing taxes on its population (2 Kings 23:34–36). Rebuked for having done "that which was evil in the sight of the Lord" (2 Kings 23:37), Jehoiakim was the antithesis of his pious father. Becoming a vassal of Nebuchadnezzar when the Babylonian king defeated Egypt, three years later Jehoiakim made the disastrous decision to rebel. Nebuchadnezzar's forces invaded the country, captured Jerusalem, and carried off Jehoiakim and many of the leaders of Judah (and much of the Temple treasury) to Babylonia (2 Chron. 36:6–7). According to Josephus, Jehoiakim's body was thrown over the gates of Jerusalem, as prophesied by Jeremiah (22:18–19).

The *aggadah* recites a litany of evil acts perpetrated by Jehoiakim. "He deliberately wore garments of *sha'atnez* (wool and linen combined); disguised his circumcision; engaged in incestuous relations with his mother, daughter-in-law, and stepmother; and murdered men whose wives he then violated and whose property he seized" (Lev. R. 19:6). Jehoiakim said, "My predecessors did not know how to anger God. Do we need anything [of His] besides His light [the sun]? But we have Parvaim gold, which we use [for light], so let him take His light!" The king's servants noted that silver and gold also belong to God, based on the verse, "The silver is Mine, and the gold is Mine, says the Lord of Hosts" (Hag. [Bible] 2:8). However, the arrogant Jehoiakim retorted, "He gave them to us long ago, as it is written, 'The heavens are the Lord's, but the earth He has given to mankind'" (Ps. 145:16). Jehoiakim was so evil that "God wished to return the entire world back into chaos [*tohu v'vohu*; formlessness and emptiness] on his account. But then God gazed at [the rest of] his generation [which was righteous] and was appeased" (Sanh. 103a).

Jehoram, fifth king of Judah (849–842 B.C.E.).

Married to Athaliah, the daughter of King Ahab of Israel, Jehoram adopted the idolatrous practices of his in-laws and renewed pagan worship in Judah (2 Kings 8:18). A vicious ruler, Jehoram slew his six brothers and other influential men in the kingdom to prevent a revolt against his disastrous policies, which resulted in rebellions by Edom and Libnah and an invasion by the Philistines. Nevertheless, Jehoram remained on the throne. "The Lord did not wish to destroy the house of David, because of the covenant that he had made with David, and his promise to give a light to him and to his sons forever" (2 Chron. 21:7). After two years of an illness that caused him severe pain, the wicked and despised Jehoram died unmourned, denied burial in the tombs of the kings in the City of David (2 Chron. 19–20).

Jehoshaphat, fourth king of Judah (870–849 B.C.E).

Jehoshaphat was the first king of Judah to enter into a close alliance with the Northern Kingdom, even betrothing his son Jehoram to Athaliah, the daughter of Ahab and Jezebel. During his reign, Jehoshaphat eradicated the pagan cults in Judah and sent priests and Levites throughout the land to teach the law of God (2 Chron. 17:7–9). He also reorganized the administration of justice, appointing judges in the cities of Judah and establishing a court of appeal in Jerusalem (2 Chron. 10:4–11).

According to the Talmud, "When he [Jehoshaphat] saw a Torah scholar, he would rise from his throne, embrace and kiss him, and call him 'my master, my master; my teacher, my teacher'" (Ket. 103b). It was from his table that the ravens brought food to sustain Elijah the prophet as he hid from the wicked Ahab (Num. R. 23:9).

Jephthah, Gileadite warrior who served as judge of Israel.

Although a mighty man of valor, Jephthah was the son of a harlot, and his father's legitimate sons drove him away from home (Judg. 11). Some years later, however, the elders of Gilead appealed to Jephthah to repel an Ammonite invasion. Jephthah agreed to return on the condition that he would remain the leader of the Gileadites after the conflict. When the time for battle arrived, Jephthah rashly vowed to sacrifice as a burnt offering to the Lord whatever would first come out of his house to meet him upon his victorious return. To his horror, it was his only daughter who rushed out first "with tambourines and dances" to greet him. Nevertheless, Jephthah felt obliged to fulfill his solemn vow. Resigned to her fate, his daughter begged to live for two months so that she might have time to mourn with her companions. At the end of this period she met her tragic end. A custom then developed among Israelite women to commemorate this event by an annual four-day mourning period.

After the war, the Ephraimites rebuked Jephthah for not having called them to take part, threatening to "burn your house upon you with fire." In turn, Jephthah accused them of cowardly failing to assist him in battle. After seizing the fords of the Jordan, Jephthah required that every fugitive attempting to cross the river pronounce the word *shibboleth*. Those 42,000 who betrayed their Ephraimite origin by saying *sibboleth* were put to death (Judg. 12:1–7).

The Rabbis attacked Jephthah for both making and fulfilling his rash vow. All were convinced that he must have been an ignorant man for failing to realize that such a vow was invalid. ("Jephthah was no more lettered than a block of sycamore wood"; Tanh. Behukotai 5.) One sage maintained that Jephthah was only required to pay a specific sum to the sacred treasury of the Temple to be absolved from the vow; another argued that he was free from fulfilling it even without any payment. According to the *aggadah*, God was angry at Jephthah's vow: "What will Jephthah do if a dog, a pig, or a camel [i.e., some unclean animal] comes out to meet him? Would he offer it to Me?" When about to be sacrificed, his daughter asked, "Is it written in the Torah that human beings should be brought as burnt offerings?" When Jephthah protested about the sacredness of his vow, she reminded her father that although Jacob had vowed to give to the Lord a tenth part of anything that God gave him (Gen. 28:22), "Did he sacrifice any of his sons?" Nevertheless, the stubborn Jephthah refused to relent (Gen. R. 60:3).

According to legend, part of the blame for the catastrophic conclusion of this episode was due to the stubbornness of Pinchas, the high priest, who had the right to absolve a person from a vow. However, as the high priest and son of a high priest, Pinchas considered it beneath his dignity to call on an ignoramus. Similarly, as chief of the tribes of Israel, Jephthah refused to demean himself by calling on a commoner. Consequently, both men were held liable for the daughter's innocent blood. Pinchas was deprived of his Divine Inspiration (spirit of prophecy). As Jephthah moved from place to place, his limbs dropped off one by one, and they were buried where they fell. Consequently, the biblical verse is: "Then Jephthah the Gileadite died and was buried in the *cities* of Gilead" (Judg. 12:7), rather than "in *a city* of Gilead" (Gen. R. 60:3).

Although considered one of the least worthy of the judges, the Torah states: "The Lord sent Jerubbaal, and Bedan, and Jephthah, and Samuel, and delivered you from the hand of your enemies on every side, and you lived in security" (1 Sam. 12:11). From this the Rabbis deduced that "Jephthah, in his generation, was like Samuel in his generation," teaching that even the most unworthy person, once appointed a leader of the community, is to be regarded as one of the greatest (RH 25b).

Jeremiah, second of the major prophets (seventh-sixth century B.C.E.).

Son of Hilkiah, a priest of Anatot (Jer. 1:1), Jeremiah witnessed the tragic events that ended in the destruction of Jerusalem. Initially, Jeremiah refused the Divine call, pointing to Moses, Aaron, Elijah, and Elisha, all of whom suffered intense sorrow and mockery at the hand of their fellow Jews. "I do not know how to speak, for I am still a boy" (Jer. 1:6). But God reassured Jeremiah with promises of both protection and verbal inspiration. "Go wherever I send you and speak whatever I command you. Have no fear of them, for I am with you to deliver you" (Jer. 1:7–8). Nevertheless, Jeremiah suffered scorn and physical threats from several kings and the general populace.

Although he began his prophecy in the thirteenth year of the reign of King Josiah (626 B.C.E.), Jeremiah barely mentioned the discovery of the Deuteronomic law five years later and the subsequent religious reforms that occurred during this time. Indeed, when a question arose about the authenticity of the scroll, it was the prophetess Huldah, rather than Jeremiah, who was consulted (2 Kings 22:14). Realizing that a new empire was rising that could not be successfully resisted militarily, Jeremiah urged voluntary submission to Babylonia. However, this pessimistic view was rejected, his writings were burned, and Jeremiah spent time in prison. After the fall of Jerusalem, Jeremiah remained in the capital until the murder of Gedaliah, the Babylonian-appointed governor. After this event, Jeremiah was taken against his will to Egypt, where he died.

Jeremiah severely castigated the people for forsaking God and the Torah and turning to idolatry. Using the relationship of husband and wife as an analogy to that between God and Israel, Jeremiah accused Israel of being unfaithful to God, like a wife betraying her husband for a lover. Therefore, he exhorted the people to worship the Lord with repentance, stressing the responsibility of each individual for his or her own acts. Jeremiah's prophecies foretold the disaster that would befall his people as punishment for their sins, but they rejected his doom-laden words. Although a prophet of apocalypse, Jeremiah emphasized the temporary nature of the destruction. He consoled the people with the assurance that God would redeem them from captivity, enabling a righteous Israel to eventually dwell in safety in its own land.

"Truly the Lord has comforted Zion, comforted all her ruins. He has made her wilderness like Eden, her desert like the Garden of the Lord. Gladness and joy shall abide there, thanksgiving and the sound of music" (Jer. 51:3).

According to tradition, Jeremiah was the author of the Book of Lamentations, the third of the *megillot* and the sixth book in the Writings section of the Bible. It describes the Babylonian destruction of Jerusalem in 586 B.C.E. and the exile of the Jewish people from their land. The Book of Lamentations is recited in a haunting melody on the fast day of Tisha b'Av. The next-to-last verse—"Turn us back, O Lord, and let us return; renew our days as of old" (Lam. 5:21)—is repeated by everyone so that even this mournful book ends on a hopeful note. This same verse is the final line sung as the ark is closed after the scroll has been returned to it following the Torah reading.

The *aggadah* relates that Jeremiah was a descendant of Rahab by her marriage with Joshua (Meg. 14b). As an early sign of his eventual prophetic mission, Jeremiah was born circumcised (ARN 2). When a newborn infant, he spoke in the voice of a youth and rebuked his mother for her unfaithfulness. Jeremiah then explained to his shocked mother that he was not actually referring to her, but rather to the inhabitants of Zion and Jerusalem (Pes. Rab. 26): "They deck out their daughters, and clothe them in purple, and put golden crowns on their heads; but the robbers shall come and take these things away."

Jeremiah was commanded by God to go to his birthplace of Anatot, because as long as he stayed in Jerusalem it could not be destroyed (due to his merits). Once he departed, the city was conquered and the Temple set on fire (PdRK 13:119). When Jeremiah returned and saw smoke rising from the Temple, he thought that "the people Israel have repented and are offering sacrifices." However, when he realized his mistake, Jeremiah wept bitterly. He accompanied the captives as far as the Euphrates, but then returned to comfort those who had been left behind (Pes. Rab. 26). Nearing the ruins of Jerusalem, Jeremiah recalled: "I raised my eyes and saw a woman sitting at the top of the mountain clothed in black, her hair uncombed. She was crying and pleading, 'Who will comfort me?' I approached her and said, 'If you are a woman, speak to me; but if you are a spirit, depart.' When she replied, 'I am your mother Zion,' Jeremiah comforted her with the promise, 'In times to come [says the Lord], I will rebuild you'" (Pes. Rab. 26). *See also* Baruch; Rachel.

Jeroboam, first ruler of the Kingdom of Israel (931–910 B.C.E.).

Jeroboam served as chief superintendent of Solomon's extensive building projects for the bands of forced laborers from the tribes of Manasseh and his native Ephraim. Jeroboam plotted against the king after falling under the spell of the prophet Ahijah, who symbolically tore his robe into twelve pieces and gave ten of them to Jeroboam to foretell his ultimate rule. When his conspiracy was discovered, Jeroboam was forced to flee to Egypt. However, following Solomon's death and the refusal of his successor, Rehoboam, to ease the unbearable burden of taxation and forced labor, the ten northern tribes declared their political independence from the House of David and appointed Jeroboam as their king (1 Kings 12:1–20). Jeroboam rebuilt and fortified Shechem as his capital. He erected two golden calves in Dan and Bethel, respectively, near the northern and southern borders of his kingdom, and transformed these sites into holy shrines in competition with Jerusalem, so that the people would have no need to make pilgrimages to worship in the Davidic capital. In the fifth year of his reign, Shishak, the king of Egypt and Jeroboam's former protector, invaded Israel and plundered many of its villages.

Using various permutations of Hebrew words that could form his name, the *aggadah* states that he was called Jeroboam either because he debased the nation, fomented strife within the nation by his introduction of calf worship, or caused friction between Israel and their Father in Heaven. His father, Nabat, saw fire emerging from his body and interpreted it as signifying that he would reign. However, he was wrong, for it was his son Jeroboam who became king.

Why did Jeroboam merit becoming king? Because he once had the courage to rebuke King Solomon for his misdeeds. Unlike his father David, who widened all the entrances in the walls surrounding the city of Jerusalem to encourage people to visit the Temple on the pilgrimage festivals, Solomon sealed all the breaches in the wall, thus forcing the people to enter only through the official gates. Even worse, Solomon's motivation for this act was to collect a special tax from anyone entering the city, which he then used to support the household of one of his wives, the daughter of Pharaoh. Although rewarded for having reproved Solomon, God later punished Jeroboam for having rebuked Solomon in public, thus shaming him in front of the people (Sanh. 101b).

Attacked for what was considered little short of idolatry, Jeroboam is described in the Bible as one "who sinned and made Israel sin" (1 Kings 14:16). The Talmud lists Jeroboam as one of the three kings, along with Ahab and Manasseh, who have "no portion in the World to Come" (Sanh. 90a).

Jesse, father of King David.

A wealthy Bethlehemite from the tribe of Judah, Jesse was the son of Obed and the grandson of Ruth and Boaz. Isaiah predicted that the Messiah eventually would come "from the root of Jesse" (Isa. 11:10). The Talmud (Suk. 52b) lists Jesse as the first of the "eight [messianic] princes among men" (Mic.

5:4), the others being Saul, Samuel, Amos, Zephaniah, Zedekiah, the Messiah, and Elijah, with some sources reversing the last two.

Jethro, priest of Midian, and the father-in-law of Moses.

Because he was also called Reuel ("friend of God"; Exod. 2:18), some modern scholars have suggested that Jethro (*Yitro* in Hebrew) was an honorific title meaning "His Excellency." According to tradition, Jethro initially was a priest to idols (Sot. 43a) and "there was not a deity in the world that he had not worshiped (Mech. Yitro 1:1). However, he later repented after seeing how God destroyed Amalek (Exod. R. 27:6). God sent down manna for him (Exod. R. 27:5), as for all Israelites, and he became a Jew (Yalkut Shimoni, Yitro 268).

Arriving at the well in Midian after fleeing Egypt, Moses came to the aid of Jethro's seven daughters who were being abused by local shepherds. After watering their sheep, he was welcomed into the home of Jethro, who gave Moses one of his daughters, Zipporah, as a wife and appointed him as shepherd of his flocks (Exod. 2:15–21; 3:1).

From the biblical narrative, it appears that Moses went to Egypt without his family when preparing to confront Pharaoh or sent them back to Midian for their protection. It was only after Moses and the Israelites had crossed the Sea of Reeds during the Exodus from Egypt or, according to some, after the Revelation at Mount Sinai, that Jethro "brought Moses' sons and wife to him in the wilderness, where he was encamped at the mountain of God" (Exod. 18:5–27). When Moses told Jethro of all the miracles that God had performed for the Israelites in delivering them from bondage, Jethro exclaimed: "Blessed be the Lord. . . . Now I know that the Lord is greater than all gods." When on the next day he saw that Moses sat "from morning until evening . . . [as] magistrate among the people," Jethro told his son-in-law that "the task is too heavy for you; you cannot do it alone." Consequently, he convinced Moses to delegate some of his responsibilities by appointing deputies to assist him in deciding minor disputes, reserving only the difficult matters for himself. Then Jethro "went his way to his own land." According to the Mechilta (Yitro 1:2), his motivation was to "convert all the people, bring them to Torah study, and draw them under the wings of the *Shechinah*."

A *midrash* relates how Jethro saved the life of the young Moses. When Pharaoh hugged and kissed the child, Moses took the royal crown and placed it on his own head. The Egyptian sorcerers warned that this act indicated that the boy was destined to take away the kingdom. Some suggested that Moses be executed by the sword, others by fire. But Jethro, who sat among them, argued that the boy simply did not understand what he was doing. He urged Pharaoh to test Moses by placing before him a plate containing gold and glowing coal. "If he reaches for the gold, he has understanding and you will kill him. If he reaches for the coal, he has no understanding and does not deserve the death penalty." The two objects were brought before Moses, who initially reached for the gold. But the angel Gabriel came and pushed away his hand, and Moses burned his fingers on the hot coals (Exod. R. 1:26). *See also* Jael.

Jezebel, wife of Ahab, the seventh king of Israel.

Daughter of Ethbaal, king of Sidon, Jezebel championed the spread of idolatry in Israel. She influenced her husband to build a pagan temple and provide support for "450 prophets of Baal and 400 prophets of [the goddess] Asherah who eat at Jezebel's table" (1 Kings 18:18–19). Hoping to have these cults replace the worship of God as the religion of Israel, Jezebel killed large numbers of the prophets of the Lord. She would have slain them all, except for the heroic efforts of Obadiah, the devout overseer of Ahab's house.

Jezebel conceived and executed the plot to kill Naboth for refusing to sell to Ahab a vineyard that the king coveted (1 Kings 21). For this heinous act, Elijah the prophet predicted the queen's violent death ("The dogs shall eat Jezebel") and the destruction of their royal line. Jezebel's corrupting influence also had a disastrous effect on the Kingdom of Judah, for her daughter Athaliah married King Jehoram, son of Jehoshaphat, and spread Baal worship and pagan cults to this land as well. Depicted by the Bible as the epitome of wickedness and ruthlessness, the name Jezebel has become synonymous with a scheming, devious, and morally corrupt woman.

According to the Talmud, Jezebel instigated all of the sins of her husband, Ahab (JT Sanh. 10:2). "Every day she would weigh out golden shekels for idols" (Sanh. 102b), and all the righteous in Israel were in hiding because of her (Hul. 4b). To excite her passionless husband, Jezebel had two paintings of harlots placed in his chariot so that he would see them and warm up (become excited) (Sanh. 39b).

Yet Jezebel did have one redeeming quality. Whenever a bride and groom passed her house next to the marketplace, she would go outside, clap her hands, sing in their honor, and walk ten steps. Whenever a dead body was carried through the marketplace, she would join in the mourning and follow the procession for a few steps. As a reward for these actions, despite Elijah's prophecy that she would be eaten by dogs, these animals did not consume the limbs that had performed acts of kindness. Consequently, "[When] they went to bury her, they found no more than the skull, the feet, and the palms of her hands [2 Kings 9:35]" (PdRE 17). *See also* Ahab.

Joab, son of Zeruiah, a sister of David, and commander in chief of the king's army.

A brave general who was loyal to David and a confidant of the king, Joab took the lead in suppressing internal revolts, such as that of the king's son Absalom. Joab ordered Absalom to be killed, despite the king's urgent command that his son's life be spared (2 Sam. 18:14). Joab also murdered Abner, either to avenge the death of his brother Asahel or to remove an obvious rival. In the dispute over the succession to David's throne, Joab supported Adonijah, unaware that David preferred Solomon. David ordered Solomon to take vengeance on Joab, arguing that one who had shed innocent blood should not be allowed to go down to the grave in peaceful old age (1 Kings 2:5–6). Realizing that his life was in danger, Joab fled to the Sanctuary and seized hold of the horns of the Altar (1 Kings 2:28). Nevertheless, Solomon ordered Joab struck down, determined to carry out his father's dying injunction to remove "guilt from me and my father's house for the blood of the innocent that he [Joab] shed without cause" (1 Kings 2:31).

According to the Rabbis, "But for David [who studied Torah constantly], Joab could not have succeeded in waging war; and without Joab, David could not have devoted himself to [the study of] Torah." His house was "like a wilderness," meaning that it was "free to all" (everyone, even the most needy, could find hospitality there) and "free from theft and immorality" (Sanh. 49a). Joab "kept alive [fed] the rest of the city" (1 Chron. 11:8) by sharing even the smallest meal with the poor (Sanh. 49a). Prior to his death, David commanded that Joab be brought to trial before Solomon for having killed Abner and Amasa (1 Kings 2:5). Joab was acquitted for the murder of Abner, since this was to avenge the blood of his brother Asahel, whom Abner had killed. However, Solomon did not accept Joab's defense of justifiable homicide in killing Amasa for treason in delaying to fulfill a royal command (Sanh. 49a).

When David decided to take a census of the people, Joab vainly tried to convince the king against this action, which resulted in God's anger against David and all Israel (1 Chron. 21:4).

Job, title figure of the biblical book, which explores the basic question of theodicy—if God is just, benevolent, and omnipresent, why do good people suffer?

A native of Uz, Job was a wealthy, pious, and upright man who had seven sons and three daughters. God taunted Satan, "Have you noticed My servant Job? There is no one like him on earth, a blameless and upright man who fears God and shuns evil." Satan cynically replied that it was easy for a rich man to love and revere God, but if Job were to lose all that he had, he would renounce and curse God (Job 1:6–11). Why did Satan make this challenge? An *aggadic* explanation is that when Satan saw God praising Job in scripture more than He had praised Abraham, he feared that Abraham's intense love for God might be forgotten, and that all of Abraham's actions for the sake of heaven might not receive their deserved reward (BB 15b–16a).

Even when his children were killed and he lost his vast possessions, Job did not reproach God. Instead, he declared God's act to be just, saying: "The Lord gave and the Lord has taken away; blessed be the Name of the Lord" (Job 1:21). Even after Job himself was afflicted with painful sores, he refused to curse God.

Most of the Book of Job consists of a poetic dialogue between Job and three of his friends who come to mourn with and comfort him. However, Job refuses to accept their traditional argument that he must have been guilty of some transgression, based on the idea that the righteous cannot perish and only the wicked suffer in just measure for their sins. Finally, God enters the scene and chastises the three friends for their arrogant assumption that they could fathom the Divine will. At the end of the book, God vindicates Job and restores his health and wealth (giving him twice as much as he had before), and Job sires a new family. Although never revealing the reason for Job's suffering, which remains a Divine mystery, God communicates directly with Job and assures him of His Presence.

When did Job live? The Rabbis had widely different opinions, based on inferences gleaned from making an analogy between two biblical words or sentences, which included the times of Abraham; Jacob (with Job marrying his daughter, Dinah); slavery in Egypt (Job was born when Jacob and his children entered Egypt and died 210 years later when the Israelites left that country); Moses (who in this view was the actual author of the Book of Job); the spies; the judges; and King Ahasuerus of Persia (BB 14b–15b). Some Rabbis said that Job was among those who returned from the Babylonian Exile (JT Sot. 8), while one even declared that "Job never was and never existed, but is only a typical figure [a parable to teach men the virtue of resignation]" (BB 15a). One view was that Job was to have lived only seventy years, but his years were doubled after his sufferings and he lived on for 140 more years (total of 210) (BB 15b).

According to one *aggadic* tale, at the time of the birth of Moses, Job was with Balaam and Jethro when the plan was made to issue a decree that all the infant Hebrew males would be drowned in the Nile. "Balaam, who devised the scheme, was slain; Job, who silently acquiesced, was afflicted with sufferings; Jethro, who fled, merited that his descendants should sit in the Chamber of Hewn Stone [i.e., in the Temple where the Sanhedrin met]" (Sot. 11a).

The Zohar (2:33a) took a different view, saying that when Pharaoh wanted to destroy the Israelites, Job suggested that instead he take their money and subject their bodies to hard labor. The Divine punishment was that the same sentence be pronounced against Job, so that his wealth was taken away and his body afflicted.

Nevertheless, the *aggadah* says that no one among the nations was more righteous than Job (Deut. R. 2:4), and that he was one of four who recognized God on their own (Num. R. 14:2) and one of seven who prophesized to the nations of the world (ARN 2). Job was a paragon of generosity and, like Abraham, built his house with four doors opening to the cardinal points of the compass, so that wayfarers did not have to walk around it to enter. He was devoted to charitable causes, such as visiting the sick, and "anyone who took a penny [of charity] from Job was blessed" (Pes. 112a).

On Tisha b'Av, the fast day commemorating the destruction of the two Temples in Jerusalem, it is forbidden to study Mishnah and Talmud or even read most parts of the Torah. Only the Book of Job, along with Lamentations and the "sad parts of Jeremiah," are permitted (Taan. 30a). According to the Talmud, "He who sees the Book of Job in a dream may anticipate a misfortune" (Ber. 57b).

When R. Yochanan finished reading the Book of Job, he used to say: "The end of man is to die, and the end of a beast is to be slaughtered, and all are doomed to die. Happy is he who was brought up in the Torah, whose labor was in the Torah, who has given pleasure to his Creator, who grew up with a good name, and departed the world with a good name. Of him [Job] Solomon said: 'A good name is better than precious oil, and the day of death than the day of one's birth' [Eccles. 7:1]" (Ber. 17a).

Jochebed, wife of Amram, and the mother of Moses, Aaron, and Miriam.

The text initially described her as simply "a Levite woman" (Exod. 2:1). Because Jochebed was Amram's aunt (she was the daughter of Levi; he was Levi's grandson), their marriage would have been forbidden according to the law given after the Revelation at Mount Sinai (Lev. 18:12).

The Talmud identifies Jochebed with Shiphrah, one of the two Hebrew midwives, either because she straightened (*meshapperet*) the limbs of the children she delivered, or because the Israelites were fruitful (*sheparu*) and multiplied in her days (Sot. 11b). The verse, "And because the midwives feared God, He established households for them" (Exod. 1:21), was interpreted as Jochebed's "houses" being the priesthood and royalty, which went to her sons Aaron and Moses, respectively (Exod. R. 48:5). *See also* Shiphrah.

Joel, second of the minor prophets.

The Book of Joel provides a vivid description of a plague of locusts of unprecedented severity that destroyed fields and vineyards and deprived the people of food. The prophet called on the people to repent and seek the Lord's mercy to save themselves from the impending punishment of the nations that had oppressed Judah. The four species of locusts that devastated the land were later seen as metaphors for the four world empires that were most destructive to the Jewish people—Babylonia, Persia, Greece, and Rome. In the final part of his book, Joel portrays a golden age when God will restore His exiled people to their land, which will be blessed with great fertility. He concludes with the promise, "Judah shall abide forever, and Jerusalem from generation to generation" (Joel 4:20).

Jonah, fifth and most famous of the minor prophets (eighth century B.C.E.).

The son of Amitai, Jonah was commanded to go to Nineveh and announce to its inhabitants that God would destroy the city because of their wickedness ("Nineveh shall be overturned"; Jon. 3:4). However, the reluctant prophet "did not know whether it was for good or for bad" (i.e., whether the "overturning" meant their spiritual repentance or their physical destruction) (Sanh. 89b). According to a *midrash*, Jonah feared that once the inhabitants of Nineveh repented, God would turn his wrath on the unrepentant Israelites. He concluded: "As if it were not enough that the Israelites call me a false prophet, even idolaters will do so" (PdRE 10).

Consequently, Jonah attempted to flee the Divine calling by boarding a ship bound in the opposite direction, toward Tarshish, a gentile country outside the Land of Israel where "the Divine Presence does not reveal itself [to prophets]" (Mech. Pesikta 25). However, God brought on a savage storm that terrified the sailors, who tossed their cargo overboard and frantically prayed to their gods. Jonah calmly fell asleep until awakened by the captain, who urged him to pray to his God for mercy. The sailors cast lots to determine who was responsible for the storm, and the lot fell upon Jonah, who disclosed that he was fleeing from a Divine mission. After the sailors futilely attempted to row back to land, Jonah convinced them to throw him overboard and the storm suddenly abated.

Jonah was swallowed by a "great fish" (often mistranslated as a whale). After spending three days and nights in the belly of the fish praying to God, the fish spewed Jonah out onto dry land. After God called Jonah a second time, he finally obeyed the Divine will and went to Nineveh to prophesy its destruction. When the people repented and God renounced the planned punishment, Jonah was greatly displeased by this Divine forgiveness (since his prophecy of destruction did not come true) and petulantly asked God to take his life.

While Jonah sat sweltering in the hot sun outside Nineveh, God caused a large plant to grow and provide welcome shade. On the following day, however, God sent a worm to attack the plant, which withered and died. As the heat of the day increased, Jonah became faint and asked for death. Then God said: "You cared about the plant, which you did not work for and which you did not grow, which appeared overnight and perished overnight. And should I not care about Nineveh, that great city, in which there are more than 120,000 persons who do not yet know their right hand from their left, and many beasts as well?" Because of its message of Divine forgiveness in response to true repentance, the entire Book of Jonah is the *haftarah* read in synagogue for the afternoon service on Yom Kippur.

Jonathan, eldest son of Saul, and the loyal friend and constant companion of David.

Soon after his father's accession to the throne of Israel, Jonathan was given command of one-third of the army (1,000 men; 1 Sam. 13:2). A brave and strong youth and a shrewd military commander, Jonathan led a bold surprise attack that routed the Philistines (1 Sam. 14:6–23). Unbeknown to Jonathan, Saul had issued a curse on anyone who would eat any food while pursuing the fleeing enemy. Coming across some wild honey, Jonathan dipped a rod into a honeycomb, put some of the honey into his mouth, "and his eyes were brightened." When Saul sentenced Jonathan to death, the people, recognizing that his courage was responsible for the victory, interceded on Jonathan's behalf, and saved his life (1 Sam. 14:24–45).

Even though he was heir to the throne, Jonathan recognized that David would succeed Saul as king ("You will be king over Israel, and I will be second to you"; 1 Sam. 23:17). When Saul threatened to kill David, Jonathan arranged for David to escape his father's wrath. However, his inadvertent oversight in failing to provide food for his fleeing friend had dire consequences: "Had Jonathan given David two loaves of bread for his travels, [David would have had no reason to ask Ahimelech for food] then Nob, the city of priests, would not have been massacred, Doeg the Edomite would not have been banished, and Saul and his three sons would not have been slain" (Sanh. 104a).

Hearing of the battlefield deaths of Saul and his sons, David wept bitterly and tore his clothes. However, his deepest grief was reserved for Jonathan, whom David eulogized as "My brother, you were most dear to me. Your love was wonderful to me, surpassing the love of women" (2 Sam. 1:26).

Joseph, firstborn son of Rachel, the favorite wife of Jacob.

After years of barrenness, Rachel named her longed-for baby Joseph, praying that God "add [*yosef* in Hebrew] another son for me" (Gen. 30:24). The name also could have derived from another Hebrew word, *asaf* (take away), implying that God had removed her disgrace. The jet-black flag of Joseph was embroidered with an outline of Egypt, in honor of his two sons that were born there (Num. R. 2:8). According to the *aggadah*, Divine inspiration rested on Joseph from his youth until his death, guiding him in all matters of wisdom (PdRE) and ensuring that "the evil eye has no power over the seed of Joseph" (Ber. 20a).

Joseph was the master biblical dreamer and interpreter of dreams. As the youngest and most beloved son of Jacob, he engendered the hatred of his brothers by relating his dreams of their sheaves bowing down to his (Gen. 37:7), and of the sun (Jacob), moon (Rachel), and eleven stars (the brothers) bowing down to him (Gen. 37:9). When the brothers exclaimed, "Would you then reign over us? Would you then dominate us?" little did they realize that this would be precisely the situation when they eventually traveled to Egypt and unsuspectingly placed themselves at the mercy of Joseph, who had become the all-powerful viceroy of the country.

Given a ceremonial robe ("coat of many colors") by his doting father, as a teenager Joseph was sent by his father to visit his shepherd brothers and report back on their welfare. Seeing their favored sibling from a distance, their hostility flared into a desire to murder him. When Joseph approached, the brothers stripped him of his robe and cast him into a pit full of deadly snakes and scorpions (Gen. R. 84:16). Rather than kill him, Judah suggested selling their brother to an approaching caravan for twenty pieces of silver (Gen. 37:25–26), and thus Joseph was carried to Egypt. Seeking to deceive their father about Joseph's fate, the brothers dipped his robe in the blood of a slaughtered kid and brought it to Jacob. Recognizing it and assuming that his son had been torn to pieces by a savage beast, Jacob mourned for Joseph with inconsolable grief.

Arriving in Egypt, Joseph was sold to Potiphar, a courtier and chief steward of Pharaoh. Joseph soon earned the complete confidence of his master, who promoted him to be his personal attendant and overseer of his estate. When Potiphar's wife attempted to seduce the handsome young Hebrew slave, Joseph resisted the temptation and rejected her advances. The *aggadah* relates that when Joseph was at the point of succumbing to her wiles, he was prevented from sinning by seeing "his father's face," possibly a reflection of his own face in a mirror (Gen. R. 87:7). In revenge, Potiphar's wife falsely accused Joseph of attacking her, whereupon Potiphar imprisoned him. Asking why Potiphar merely threw Joseph into prison rather than having him executed, the Rabbis envisioned him saying to Joseph: "I know that you are innocent, but [I must do this] lest a stigma fall on my children [i.e., as the children of a harlot, if he did not pretend to believe her]." Had Potiphar really believed her, he surely would have put Joseph to death (Gen. R. 87:9).

While in prison, Joseph successfully interpreted the dreams of two fellow inmates—the cupbearer of Pharaoh, who had been cast into prison because "a fly was found in the goblet he prepared," and the baker, because "a pebble was found in his confection" (Gen. R. 88:2). Stressing that "interpretations belong to God," Joseph correctly explained that within three days the cupbearer would be restored to his former position, but the baker would be executed (Gen. 40:5–23). Joseph's request that the butler intercede with Pharaoh on his behalf was criticized by the Rabbis, who argued that he should not have placed his trust in a mortal man and thus was forced to remain in prison for two more years (Gen. R. 89:2).

When Pharaoh dreamed of seven robust cows eaten by seven scrawny ones and seven full ears of corn swallowed up by seven withered ones, the court magicians were unable to interpret the meaning (Gen. 41:17–24). The cupbearer belatedly remembered Joseph's skill at dream interpretation and had the Hebrew prisoner brought to the palace. According to Joseph, these were two versions of a single dream, in which God was revealing to Pharaoh that there would be seven years of abundance followed by seven years of famine (Gen. 41:25–32). Not only did Joseph provide an interpretation, he also urged Pharaoh to select someone to amass food during the years of plenty that could be used during the famine years. Pharaoh selected Joseph himself for the task, noting that "since God has made all this known to you, there is none so discerning and wise as you" (Gen. 41:39). So Joseph became the viceroy of Egypt, second in command only to Pharaoh. He was given a wife, Asenath, whom the Bible described as the daughter of Poti-Phera, priest of On (Gen. 41:45). A *midrash* identifies her as the daughter of Dinah, and thus Joseph's niece, who was later adopted by Potiphar (PdRE 38).

During the famine, Joseph's brothers were forced to go down to Egypt to purchase grain. Joseph recognized them but did not reveal himself, instead speaking harshly to them, interrogating them and accusing them of spying, and confining them for three days before sending them home with food, while keeping Shimon as a surety. Joseph insisted that they bring Benjamin to Egypt, and he arranged that the money used for purchasing grain be put back into the brothers' sacks (Gen. 42:7–26). Though fearing the loss of his youngest son, Jacob agreed to permit the brothers to return with Benjamin to Egypt. Joseph freed Shimon and received gifts from the brothers, who offered to repay the cost of the original purchases. Upon seeing Benjamin, Joseph was overcome with emotion and rushed from the room to weep (Gen. 43). Once again, Joseph instructed his steward to restore the purchase money in each bag of grain and to put his personal silver divining goblet into the sack of Benjamin. Then he sent his steward to chase after the brothers and accuse them of having stolen the goblet. Unaware of the true situation, the brothers vigorously protested their innocence, offering to become slaves if it be found in their possession.

Although the steward insisted that only the culprit would be enslaved, when a search disclosed the goblet in Benjamin's sack, they all returned to Joseph and begged for mercy (Gen. 44:1–17). After Judah's impassioned plea volunteering to be imprisoned in place of Benjamin, lest the loss of his youngest son cause Jacob's death, Joseph realized that his brothers had learned from their previous actions toward him. So Joseph finally revealed his identity, assuring his frightened brothers that their selling him years previously had actually been an act of Providence to provide for the survival of their family during the years of famine. After this dramatic narrative, the elderly Jacob joined the family in Goshen (Gen. 47:11–12). Joseph was separated from his father (Jacob) for twenty-two years, the same length of time that the patriarch Jacob had been separated from his father, Isaac (Meg. 17a). Jacob adopted Joseph's two sons, giving each of them a portion of his inheritance but transferring the birthright from the elder, Manasseh, to the younger, Ephraim (Gen. 48:1–20). After the death of Jacob, his brothers claimed that their father asked Joseph to forgive them for having sold their younger brother into slavery (Gen. 50:16). Although Jacob never made such a statement, the Rabbis forgave the brothers this "white lie," since their words were only meant to serve the valuable purpose of maintaining family harmony (Yev. 65b).

On his deathbed, Joseph made his brothers swear that, when the time was ripe, they would transfer his remains to the Promised Land. The Book of Genesis concludes: "Joseph died at the age of 110 [considered an ideal age among the Egyptians], and he was embalmed and placed in a coffin in Egypt" (Gen. 50:26). Interpreting the verse, "And Joseph died and all his brothers" (Exod. 1:6), the Talmud notes that Joseph was mentioned as dying first "because he assumed airs of authority" (Ber. 55a). The tragedy of the slave experience of the Israelites in Egypt began with the opening of the Book of Exodus, when "a new king arose over Egypt who did not know Joseph" (Exod. 1:8). *See also* Benjamin; Ephraim; Manasseh; Potiphar.

Joshua, son of Nun, chieftain of the tribe of Ephraim, and the successor of Moses.

Originally known as Hoshea, shortly before he was sent with the other eleven spies to scout the land of Canaan, his name was changed by Moses to Joshua by adding a *yud*, half of a Divine name. As the Talmud relates, the *yud* that God had removed from Sarah (when her name was changed from Sarai) continuously cried out for many years in protest of this act until God added it to Joshua's name, to convert it from Hosea to Joshua (Sanh. 107a). According to a *midrash*, his new name (meaning "may God save") reflected the hope that God would prevent Joshua from joining the future conspiracy of the spies (Sot. 34b). Risking their lives by refuting the negative report of the majority, Joshua and Caleb tried to convince the people that with God's help they could overwhelm the giant inhabitants and conquer the land (Num. 14:6–10). As a reward for their faith in the Divine promise, of all the Israelites twenty years old and upward at the time, only Joshua and Caleb were allowed to enter the Promised Land (Num. 14:29–30). When the Israelites finally entered the Land of Israel, Joshua ordained the blessing for the land in the *Birkat ha-Mazon* (Grace after Meals) (Ber. 48b).

Joshua first appeared as a military leader in the victory over the Amalekites, who attacked the Israelites shortly after the Exodus from Egypt (Exod. 17:9–13). Described as the "attendant" (lit., "servant") of Moses (Exod. 24:13; 33:11), Joshua accompanied Moses part of the way when he ascended Mount Sinai to receive the Ten Commandments. Thus Joshua was able to warn Moses of what he termed "a cry of war in the camp," related to the idolatrous revelry about the Golden Calf (Exod. 32:17). When Eldad and Medad prophesied in the camp, Joshua urged Moses to "restrain them" in an attempt to defend the honor of his master (Num. 11:27–29).

After receiving the unequivocal decree that he would not be permitted to enter the Promised Land, Moses asked God to appoint his successor. "And the Lord answered Moses, 'Single out Joshua son of Nun, an inspired man [lit., "a man in whom there is spirit"], and lay your hand upon him. Have him stand before Eleazar the priest and the whole community, and commission him in their sight. Invest him with some of your authority, so that the whole Israelite community may obey'" (Num. 27:16–23). Before Moses gave his final address to the people, God spoke directly to Joshua for the first time: "Be strong and resolute; for you shall bring the Israelites into the land that I swore to them, and I will be with you" (Deut. 31:23).

The Book of Joshua describes the story of Israel's military conquest of the land of Canaan and its allocation among the various tribes. With the priests leading the way carrying the Ark of the Covenant, which contained the tablets on which the Ten Commandments were written, the waters of the Jordan miraculously stopped flowing while the people crossed to the western bank on dry ground. To commemorate this event, a monument of twelve stones (one for each tribe) was erected where the priests had stood, and twelve stones taken from that spot were deposited on the western bank as a memorial (Josh. 4:1–8). After the capture of Jericho, whose great walls came tumbling down (Josh. 6), Joshua fulfilled the command from Deuteronomy (27:11–13) to proclaim a series of blessings and curses on Mounts Gerizim and Ebal, representing respectively the Divinely imposed consequences of fulfilling or disobeying the terms of the covenant.

Sometime later, the five kings of the Amorites launched a war against Gibeon, which had made a treaty with the Israelites. Joshua rushed to help

Gibeon, and God assured him of victory. As promised, the Israelites were defeating the Amorites but could not completely overcome them before the approaching darkness of evening. Then Joshua called out before the Israelites: "Sun, stand still upon Gibeon; and you, Moon, in the valley of Ayalon" (Josh. 10:12). According to the *aggadah*, the sun was furious that a youngster could open his mouth and demand something from his elder. "I was created on the fourth day and you only on the sixth?" Joshua responded sharply, "You upstart slave! Are you not a mere chattel of one of my forebears? Did not my ancestor Joseph see you as a slave in a dream, in which 'the sun and the moon and eleven stars bowed down to me' [Gen. 37:9]?" (Gen. R. 6:9; 84:11). Only then did these heavenly bodies heed Joshua's call, so that the Israelites had time to avenge themselves upon their enemies. "And there was never a day like that before or since, when the Lord listened to the voice of a man; for the Lord fought for Israel" (Josh. 10:14). Joshua later moved the Tabernacle and Ark of the Covenant from Gilgal to Shiloh, residing there until his death at the age of 110 (Josh. 24:29).

In describing the chain of tradition, the opening *mishnah* of Pirkei Avot states: "Moses received the Torah at Mount Sinai and transmitted it to Joshua, and Joshua [transmitted it] to the elders . . ." (Avot 1:1). As a military hero, prophet, and faithful servant of Moses, Joshua was a worthy successor to the Lawgiver. Nevertheless, for the Rabbis, "The countenance of Moses was like that of the sun; that of Joshua was like the moon" (BB 75a), since his glory was inferior to that of Moses. According to legend, Joshua married Rahab after she converted. Although only having daughters and no sons, they were the progenitors of eight prophets and priests, including the prophet Jeremiah and the prophetess Huldah (Meg. 14b).

One Rabbi observed, "Had Israel not sinned, they would have been given only the Five Books of Moses and the Book of Joshua, [the latter] because it is the record of the disposition of the Land of Israel [among the tribes; the other books, consisting mostly of the prophets rebuking the people, would have been unnecessary]" (Ned. 22b).

Josiah, fifteenth king of Judah (640–609 B.C.E.).

Assuming the throne at age eight after the assassination of his father, Amon, Josiah presided over a great national and religious reformation that represented the final flourishing of the kingdom of Judah before its collapse and the fall of Jerusalem two decades after his death. As the Bible relates (2 Kings 22), during repair work on the Temple, Hilkiah, the high priest, discovered the "Book of the Law," which most scholars consider to be a large part of the current Book of Deuteronomy. Realizing that for decades the people of Judah had blissfully neglected the commandments, Josiah was frightened by the catastrophes predicted for failure to observe them. He instituted a sweeping series of religious reforms that included the destruction of corrupt local sanctuaries ("high places") throughout the land and the centralization of religious worship in Jerusalem (2 Kings 23). "Before him there was no king like him, who turned back to the Lord with all his heart, and soul, and might, in full accord with the Torah of Moses; nor did any like him or after him" (2 Kings 23:25). However, even Josiah's praiseworthy actions were not sufficient to quell "the fierceness of his [God's] great wrath against Judah because of all the provocations of Manasseh." God vowed to "also remove Judah from My Presence, as I have removed Israel [the Northern Kingdom, in 721 B.C.E.], and I will reject the city of Jerusalem which I have chosen, and the House where I said My name would abide" (2 Kings 23:26–27).

The *aggadah* explains that the biblical verse about Josiah's "return to God" (2 Kings 23:25) did not imply any sin by the king, who was described as having done "that which was right in the eyes of the Lord and walked in the ways of David, his father" (2 Kings 22:2). Instead, it taught that, "He revised every [legal] judgment that he had made from his ascent to the throne [at age 8] until finding the Book of the Law [at age 18]," for fear that he had erred out of ignorance before he had delved into the laws of the Torah. Moreover, he "returned" from his own money ("with all his [own] wealth") any monetary judgments that he had imposed in error. Consequently, "There was no penitent greater than Josiah in his generation" (Shab. 56b).

When Josiah first glanced at the newly discovered Book of the Law, the first verse he saw was: "God will lead you and your king into exile, into a nation that you have not known" (Deut. 28:36). Understanding this as a portent of the future destruction of the Temple, it was Josiah who hid the Holy Ark (with the container of manna, the flask of anointing oil, the staff of Aaron with its almond and flowers, and the box that the Philistines had sent as a gift to the God of Israel) to prevent these items from being desecrated as the hands of the enemy (Yoma 52b). Josiah also called upon the prophetess Huldah to intercede with God on behalf of Israel, choosing her rather than Jeremiah in the belief that a woman would be more compassionate (Meg. 14b).

Josiah did not realize that the entire generation of Israel worshiped idols. While his sweeping religious reforms were successful in preventing public idolatry, the people had little interest in changing their ways. When Josiah sent out pairs of scholars to rid the land of images, the people would inscribe half an image on each pair of doors. In this way, the images were not recognizable when the scholars entered and opened the doors, so they could honestly report finding nothing amiss, but reappeared when the doors were closed (Lam. R. 1:63).

Although Josiah's reforms did not last, their great significance for the history of Judaism was the beginning of a focus on seeking the word of God in the book of Torah. The pledge of the people to observe the law "as written in the book" brought about a metamorphosis in Israelite religion. Observing the law required that one study it. As a result, the Second Temple period saw the rise of scribes and scholars alongside the temple cult and the gradual eclipse of prophecy. By the time of the destruction of the Second Temple, other sacred books had joined the Torah to make up the Holy Scriptures (*kitvei ha-kodesh*; Yad. 3:5), whose study and exposition led to the crystallization of Rabbinic Judaism, which has survived for almost 2,000 years.

Jotham, tenth king of Judah (752–735 B.C.E.).

According to the Bible, for eight years Jotham served as co-regent because his father, Uzziah, suffered from *tzara'at* (a skin disease mistranslated as leprosy). Uzziah had contracted this disorder after having sacrilegiously attempted to usurp the priestly function of offering incense in the Temple (2 Chron. 26:16–21) and was unable to perform his royal duties. This led the *aggadah* to label Jotham as one of the most righteous kings of Judah, since he loyally observed the fifth Commandment by being content to act as regent during his father's reign without even aspiring to the throne.

When Jotham became the sole ruler, he defeated the Ammonites (2 Chron. 27:5), fortified the wall of the Ophel in Jerusalem (2 Chron. 27:3), and constructed the upper gate of the House of the Lord (2 Kings 15:35). Unlike his father, Jotham "did not enter into the Temple of the Lord" (2 Chron. 27:2).

Jubal, son of Lamech and descendant of Cain.

As "the ancestor of all who play the lyre [stringed instruments] and the pipe [wind instruments]" (Gen. 4:21), Jubal was the founder of the art of music.

Judah, fourth son of Jacob and Leah.

When he was born, his mother exulted, "This time I will praise [*odeh*] the Lord" (Gen. 29:35) and therefore named him Judah. The flag of the tribe of Judah was the "color of the heavens," on which was embroidered a lion based on the verse in Jacob's final blessing, "Judah is a lion's cub" (Gen. 49:9). According to the *aggadah*, this meant that Judah received the strength of a lion and the boldness of its cubs (Gen. R. 98:7). The patriarch continued, "The scepter shall not depart from Judah, not the ruler's staff from between his feet"—and from this tribe came the royal House of David.

Judah married Shua, the daughter of a Canaanite, and she bore him three sons (Gen. 38:1–5). After the death of his two elder sons, Er and Onan, in childless marriages with Tamar, Judah refused to permit his third son, Shelah, to fulfill the levirate obligation to marry her (Gen. 38:11). Unwittingly, Judah himself accomplished this role, and his relations with his disguised daughter-in-law resulted in the birth of Perez and Zerah, the main ancestors of the tribe of Judah (Gen. 38:12–30).

When Joseph retained Shimon to ensure that the brothers would return to Egypt with Benjamin, Jacob was reluctant to permit his beloved youngest son to make the trip. "When there was no more bread, Judah urged him: 'If Benjamin goes with us, he may or may not be seized. But if he does not go with us, all of us will die of famine. It is better to act on a certainty than on doubt.'" So Judah promised himself as a surety for his youngest brother (Gen. R. 91:6). When the royal goblet was found in Benjamin's sack and Joseph declared that the culprit would be his slave, Judah bravely offered to substitute himself to secure Benjamin's freedom (Gen. 44). It was at this point that Joseph revealed his identity to the brothers.

After the Israelite conquest of the Land of Israel, the tribe of Judah received territory extending westward from the Dead Sea to the Mediterranean. When the monarchy split following the death of Solomon, Judah was the predominant tribe in the south, which became known as the Kingdom of Judah. Eventually, the name of the tribe of Judah gave rise to the Hebrew word "*Yehudi*," which has become the generic term for "Jew." *See also* Tamar.

Keturah, second wife of Abraham, whom he married after the death of Sarah (Gen. 25:1).

Neither the parentage nor origin of Keturah is given in the text. However, since her name was related to the Hebrew word for "spices" (*ketoret*), many scholars believe that the six sons she bore to Abraham and their descendants, such as Midian and Sheba, were members of a group of tribes that traded in spices, gold, and precious stones coming from southern Arabia. According to the biblical text, Abraham gave gifts to these children when he sent them away to the east, ensuring that they would have no claims to rival Isaac, to whom "he gave all he had" (Gen. 25:5–6).

The *aggadah* relates the connection of her name with incense as indicating that her good deeds gave off a fragrance like incense, or that she combined (*kitrah*) within herself piety and nobility (Gen. R. 61:4). This source also states that "Keturah is Hagar," a view taken by Rashi and other major commentators that Abraham remarried his former concubine. *See also* Hagar.

Kohath, second son of Levi, and the grandfather of Moses, Aaron, and Miriam.

Under the direction of Eleazar, the third son of Aaron, his clan (Kohathites) carried on their shoulders the most sacred elements of the Tabernacle, such as the Ark and its coverings, Golden Menorah, Golden Altar (for incense), and screening curtain that separated the Holy of Holies from the rest of the Sanctuary (Num. 4:4–14). However, the Kohathites served only as the porters of these most holy objects, which were covered before transport and could be dismantled and reassembled only by the priests, the sons of Aaron and their descendants, because the Kohathites were forbidden to actually touch them under pain of death (Num. 4:15).

A grandson of Kohath was Korach, who led the rebellion in the wilderness against the leadership of Moses and Aaron (Num. 16). After the Israelites entered into the Promised Land, the Kohathites received twenty-three cities from the tribes of Judah, Shimon, Benjamin, Dan, and the half-tribe of Manasseh (Josh. 21:4–5). Kohathites played important roles in instituting the cultic reform and cleansing the Temple under Hezekiah (2 Chron. 29:12–19) and in repairing the Temple during the time of Josiah (2 Chron. 34:12).

The *aggadah* relates that Kohath was one of the seven righteous men who helped bring the *Shechinah* (Divine Presence) back to earth after it had ascended to heaven because of the sins of previous generations (PdRK 1:22). Although the family of Kohath was awarded the privilege of carrying the Ark in the wilderness, this indirectly led to a decrease in their numbers due to two factors—a fire that occasionally emerged from the Ark and killed those who carried it, and deaths resulting from the crush of family members wanting to be granted this special privilege (Num. R. 5:1). The Rabbis praised the humility of the Kohathites: "Although they [family of Kohath] were aristocrats, they carried the Ark [on their shoulders] like ordinary slaves," while walking backward as a sign of respect (Num. R. 5:8).

Korach, son of Izhar of the family of Kohath, and the great-grandson of Levi.

During the journey through the wilderness, Korach led a rebellion of 250 "men of repute" against the leadership of Moses and Aaron, his first cousins. Although the cause of Korach's revolt was not specifically given in the text, the Rabbis attributed it to his anger at Moses for naming Elizaphan, son of Uzziel, as prince over the Kohathites (Num. 3:30). This seemed patently unfair to Korach, who was convinced that since "the two sons of Amram, Kohath's eldest son, took for themselves the kingdom and the priesthood," he should have been next in line rather than the son of Kohath's youngest son (Num. R. 18:1). According to the *aggadah*, Korach challenged Moses with several questions aimed at inciting controversy, not for "the sake of Heaven" (Avot 5:17) but solely to embarrass Moses and enhance his own status in the community. "Does a *tallit* made entirely of blue wool need fringes?" When Moses replied in the affirmative based on Torah law (Num. 15:38), Korach retorted: "The blue color of the *tallit* does not make it ritually correct, yet according to your statement four blue threads do so!" Korach continued, "Does a house filled with books of the Law need a mezuzah?" When Moses answered that it did, Korach ridiculed his response: "The presence of the whole Torah, which contains 275 chapters, does not make a house fit for habitation, yet you say that one chapter from it does so. It is not from God that you have received these commandments; you have invented them yourself!" (Num. R. 18:2).

Attempting to turn the people against Moses, Korach told a parable to prove that it was impossible to adhere to the laws that Moses had established. "A widow, the mother of two young daughters, had a field. When she came to plow it, Moses told her not to plow it with an ox and an ass together (Deut. 22:10); when she came to sow it, Moses told her not to sow it with mingled seeds (Lev. 19:19). At the time of harvest, she had to leave unreaped the parts of the field prescribed by the law, while from the harvested grain she had to give the priest the share due to him. The woman sold the field and with the proceeds bought two sheep. But the first-born of these she was obliged to give to Aaron the priest; and at the time of shearing he also required the first of the fleece (Deut. 18:4). The widow said: 'I cannot bear this man's demands any longer. It will be better for me to slaughter the sheep and eat them.' But Aaron came for the shoulder, the two cheeks, and the maw (Deut. 18:3). The widow then vehemently cried out: 'If you persist in your demand, I declare them devoted to the Lord.' Aaron replied: 'In that case the whole belongs to me' (Num. 18:14), whereupon he took away the meat, leaving the widow and her two daughters wholly unprovided for" (Num. R. 18:2–3).

Moses tried in vain to appease Korach and his followers (Num. R. 18:4). However, when they proclaimed, "The Torah was not given by God, Moses is not a prophet, and Aaron is not the high priest" (JT Sanh. 10:1), Moses realized that he had to publicly confront them to protect the integrity of the Torah. He ordered Korach and his company to appear in the Tabernacle on the following day, each bearing a fire pan filled with lighted incense, so that the Lord could decide who were the rightful leaders of the people (Num. 16:4–17). When the congregation separated itself from Korach and his fellow rebels as God commanded, "the earth opened its mouth and swallowed them up. . . . They went down alive into Sheol, with all that belonged to them; the earth closed over them and they vanished from the midst of the congregation" (Num. 16:32–33). His repentant sons were spared, and one became the progenitor of Samuel (Num. R. 18:8).

As a postscript, the Talmud relates that a Rabbi was traveling in the desert when an Arab showed him where Korach and his company had been swallowed up by the earth. Bending down and placing his ear to a small slit in the ground, he heard voices cry out: "Moses and his Torah are true, and we are liars" (BB 74a).

L

Laban, son of Bethuel, and the grandnephew of Abraham.

Through his sister Rebecca and daughters Rachel and Leah, Laban was the uncle and later the father-in-law of Jacob. When Eliezer, the servant of Abraham, came to Padan-Aram in the province of Haran to find a wife for Isaac, Laban offered hospitality that the sages deem was motivated by pure greed. Seeing the gold nose-ring and bracelets that Eliezer had given Rebecca, Laban was convinced that if his young sister had received such extravagant gifts, how much more expensive tokens would be his. Years later, when escaping the wrath of his brother, Esau, Jacob fled to the home of the greedy Laban. Laban contemplated the riches that Abraham's grandson must have with him since Eliezer, a mere servant, had previously brought ten heavily laden camels (Gen. 24:10). Crestfallen that Jacob was empty-handed, Laban was convinced that he must be hiding money in his cloak or even in his mouth (Gen. R. 70:13). Therefore, "Laban ran to greet him; he embraced him [to feel whether he had any hidden treasures on his person] and kissed him [to see whether Jacob had any jewels hidden in his mouth]" (Gen. 29:13).

Jacob agreed to work seven years to marry his beloved Rachel, but Laban deceived him by substituting Leah on their wedding night, explaining: "It is not the practice in our place to marry off the younger before the older" (Gen. 29:26). According to the *aggadah*, Jacob had already been suspicious of his future father-in-law. Interpreting the biblical verse in which Jacob said, "I will work . . . for Rachel your younger daughter" (Gen. 29:18), a *midrash* observed that, knowing the deceitful reputation of the inhabitants of the place, he spelled out the terms of the agreement: *for Rachel* and not Leah; *your daughter*, rather than another girl named Rachel from the marketplace; and the *younger*, so that he would not switch the names of Rachel and Leah (Gen. R. 70:17).

According to the *aggadah*, before the wedding Laban gathered together all the men of the place and said, "You know how we were short of water, but as soon as this righteous man came the water was blessed [i.e., the land was blessed with an abundance of water since Jacob's arrival]." They agreed to Laban's plan to substitute Leah for Rachel, since this would mean that Jacob would continue to work for him. Laban forced them to promise not to reveal his scheme and to deposit a pledge with him, but the wily Laban also deceived them and used the money for the purchase of wine, oil, and meat for the wedding feast. The men of the town attempted to inform Jacob of his father-in-law's devious act by singing an exclamation of joy—"*Hi Leah, hi Leah*" (lit., "it is Leah")—but Jacob did not understand their hints (Gen. R. 70:19). Although Laban continued to be deceitful in his dealings, Jacob outwitted him and eventually left with his wives, children, and flocks to return to Canaan.

The Rabbis used the verse "And God came to Laban the Aramean in a dream at night" (Gen. 31:24) to explain the difference between the prophets of Israel and those of other nations. "God reveals Himself to heathen prophets with half speech only . . . but to the prophets of Israel He speaks with complete speech, in terms of love and sanctity, with language in which the ministering angels praise Him. . . . God appears to heathen prophets only in the hour when people generally take leave of each other [i.e., at night]." The text continued, "It may be compared to a king and his friend sitting together in a chamber. Whenever he wishes, he speaks with his friend. . . . It may be compared to a king who has a wife and a concubine. To his wife he goes openly, but to his concubine he goes only in stealth. Similarly, God appears to the heathen prophets only at night" (Gen. R. 74:7).

Arami oveid avi were the opening Hebrew words of the declaration made by a farmer bringing the first fruits to the Temple in Jerusalem (Deut. 26:5–8). This is usually translated as "a wandering Aramean [Jacob] was my father," probably reflecting his unsettled life and related to the verse, "Jacob fled into the field of Aram" (Hos. 12:13). However, since the Hebrew word meaning "wandering" can also be translated as "ready to perish," the Passover Haggadah often translates it as "an Aramean [the deceitful Laban] tried to destroy my forefather [Jacob]." *See also* Jacob.

Lamech, sixth generation of the descendants of Cain.

Lamech was the first biblical figure to have two wives, Adah and Zillah, "one for childbearing and one for pleasure. The one for childbearing sat [alone, mourning] like a widow, whereas the one for pleasure was given a sterility potion and she sat beside him adorned like a harlot" (Gen. R. 23:2). Lamech's song to them is one of the most ancient examples of Hebrew poetry: "O wives of Lamech, give ear to my speech. I have slain a man for wounding me, and a lad for bruising me. If Cain is avenged sevenfold, then Lamech is seventy-seven fold" (Gen. 4:23–24). Although possibly a mere boast of his physical prowess and ability to use the implements of war forged by his son Tubal-cain, an *aggadic* explanation developed. The blind Lamech went out hunting, with his son leading him by the hand. Tubal-cain mistook

Cain for an animal and urged his father to shoot an arrow that killed their ancestor. When the distraught Lamech realized what he had done, he clapped his hands together in sorrow, accidentally striking his son and killing him. His angry wives, fearing Divine punishment of their husband, refused to live with him. In his song, Lamech stressed that if the punishment of Cain, who murdered intentionally, had been delayed until the seventh generation, then Lamech's punishment would be delayed far longer, since his killings had been accidental.

Lamech's other two sons were Jabal and Jubal, respectively the founders of the nomadic way of life and the musical arts, which represented advances in the development of human civilization.

Lamech, father of Noah.

The son of Methuselah and a descendant of Seth (Adam's third son), Lamech lived for 777 years (Gen 5:31). *See also* Cain.

Leah, elder daughter of Laban, first wife of Jacob, mother of Reuben, Shimon, Levi, Judah, Issachar, Zebulun, and Dinah, and the third matriarch of Israel.

Described as having "weak [or gentle] eyes" (Gen. 29:17), the Rabbis deemed these not a disgrace but rather a mark of praise. Leah used to hear people say that because Rebecca had two sons (Esau and Jacob) and Laban two daughters (Leah and Rebecca), the elder son should marry the elder daughter and the younger ones should do likewise. When Leah asked about the character and deeds of Rebecca's older son, Esau, she was told that he was "a wicked man, a highway robber," whereas the younger son, Jacob, was "a quiet man dwelling in tents." At this news, Leah "wept until her eyelashes dropped [from their lids]" and prayed that God not let her "fall to the lot of that evil man." Referring to her eventual marriage to Jacob rather than Esau, R. Huna said: "Great is prayer, that it annulled the decree [i.e., her natural destiny], and she even preceded her sister [in marrying Jacob]" (BB 123a; Gen. R. 70:16).

Jacob was passionately in love with Leah's younger sister, Rachel, and had worked seven years for her hand in marriage. However, on the morning after his wedding, he discovered Laban's trickery in substituting Leah as his bride (Gen. 29:25). According to a *midrash*, Jacob and Rachel were aware of Laban's deceitful nature and devised a code so that no substitution could occur. However, Rachel had such pity and compassion for her elder sister that on the wedding night she shared the code with Leah to prevent her from being shamed (Meg. 13b; BB 123a). Jacob confronted Leah, "O deceiver and daughter of a deceiver! Did I not call you Rachel all night long and you answered to that name?" Leah calmly replied, "Is there a teacher who has no pupils? Did not your father call you Esau, and did you not answer to that name?" (Gen. R. 70:17, 19). As the Rabbis noted, just as Jacob had deceived his blind father, Isaac, to gain the major blessing instead of Esau, so Jacob was deceived in the darkness.

Jacob's experience is the basis for the tradition of *bedeken* (*di kalla*), or "covering (the bride)." In this ritual, the groom lets down the veil over the face of his bride before the marriage ceremony so that he can clearly identify her and not be fooled. When Jacob rebuked Laban for this fraud, his new father-in-law simply stated, "It is not the practice in our place to marry off the younger before the older" (Gen. 29:26). However, Laban offered a compromise: "Wait until the bridal week of this one [Leah] is over and we will give you that one [Rachel] too, provided you serve me another seven years" (Gen. 29:27). This is the basis, in traditional communities, for the wedding celebrations to continue for an entire week. The *Shevah Berachot* (seven blessings) are recited as part of the *Birkat ha-Mazon* (Grace after Meals) whenever there is a *minyan* and a new guest present, as a way of extending the joyous festivities associated with the wedding.

To compensate for Leah being "unloved," God "opened her womb" and she became the mother of six sons and a daughter, while the favored Rachel remained childless for years. As the elder daughter who deserved the better inheritance, both the priesthood and the monarchy were descended from her (Aaron from her son Levi, and David from Judah). Leah later gave Jacob her handmaiden Zilpah as a concubine, and her two offspring (Gad and Asher) were considered as Leah's legitimate sons as well. When Rachel requested the aphrodisiac mandrakes, Leah asked for an extra night with Jacob in return. Knowing that her intentions were honorable (Gen. 30:16), God blessed her with two additional sons, Issachar and Zebulun (Gen. R. 72:5). Leah's seventh child was also destined to be a son, but a *midrash* related that the embryo was changed into a female (Dinah) because Leah, knowing that Jacob was destined to have twelve sons, prayed that her sister Rachel be granted a second son so that she would have at least as many as their handmaids (Ber. 60a). Leah was buried next to Jacob in the family tomb in the Cave of Machpelah (Gen. 49:31). *See also* Asher; Dinah; Gad; Issachar; Judah; Levi; Reuben; Shimon; Zebulun; Zilpah.

Levi, third son of Jacob and Leah.

The reason for the name of Levi was given in the verse, "This time my husband will become attached to me [*yilaveh*], for I have borne him three sons" (Gen. 29:34). According to a *midrash*, the name Levi was prophetic since his tribe would lead (*laveh*; "to escort/accompany") the Israelites to their Father in heaven (Gen. R. 71:4). The flag of the tribe of Levi, which was one-third white, one-third black, and one-third red, was embroidered with the breastplate of the high priest and the *Urim* and *Thumim*.

After the rape of his sister Dinah, Levi joined Shimon in exacting revenge by slaying the men of Shechem and plundering their city (Gen. 34), an act that aroused Jacob's anger against them (Gen. 49:5–7). However, the zeal that earned this rebuke later became channeled to the service of God. Moses and Aaron came from the tribe of Levi, and the descendants of the latter became the *kohanim* (priests) of Israel. At the time of the shameful episode of the Golden Calf, only the Levites remained faithful to the Divine covenant and responded wholeheartedly when Moses said, "Whoever is for the Lord, come here!" (Exod. 32:26). Although the tribe of Levi was the smallest among the Israelites, its members were consecrated to render service at the Sanctuary, where the Israelites worshiped God by bringing sacrifices to the altar. The Levites were the gatekeepers and caretakers of the Sanctuary and its furnishings; the judges, teachers of the law, and scribes; the Temple musicians; and assistants to the priests. Unlike the other tribes, the Levites received no allotment of land in Canaan. Instead, they were dispersed among the people in forty-eight levitical cities and were sustained by a portion of the tithes brought by the people to the Temple in Jerusalem. Consequently, the Levites are repeatedly reckoned in the Bible among those needing support, along with "the stranger, the orphan, and the widow."

Each morning in the Temple, the Levites chanted a psalm appropriate to that day of the week. As a memorial to the destroyed Temple, the Rabbis added these psalms to the daily morning service in the synagogue. In honor of their major role in the Temple service, in traditional synagogues a Levite is the second person called for an *aliyah* to the Torah. A ewer and basin or musical instruments are often carved on the tombstone of a Levite as a symbol of the ancient duties of their tribe.

The *aggadah* relates that when Shimon and Levi were born, Leah prophesied that Shimon would produce an enemy of God (Zimri), but from Levi would come Pinchas and heal the wound inflicted through Zimri (Gen. R. 71:4). The proposal to kill Joseph (Gen. 37:20) came from Shimon and Levi. When the brothers came to Egypt, they were separated by Joseph, who imprisoned Shimon (Gen. 42:24), since together they would have destroyed the country. During the years of Egyptian slavery, the tribe of Levi was the only one that practiced circumcision and did not engage in idolatry (Exod. R. 15:1; 19:5); it also was the only tribe not put to degrading work (Exod. R. 5:16). The children of the other tribal ancestors did not uniformly produce righteous descendants, but the descendants of Levi's three sons (Gershon, Kohath, and Merari) were all righteous (Num. R. 3:7). *See also* Shimon.

Lot, son of Haran, and the nephew of Abraham.

Emigrating with his grandfather, Terah, from Ur of the Chaldees to Haran (Gen. 11:31), Lot joined Abraham in traveling to Canaan in response to the Divine command (Gen. 12:4–5) and then went with the patriarch to Egypt in time of famine (Gen. 12:10; 13:1). Lot and Abraham were so rich in cattle that "the land could not support them staying together" (Gen. 13:6). Following quarrels between their respective herdsmen, the two agreed to separate. Offered his choice of territory by his uncle, Lot selected the fertile and well-watered Jordan Valley to the east. Thus, "Abram remained in the land of Canaan, while Lot settled in the cities of the Plain, pitching his tents near Sodom" (Gen. 13:17). Soon Lot was taken captive in a local conflict, but was rescued by Abraham (Gen. 14:12–16).

While living in the depraved city of Sodom, Lot offered hospitality to two visiting angels. When the men of Sodom demanded that the guests be handed over "so that we may be intimate with them" (Gen. 19:5), Lot refused and instead offered them his "two daughters who have not known a man" (Gen. 19:8), preferring to allow them to be dishonored rather than violate the rules of hospitality. The angels caused the men of Sodom to be blinded, informed Lot that their mission was to destroy the wicked city (and Gomorrah), and seized Lot, his wife, and two daughters by their hands as they led them out of Sodom before fire and brimstone rained down upon it. Although warned not to look back while they were fleeing to the mountains, Lot's wife disobeyed and was turned into a pillar of salt (Gen. 19:26).

While hiding in a cave and fearing that they were the only human beings remaining on earth, Lot's two daughters made their father drunk and then had intercourse with him to continue the human race (Naz. 23a). In this way, Lot became the ancestor of the nations of Moab ("from my father") and Ammon (from Ben-Ami, "son of my people") (Gen. 19:30–38). One Rabbi stated that, as a reward for performing the mitzvah of beginning to repopulate the earth by having sexual relations with her father the night before the younger, the older daughter was privileged to appear in the record of the royal house of Israel four generations earlier (i.e., Obed, Jesse, David, and Solomon descended through Ruth the Moabitess, while Rehoboam [the first king of Judah] was a son of Naamah, the Ammonitess) (Naz. 23b–24a).

Why was Lot spared? According to one *midrash*, Lot deserved to perish with the people of Sodom, but was saved because of the merit of Abraham (Gen. R. 41:4). Another maintained that it was a reward for not having betrayed Abraham when he told Pharaoh that Sarah was his sister (Gen. R. 51:8). Unlike his daughters, whose actions were purely motivated (Hor. 10b), Lot was criticized by the commentators. First, the angels had informed him that the Divine devastation had affected only a few cities. Second, even though he was so drunk that he was unaware of what was happening on the first night, Lot realized what had occurred in the morning and could have stayed sober and prevented its repetition.

Biblical law explicitly states, "An Ammonite or a Moabite shall not enter into the congregation of the Lord forever" (Deut. 23:4). However, the Mishnah (Yev. 8:3) later restricted this prohibition to males, noting that the biblical proscription used the masculine gender. Eventually, the restriction was completely abolished when Judah, an Ammonite proselyte, asked whether he was permitted to enter the assembly by marrying a Jewess. The Rabbis acceded to this request, noting that the current inhabitants of these countries were not descended from the Ammonites and Moabites of biblical times, since Sennacherib (king of Assyria) had long ago "mixed up all the nations" (Ber. 28a).

Malachi, twelfth and last of the minor prophets.

Malachi lived in Jerusalem in the middle of the fifth century B.C.E., probably about fifty years after the rebuilding of the Temple by the Jewish exiles who had returned from Babylonia. Malachi stressed obedience to ritual and law, but his prophecies also taught the universality of God and the natural worth of all people. The prophet fiercely condemned moral and social offenses, while emphasizing the concept of the brotherhood of all Jews under one Heavenly Father.

On the Sabbath before Passover (*Shabbat ha-Gadol*), the special *haftarah* comes from Malachi (3:4–24). It concludes with the announcement that God will send Elijah the prophet as the herald of the Messianic age: "Behold, he shall reconcile [lit., 'turn the heart of'] parents with children and children with their parents, so that when I come I do not strike the whole land with utter destruction" (Mal. 3:24). This reference to the promise of ultimate messianic redemption is most appropriate to the upcoming festival of Passover, which celebrates the historical redemption of the Jewish people from slavery in Egypt.

Malachi was considered by some traditional authorities to be an anonymous prophet, because the name can simply mean "my messenger." Others identified him with Mordechai or Ezra (Meg. 15a). According to the Talmud, "After the death of the last prophets—Haggai, Zechariah, and Malachi—the Holy Spirit [of prophecy] departed from Israel" (Yoma 9b).

Manasseh, elder son of Joseph, and the grandson of Jacob.

According to the Bible, Joseph gave Manasseh his name because "God has made me forget completely [*nashani*] my hardship and my parental home" (Gen. 41:51). The flag of Manasseh contained a wild ox, based on the verse, "He has horns like the horns of the wild ox" (Gen. 33:17). The *aggadah* deemed this to be an allusion to Gideon, the judge of Israel who came from this tribe (Num. R. 2:8). Before his death, Jacob adopted both Manasseh and his younger brother Ephraim as his sons on a par with Reuben and Shimon, thereby ensuring that each would become the ancestor of an entire Israelite tribe rather than of half a tribe (Gen. 48:5). Manasseh and Ephraim were geographically contiguous, with Manasseh farther north, occupying the fertile mountains and small plains extending northward from Bethel to the plain of Jezreel in the region later known as Samaria. According to the biblical account, after assisting their fellow Israelites to conquer the land of Canaan, half the tribe of Manasseh chose to remain with the tribes of Reuben and Gad in the highlands east of the Jordan River.

The *aggadah* relates that Manasseh played a major role in the encounters between Joseph and his brothers in Egypt. He was sent by Joseph to spy on his brothers after they entered Egypt, served as the interpreter between Joseph and his brothers (Gen. 42:23) when his father feigned ignorance of Hebrew (Gen. R. 91:8), and had the strength to overcome Shimon and throw him into prison as surety for the brothers returning with Benjamin. As the steward of his father's house, Manasseh prepared the meal for Joseph's brothers (Gen. 43:16). He later was sent to search their sacks for the "stolen" silver cup, finding it in the one belonging to Benjamin (Gen. 44:4–13). Because Manasseh caused the brothers to tear their garments in grief after this episode, his inheritance was also torn, with half the tribe living in the land of Canaan and half dwelling east of the Jordan (Gen. R. 84:20).

On Sabbath eve, fathers traditionally invoke a blessing over their sons that God make them "like Ephraim and Manasseh." These two sons of Joseph had the courage and commitment to maintain their Jewish heritage despite both the antagonism and allure of Egyptian culture and society—a valuable trait during the millennia of dispersion when Jewish parents prayed that their sons would show a similar dedication to the tradition. *See also* Ephraim; Gideon.

Manasseh, thirteenth king of Judah (687–642 B.C.E.).

Ascending the throne at age twelve and ruling for fifty-five years, the most of any king of Judah, Manasseh was a wicked and depraved ruler who abolished the religious reforms of his father, Hezekiah. In addition to reintroducing foreign pagan cults into Judah, especially the worship of Baal and the rite of child sacrifice to Molech, Manasseh persecuted and killed the prophets of God and "shed much innocent blood, until he had filled Jerusalem from one end to another" (2 Kings 21:16).

The *aggadah* uses several Hebrew roots to conclude that Manasseh received his name either because "he forgot God" or "he caused Israel to forget [or be forgotten by] their Father in Heaven" (Sanh. 102b). Manasseh's mother was the daughter of the prophet Isaiah, who married Hezekiah after the king had recovered from his illness. However, when Hezekiah was carrying his sons Manasseh and Rabshakeh on his shoulders to the House of Study, they showed how different they were from their righteous parents. One said, "Father's [bald] head is a good place for frying fish." The other added, "It would be a good place to offer sacrifices to idols." Enraged by hearing these words, Hezekiah threw his sons to the ground. Rabshakeh was killed by the fall, but Manasseh was unhurt.

Manasseh destroyed the altar and set up in the Temple an idol with four faces (copying the pattern of the four figures on the Throne of God from the vision of Ezekiel), either "so that the *Shechinah* might see it and be angered" (Sanh. 103b) or so that anyone coming from the four corners of the earth should bow down to the image (Deut. R. 2:20). Rashi said that one of Manasseh's idols was so heavy that it required 1,000 men to carry it, and each day they all were killed by collapsing under its weight (Sanh. 103b). The wicked Manasseh expounded the Torah falsely (Sanh. 99b), erased the Name of God from the Torah, and committed incest by consorting with his sister (Sanh. 103b).

Manasseh sat in judgment on Isaiah and condemned him to death. "Your teacher Moses said, 'No man shall see Me and live' (Exod. 33:20). But you say, 'I saw the Lord sitting on a throne, high and exalted' (Isa. 6:1). Your teacher Moses said, 'The Lord our God, whenever we call to Him [i.e., all the time]' (Deut. 4:7). But you say, 'Seek the Lord when he may be found [implying "not always"]'" (Isa. 55:6). Isaiah refused to defend himself. He realized that anything he said would fail to convince the king that he was in error, and he preferred that the king act out of ignorance rather than be a willful murderer. Therefore, Isaiah pronounced the Ineffable Name and was swallowed up by a cedar tree. However, Manasseh ordered that the cedar tree be sawed in two, causing the prophet's death (Yev. 49b).

Manasseh was captured by the Assyrians, who placed him in a copper cauldron and lit a fire underneath it. The king vainly sought salvation from all the deities he had worshiped. Finally, he remembered the words of his father, Hezekiah: "In your distress, when all these things come upon you . . . God will neither fail you nor destroy you" (Deut. 4:30–31). Manasseh thought, "If I call to Him and he answers me, very well; if not, they are all the same." The ministering angels closed all the windows [of Heaven], so that Manasseh's prayer would not ascend before God: "Will You accept the repentance of one who erected an idol in the Temple?" God replied, "If I do not accept his repentance, I will be closing the door before all penitent sinners." Immediately God made an opening for Manasseh beneath the Throne of Glory and accepted him, before sending a wind to transport Manasseh back to Jerusalem. Then Manasseh said, "There is justice and there is a Judge" (JT Sanh. 10:2). *See also* Boaz.

Manoah, father of Samson.

A man of the tribe of Dan, his unnamed wife was barren until an angel of the Lord appeared and informed her that she would conceive and bear a son (Judg. 13:2–24). She was to "drink neither wine nor strong drink, and eat not any unclean thing . . . [and] no razor shall come on his [her son's] head; for the child shall be a Nazirite to God from the womb. He will begin to save Israel from the hand of the Philistines." The woman related this experience to Manoah, who begged that "the man of God whom you sent come back to us and teach us what we shall do with the child who is to be born." When the messenger returned and repeated his commands, Manoah invited him to have something to eat. However, the angel of the Lord replied: "Though you detain me, I will not eat your food; and if you present a burnt offering, offer it to the Lord." Not realizing that the messenger was an angel, Manoah "took a kid and the meal offering and offered them up on a rock to the Lord." Manoah and his wife were stunned when the angel ascended to heaven in the flame rising from the altar. Fearing that "we shall surely die, because we have seen a divine being," Manoah was assured by his wife that had the Lord wished to kill them, He would not have accepted their offerings or related such welcome tidings. As promised, the woman bore a son and named him Samson.

According to a *midrash*, Manoah and his wife quarreled because of their lack of a child. He claimed that she was barren, while she argued that he was sterile. The Rabbis concluded that having the angel speak to Manoah's wife indicated that she was a righteous woman, since it was she who was privileged to have an angel speak with her, to make peace between husband and wife and to inform her that it was her barrenness that was preventing conception (Num. R. 10:5).

Medad, one of the two elders who "prophesied" in the wilderness encampment of the Israelites. *See also* Eldad.

Melchizedek, king of Salem.

With his name coming from two Hebrew words meaning "righteous" or possibly "legitimate" king, Melchizedek warmly welcomed Abraham after he had defeated the four kings who had captured his nephew, Lot (Gen. 14:18–20). Melchizedek brought out bread and wine and blessed Abraham. According to the *aggadah*, "bread" alluded to the showbread and "wine" to libations, meaning that Melchizedek instructed Abraham in the laws of the high priesthood. Another explanation was that Melchizedek revealed to Abraham words of the Torah, which was called bread and wine in Proverbs (9:5) (Gen. R. 43:6).

Melchizedek was identified with Shem, the son of Noah (Gen. R. 56:10). The Bible describes him as "priest of the Most High God," suggesting to the Rabbis that God intended to allot the priesthood to Shem (i.e., Melchizedek). However, the Talmud (Ned. 32b) explains that the priesthood was taken away from Melchizedek because he blessed Abraham before God ("Blessed be Abram of the Most High God [*el elyon*], Creator of heaven and earth, and blessed be the Most High God"). Hearing these words, Abraham said, "Is the blessing of a servant to be given precedence over that of his master?" Immediately God gave the priesthood to Abraham, based on the verse in Psalms (110:4), "You are a priest forever because of the words of Melchizedek." Thus it was written of Melchizedek, "And *he* was a priest of the Most High God," implying that his descendants were not.

Merari, third son of Levi.

Under the direction of Ithamar, the youngest son of Aaron, his clan (Merarites) was in charge of carrying the less important components of the Tabernacle: "the planks of the Tabernacle, its bars, posts, and sockets, and all its furnishings, . . . also the posts around the enclosure and their sockets, pegs, and cords (Num. 3:36–37). After the Israelites entered the Promised Land, the Merarites received twelve cities scattered throughout the territories of the tribes of Reuben, Gad, and Zebulun (Josh. 21:7). Merarites participated in cleansing the Temple under Hezekiah (2 Chron. 29:12) and in repairing the Temple during the reign of Josiah (2 Chron. 34:12).

Methusaleh, son of Enoch, father of Lamech, and the grandfather of Noah.

Methuselah lived for 969 years (Gen. 5:27), the longest of anyone in the Bible, and he died at the onset of the Flood. Although his longevity is extreme by our standards, it pales in comparison with the Babylonian tradition, whose heroes were said to have lived for tens of thousands of years. *See also* Noah.

Micah, sixth of the minor prophets (ca. 730–705 B.C.E.).

A peasant from a tiny village in Judah, Micah railed against the social corruption of the cities, the injustice of the rulers, and the oppression of the poor. He predicted the destruction of the Temple and the beloved city of Jerusalem. According to the Talmud, Micah reduced the 613 commandments given to Moses to only three (Mic. 6:8): "What does the Lord require of you? To do justice, to love mercy, and to walk humbly with your God" (Mak. 24a). His appeal that God "cast out (*tashlich*) all our sins into the depths of the sea" (Mic. 7:19) is the basis for the Tashlich ceremony on the first day of Rosh Hashanah, when Jews symbolically rid themselves of their sins by throwing bread crumbs into a fish-containing body of water. Reminding the people of

God's love for Israel, Micah prophesied an era of universal justice at the end of days, when "every man shall sit under his vine and under his fig tree, and none shall make them afraid" (Mic. 4:4).

Michal, youngest daughter of King Saul, and the first wife of King David.

Michal loved David, but was given to him in marriage only after he had killed 200 Philistines. Saul, Michal's father, had insisted on this as the condition ("a hundred Philistines' foreskins") for the marriage contract instead of a dowry (1 Sam. 18:25), hoping that David would be killed while attempting to collect them.

When Saul sent men to murder David at home, Michal demonstrated her loyalty to her husband by helping him escape (1 Sam. 19:11–18). However, when David leaped and danced in front of the Ark as it was brought to Jerusalem, Michal haughtily accused him of immodesty and even indecent exposure. David retorted in anger, "But it was done in the presence of the Lord, who chose me instead of your father and his family" (2 Sam. 6:16–21). As a consequence of her intemperate words, Michal "had no child to her dying day" (2 Sam. 16:23).

Both of Saul's children loved David: "Michal helped him escape from inside the house, while Jonathan helped from outside" (Mid. Ps. 59:1). She was also called "Eglah [calf]" (mentioned as David's wife in 2 Sam. 3:5), "because she was as precious as a calf to him" (Sanh. 21a). However, this name also reflected that Michal loved David more than her father Saul. Just as a calf does not accept a yoke on its neck, so Michal refused to accept the yoke of her father, instead rebuking him for his hatred of David (Mid. Ps. 59:3–4). According to the Talmud, Michal "wore *tefillin* and the sages did not attempt to prevent her" (Er. 96a).

Miriam, daughter of Amram and Jochebed, sister of Moses and Aaron, and prophetess of Israel (Meg. 14a).

When Jochebed could no longer hide her son, Moses, she "put the child into [a caulked wicker] basket and placed it among the reeds by the bank of the Nile" (Exod. 2:3). Miriam, who had "stationed herself at a distance to learn what would befall him," saw that Pharaoh's compassionate daughter had found her baby brother. Proposing to the Egyptian princess to find "a Hebrew nurse to suckle the child for you," she returned with Jochebed, her mother (Exod. 2:4–7). At the conclusion of the victory song celebrating the Israelite crossing of the Sea of Reeds (*Shirat ha-Yam*; Exod. 1–18), Miriam "took a timbrel in her hand" and led a chorus of women in chanting the opening lines of the poem: "Sing to the Lord, for He has triumphed gloriously; horse and driver He has hurled into the sea" (Exod. 15:20–21).

Later, Miriam and Aaron (though since the verse is in the feminine singular, the Rabbis deemed her the instigator) "spoke against Moses because of the Cushite woman he had married" (Num. 12:1). Although the text suggests that the true reason she and Aaron slandered their brother was because they jealously sought a share of Moses' leadership (Num. 12:2), Rashi quoted a *midrash* that Miriam's motivation was concern that Moses' endless public duties were forcing him to neglect his wife and children (Deut. R. 6:6). Regardless of the cause, Miriam and her brother were immediately summoned by God to the Tent of Meeting, where she was punished with the snow-white scales of *tzara'at*, a skin condition often mistranslated as "leprosy." Miriam was healed after the terse prayer of Moses—"God, please heal her" (Num. 12:13)—but she was required to remain outside the Israelite camp for seven days. The people waited for Miriam (Num. 12:14–16), just as she had waited for Moses by the Nile (Sot. 9b).

As soon as Miriam died and was buried in the wilderness at Kadesh (Num. 20:1), "the community was without water" (Num. 20:2). The *aggadah* relates that, as a tribute to Miriam's piety, a well miraculously appeared whenever the Israelites made camp and accompanied them throughout their wanderings in the wilderness (Exod. R. 26:1). However, this well, which was created during the twilight on the eve of the first Sabbath (Avot 5:6), disappeared after her death (Taan. 9a). This led to the episode of Moses striking instead of speaking to the rock to obtain water, the biblically stated reason why he was not permitted to lead the people into the Promised Land (Num. 20:6–13).

One *midrashic* tradition identifies Miriam as Puah (Exod. 1:15), one of the midwives who bravely refused to obey Pharaoh's order to kill all the newborn Israelite boys (Sot. 11b). The *aggadah* described Miriam as the wife of Caleb. Their son, Hur, was the grandfather of Bezalel, the architect of the Sanctuary who inherited the wisdom of his great-grandmother. Although Miriam was punished with *tzara'at* after speaking against Moses, God Himself officiated as the priest who definitively declared her cleansed of this condition (Zev. 102a). Like Moses and Aaron, Miriam also died by the kiss of God rather than by the sword of the Angel of Death (BB 17a). *See also* Amram; Puah; Zipporah.

Mishael. *See* Hananiah, Mishael, and Azariah.

Moab, son of Lot and his unnamed elder daughter, and ancestor of the tribe bearing his name.

After fleeing the destruction of Sodom, Lot's daughters reasonably feared that this devastation had extended to the entire world and that they were the only ones remaining. "And the older one said to the younger, 'Our father is old, and there is not a man on earth to consort with us in the way of all the world [to propagate the human race]. Come, let us make our father drink wine, and let us lie with him, that we may maintain life through our father'" (Gen. 19:31–32). This relationship resulted in the birth of a son, Moab (Gen. 19:37), whose name presumably derived from the Hebrew *mei-avi* ("from my father"). Because her intentions were purely motivated, the Torah does not explicitly condemn Lot's daughter or label the relationship as incestuous. Indeed, she merited being the ancestress of Ruth, the great-grandmother of King David. *See also* Lot.

Mordechai, hero of the Purim story.

Mordechai was a descendant of one of the members of the upper class of Israelite society who, in 597 B.C.E., were taken into Babylonian exile along with King Jehoiachin of Judah by Nebuchadnezzar. Although the name Mordechai bears a close resemblance to the Babylonian god Marduk, the Talmud interpreted his name as coming from the two Hebrew words *mor* (myrrh) and *decai* (pure), which reflected his noble character (Meg. 10b). The foster father of his cousin Esther (Esth. 2:5), Mordechai was one of Ahasuerus's consultants who "sat in the king's gate" (Esth. 2:21). In this position, Mordechai was able to inquire daily about Esther's welfare when she entered the palace to become Queen of Persia (Esth. 2:10–11).

Mordechai was the only official who refused to bow down to Haman (Esth. 3:1). This refusal has often been explained incorrectly on religious grounds. However, not only does Judaism not forbid, it actually requires the showing of respect to highly placed persons, Jewish or otherwise. When asked the reason for his behavior, Mordechai simply stated that he was a Jew, and the narrator of the tale evidently assumed that all readers would be aware of the eternal enmity between the Jews and the descendants of Amalek. When Haman's plot to destroy the Jews became evident, Mordechai "tore off his clothes and put on sackcloth and ashes." He urged the initially hesitant Esther to intercede with Ahasuerus on behalf of her people: "Who knows whether it is not for a time like this that you have come to the royal estate?" (Esth. 4:14). He argued that if Esther failed to act decisively, "Do not imagine that you alone of all the Jews will escape because you are in the royal palace. If you remain silent . . . relief and deliverance for the Jews will appear from another quarter, but you and your father's family will perish" (Esth. 4:13–14).

Mordechai previously had discovered a plot to assassinate Ahasuerus and informed Esther, who passed the information to the king in Mordechai's name. However, Mordechai was not immediately rewarded for saving the king's life. One evening when Ahasuerus could not sleep, he ordered his servants to read to him from the book of records and they fortuitously picked the passage describing how Mordechai had foiled the plot against the king. When Ahasuerus asked, "What honor or advancement has been conferred on Mordechai for this?" he was told that "nothing at all has been done for him." At this moment, Ahasuerus heard someone in the outer court of the royal palace and was informed that it was Haman, who had come to speak to the king about hanging Mordechai on the gallows he had prepared for him. The king ordered Haman to enter and asked, "What should be done for a man whom the king desires to honor?" Convinced that this must be referring to him, Haman replied that he should be dressed in royal attire and diadem and paraded around the city on a royal steed led by a noble courtier proclaiming before him, "This is what is done to the man whom the king desires to honor!" Devastated when he learned that the honor was meant for Mordechai, Haman was forced to do as he had recommended for the honor of his archenemy (Esth. 6).

When Esther divulged to Ahasuerus that she was a Jewess and that the edict he had signed for Haman was for the destruction of her people, the outraged king ordered Haman's execution and put Mordechai in charge of his property. Esther requested that Ahasuerus send written dispatches to the provinces countermanding those written by Haman to destroy the Jews, "for how can I bear to see the disaster which will befall my people!" (Esth. 8:5). However, Ahasuerus replied that "an edict that has been written in the king's name and sealed with the king's signet may not be revoked" (Esth. 8:8). Nevertheless, Ahasuerus did write a letter to all his officials, "written at Mordechai's dictation," that "permitted the Jews of every city to assemble and fight for their lives; if any people or province attacks them, they may destroy, massacre, and exterminate its armed force together with women and children, and plunder their possessions" (Esth. 8). The Jews repelled their enemies, and Mordechai became second in command of the Persian Empire. *See also* Esther; Haman.

Moses, son of Amram and Jochebed, and the younger brother of Aaron and Miriam.

By far the dominant individual in the Bible, in obedience to Divine commands, Moses unleashed the ten plagues before leading the Israelites in the Exodus from Egypt, received the Torah at Mount Sinai and taught it to the newly freed slaves, and guided the often quarrelsome people during the forty years that they wandered through the wilderness until they were about to enter the Promised Land. Indeed, the entire Pentateuch, *Humash* in Hebrew, is known as the Five Books of Moses.

Moses was born after the enactment of Pharaoh's decree that all male Israelite infants be drowned at birth. After his mother placed him in a basket that was set afloat in the Nile, Moses was discovered by Pharaoh's daughter, who took pity on the crying baby and adopted him as her own, raising him as a prince in the palace. She named the boy "Moshe," which the text explained as meaning "I drew him out of the water." Although the Bible provides a Hebrew origin for his name, "Mose" was frequently appended to the name of a god in ancient Egyptian personal names, such as Ptahmose, Thutmose, and even Ramses (Ra-Mose).

As a young man, Moses was forced to flee Egypt after killing an overseer who was beating an Israelite slave, escaping to the Sinai Desert. There he was given refuge by the Midianite priest Jethro, who gave him his daughter Zipporah to wed. While shepherding the flocks of his father-in-law, Moses experienced the defining moment in his life—the encounter with the Divine at the bush that "burned but was not consumed" (Exod. 3–4). When informed that he had been chosen to lead his people out of bondage, Moses was reluctant to accept the role of prophet, humbly pleading that he was not worthy of the task. In response to Moses' argument that the Israelites would not believe him, God gave him signs to convince the people that he had been assigned a Divine mission. When Moses complained that he was "slow of speech" and lacked the eloquence to persuade the people to follow his lead, God told Moses that his brother Aaron would be his spokesman.

Returning to Egypt, Moses requested that Pharaoh permit the Israelites to go out into the desert and serve God. When Pharaoh refused, God "hardened the heart" of the Egyptian ruler (Exod. 5). As Divine agent, Moses brought ten plagues upon Egypt: blood, frogs, vermin (lice), wild beasts, pestilence, boils, hail, locusts, darkness, slaying of the firstborn (Exod. 7–10). After the last plague, the slaying of the firstborn, Pharaoh finally set the Israelites free (Exod. 12). When Pharaoh changed his mind and sent chariots to recapture the escaping slaves, God instructed Moses to stretch out his hand and the water of the Sea of Reeds parted. The Israelites crossed on dry land, but when the Egyptian forces followed, the water returned and they were drowned (Exod. 14).

En route to the Promised Land, Moses ascended Mount Sinai to receive the tablets of the Ten Commandments (Exod. 20). But when witnessing the shameful episode of the Golden Calf, he angrily flung them to the ground (Exod. 32). Ascending Mount Sinai for a second time, Moses brought down a second set of tablets, carved by the hands of man rather than by the finger of God (Exod. 34). Throughout the forty years of wandering in the wilderness, brought about because of the evil report by ten of the twelve Israelite princes sent to "spy out" the land (Num. 13–14), the people repeatedly complained. Despite his frustration, Moses remained a champion of their cause. On one occasion, when God irately declared the decision to blot out the Israelites and make a new nation from Moses, the Lawgiver of Israel answered, "Then erase me from the record which you have written!" (Exod. 32:32).

However, Moses was not permitted to join the Israelites in crossing the Jordan into Canaan—ostensibly because of his actions when the people demanded that he supply them with water. Instead of ordering the nearby rock to yield its water, Moses castigated the people as "rebels" and angrily struck the rock twice (Num. 20). Moses vainly pleaded with God to reverse this decree: "The people have been given many precepts that can be fulfilled only in the Land of Israel. Let me enter the land so that I can fulfill all of them" (Sot. 14a). Moses was only permitted to ascend Mount Nebo, across the Jordan from Jericho, where God showed him the entire land that constituted the Divine promise to the patriarchs (Deut. 34). When informed that his death was imminent, Moses conferred his authority on Joshua (Deut. 31) and delivered a powerful farewell address that recounted the history of the people and urged them to preserve their allegiance to God (Deut. 32–33). Moses died at the age of 120, in full command of his faculties, with "his eyes undimmed and his vigor unabated" (Deut. 34:7). His place of burial (by God Himself; Sot. 9b) remained unknown to prevent the possibility of a cult developing in relation to his gravesite.

Moses was the ultimate prophet, the "father of all the prophets" (Deut. R. 3:9), who spoke with God "face to face" (Exod. 33:11). According to the *aggadah*, others saw their prophetic visions through dim glass, whereas Moses saw through a clear one (Lev. R. 1:14). He was a faithful messenger who did not add or subtract or offer any explanation other than that which had been told to him at Sinai. Moses also was the great religious leader who transformed the disparate tribes of Israel into a nation, with a unified legal and moral system based on a Divine covenant. When Moses was angry with Israel, God appeased him; conversely, when the Lord was angry with Israel, Moses appeased Him (Exod. R. 45:2).

"Moses instituted the formula of prayer [that opens the *Amidah*]—the Great, Mighty, and Awesome God" (Deut. 10:17; JT Ber. 7:3). He composed the first blessing of the Grace after Meals, which praises God for providing food, in response to the manna that sustained the people in the wilderness (Ber. 48b). He also ordained that the Torah be read publicly on Sabbaths, festivals, New Moons, and the intermediate days of the festivals (JT Meg. 4:1). After the episode of the Golden Calf, God "wrapped Himself in a *tallit* like the reader [one who leads the prayers] of a congregation and showed Moses the order of prayer [the Thirteen Attributes of God, which when recited evoke Divine Mercy; Exod. 34:6–7]" (RH 17b).

When a kid ran away while he was tending Jethro's flock, Moses pursued it to a pool of water where the animal was drinking. "I did not know that you were running because of thirst! You must be tired." So Moses carried the kid on his shoulders on his return. Impressed by this kind gesture, God said:

"Because you have shown such compassion in tending the flocks, you will tend My flock, Israel" (Exod. R. 2:2).

The Bible notes that when Moses came down from Mount Sinai with the second set of tablets, his face emitted a radiance reflecting the afterglow of his encounter with the splendor of the Divine Presence (Exod. 34:29–35). According to one legend, these "rays of glory" arose from the sparks that emanated from the mouth of the *Shechinah* when God taught him Torah; in another, their origin was a bit of ink left in the pen used by Moses when writing the Torah, which he then passed over his head. A third opinion was that the Divine radiance came from the cave in which Moses hid to comply with the statement of God, "When My glory passes, I will place you [Moses] in a cleft of the rock" (Exod. 33:22). The Hebrew word used, *keren*, also means "horn," the source of the "horned" Moses in the classic statue by Michelangelo. *See also* Aaron; Jethro; Joshua; Korach; Nachshon; Zelophehad; Zimri; Zipporah.

N

Nabal, first husband of Abigail, who later became the wife of King David.

A wealthy man from the family of Caleb who "had 3,000 sheep and 1,000 goats," Nabal was "churlish and evil in his doings" and an extreme miser (1 Sam. 25). Although he resided in Maon, about eight miles south of Hebron, Nabal's flocks pastured in the Judean desert. At the time, David and his men were wandering through the hills of Judah, often protecting the shepherds of Nabal from robbers. When he was informed that Nabal was shearing his sheep, David sent ten of his men to greet Nabal and request that he "give whatever your generosity permits you to my servants" on this festive day (i.e., some payment in return for protecting his sheep while grazing). When Nabal not only refused to pay but even accused David of being a mere rebellious servant, David assembled 400 well-armed men to take revenge. However, on the way they met Nabal's wife, Abigail, who brought food and wine and begged David to spare her worthless husband and his servants lest he, the future king, shame himself by shedding blood without cause. That night, Nabal feasted like a king and his "heart was merry within him, for he was very drunk." The next morning, however, when "the wine was gone out of Nabal" and Abigail told him what had occurred, "his heart died within him and he became as a stone" and died ten days later.

The *aggadah* describes Nabal as one who had forbidden relations, idolatrous thoughts, and denied God. Playing on the rearranged letters of their names, Nabal was identified with Laban, both sharing the same deceitful qualities (Mid. Ps. 53:1). Why did God wait ten days to kill Nabal (1 Sam. 25:38)? According to one opinion, "They correspond to the ten dishes [one to each] that Nabal gave to the servants of David." Another said, "These are the ten days between Rosh Hashanah and Yom Kippur," thus suspending the punishment and offering Nabal a chance to repent, which he failed to accept. A final thought was that God suspended Nabal's punishment during the seven days of mourning for Samuel, to prevent any confusion between the mourning for a righteous man (Samuel) and any lamentations for a scoundrel. Consequently, Nabal was permitted to live three days longer and then died in a plague (JT Bik. 2:1).

Naboth, owner of a vineyard close to the palace of Ahab, king of Israel.

Ahab coveted the vineyard of Naboth "for a vegetable garden" and offered to provide either a "better vineyard" or monetary compensation (1 Kings 21). However, Naboth refused to sell or exchange what he considered as his family's inheritance. Jezebel, Ahab's wicked queen, brought a false accusation that Naboth had blasphemed God and the king, resulting in Naboth's death and the confiscation of his property by the crown. Ahab even arranged to have Naboth's children killed, so that the king (who was Naboth's cousin) could inherit the vineyard as the next of kin (Sanh. 48b). Ahab's brazen actions led Elijah to condemn him as a murderer and robber, and the prophet foretold the destruction of his royal house (1 Kings 21:17–24).

Nachshon, son of Aminadav and prince of the tribe of Judah.

Nachshon's sister, Elisheba, was the wife of Aaron (Exod. 6:23). As the most renowned of the Israelite tribal leaders, Nachshon was accorded the honor of being the first of the twelve princes to bring an offering at the dedication of the Tabernacle (Num. 7:12–17). As the head of the tribe of Judah, Nachshon led the Israelites on their journeys through the wilderness (Num. 10:14). According to the Book of Ruth (4:20–22), Nachshon was the grandfather of Boaz, who in turn was the great-grandfather of King David.

When the Israelites, camped by the Sea of Reeds, saw the army of Pharaoh looming on the horizon, they were thrown into a frightened frenzy. They complained to Moses: "Was it for want of graves in Egypt that you brought us to die in the wilderness?" (Exod. 14:11). The Bible described God as castigating Moses—"Why do you cry out to me?"—ordering him to "tell the Israelites to go forward. And lift up your rod and hold out your arm over the sea and split it, so that the Israelites may march into the sea on dry ground" (Exod. 14:15–16).

According to the Talmud, "Each tribe was unwilling to be the first to enter the water." Firmly believing that God would redeem the people, Nachshon bravely jumped into the sea. Even when the waters reached his neck and nearly drowned him, Nachshon remained resolute in his faith and kept moving forward. Only when the water lapped over Nachshon's nostrils and his life was in danger did the sea split so that Israelites could cross over in safety (Sot. 37a). The Rabbis ascribed this miracle to the courageous actions of this prince of Judah, whose tribe was rewarded with the eternal kingship of Israel.

Nadab, eldest of the four sons of Aaron and Elisheba.

Immediately after the ceremonies at which he and his brothers were consecrated as priests and their father Aaron was anointed as high priest, Nadab and his brother Abihu took their fire pans and incense and offered "alien fire" before the Lord. This unauthorized service, an action "which He [God] had not enjoined upon them," resulted in Nadab and Abihu being consumed by a fire that "came forth from the Lord" (Lev. 10:1–2).

This brief passage has been the focus of extensive commentary, attempting to discover the explicit reason why they were struck down and to reconcile Divine justice with their summary execution for what seemed like a trivial offense. The most common explanation was that they entered the Sanctuary while drunk, based on the subsequent warning to the priests, "Drink no wine or other intoxicants, you or your sons, when you enter the Tent of Meeting, that you may not die" (Lev. 10:9). Related to this was the idea that they entered the Sanctuary "so casually dressed that they showed disrespect for their surroundings." Others related the "strange fire" to overwhelming ambition, suggesting that Nadab and Abihu could not wait to succeed Moses and Aaron as the leaders of the people, or that they "disregarded the tradition of their elders." According to the *aggadah*, "Moses and Aaron once walked along, with Nadab and Abihu behind them and all Israel following in the rear. Then Nadab said to Abihu, 'When will these two old men die, so that you and I become the leaders of our generation?' But God said to them: 'We shall see who will bury whom.'" This led R. Papa to observe, "Many an old camel is laden with the hides of younger ones" (Sanh. 52a).

Based on the phrase "each took his fire pan," some blamed Nadab and Abihu for their excessive egotism in not consulting each other or their father Aaron (*Sifra*). According to a *midrash*, Nadab and Abihu had no wives because they were arrogant. Although many women remained unmarried waiting for them, they haughtily declared: "Our father's brother [Moses] is king, our mother's brother [Nachshon] is prince [of his tribe], our father [Aaron] is high priest, and we are assistant high priests. What women are suitable for us?" (Lev. R. 20:10). Taking the opposite extreme, some commentators have argued that Nadab and Abihu were too pious, so inflamed with love for God that they attempted to come too close to Him and thus were consumed by the Lord, who is compared to a "raging fire." This view was supported by the frequent instructions to Aaron about precisely when and how to enter the Tabernacle, lest he be struck down in similar fashion while trying to "be one with God."

According to a legend, the death warrant for Nadab and Abihu was actually drafted at Mount Sinai, based on the biblical verse, "They beheld God, and then they ate and drank" (Exod. 24:11). This was interpreted as meaning that they feasted their eyes on the *Shechinah* like a person who looks at his friend while eating and drinking. The Rabbis offered the parable of a king who, while celebrating the marriage of his daughter, learned of something disreputable about her best man. The king [God] thought: "If I kill him now, it will disturb my daughter's joy [Israel when receiving the Torah]. At some later time, my own joyous celebration [the consecration of the priests] will arrive, and it will be better to do the deed [kill Nadab and Abihu] at that time" (Lev. R. 20:10).

Nadab and Abihu left no sons (Num. 3:4), and thus their priestly lines ended with their deaths.

Nahor, son of Terah, and the brother of Abraham and Haran.

Married to his niece Milcah, the daughter of his late brother, Haran (Gen. 11:26–29), Nahor was the progenitor of twelve Aramean tribes. His son, Bethuel, was the father of Rebecca and Laban. When Bethuel died young, his children came under the protection of their grandfather. Consequently, the Torah described Laban as the "son of Nahor" (Gen. 29:5).

At the covenant ceremony between Jacob (Abraham's grandson) and Laban (Jacob's brother-in-law), the latter stated: "May the God of Abraham and the god of Nahor judge between us [in any dispute]" (Gen. 31:53), thus invoking the name of the patriarchal deity of each family as witnesses to the pact.

Nahum, seventh of the minor prophets.

Nahum prophesied the coming of Divine vengeance on Nineveh and provided a vivid description of the city's destruction by the Babylonians and the Medes in 612 B.C.E.

Naomi, wife of Elimelech, and the mother-in-law of Ruth.

During a time of famine, Naomi left her family home in Bethlehem and accompanied her husband and two sons to the land of Moab. There Elimelech died, and his two sons married Moabite women, Mahlon marrying Ruth and Hilion wedding Orpah. Ten years later, after the death of her two sons, Naomi heard that the famine in Judah had passed and decided to return to her homeland. She urged her daughters-in-law to return to their families: "May the Lord deal kindly with you, as you have dealt with the dead and with me. May the Lord grant that each of you find security in the house of a husband" (Ruth 1:8–9). After some reluctance, Orpah chose to remain in Moab and kissed Naomi farewell (Ruth 1:14). However, Ruth refused to be dissuaded from going with her beloved mother-in-law, saying: "Do not urge me to leave you. . . . For wherever you go, I will go; wherever you lodge, I will lodge; your people shall be my people, and your God my God" (Ruth 1:16).

The *aggadah* expands the biblical text. Ruth added, "In any case I intend to convert [to Judaism], and it is better for my conversion to be at your hand than at another's." When Naomi heard this, she began to teach Ruth the laws of proselytes. In one version, she said, "My daughter, daughters of Israel do not go to theaters and circuses." Ruth replied, "Wherever you go, I will go." "The people of Israel do not dwell in a house without a *mezuzah*." Ruth responded, "Where you lodge, I will lodge" (Ruth R. 2:22). In another version, Naomi said: "On the Sabbath we are forbidden to walk further than the 2,000 cubit Sabbath limit [from one's town or resting place]." Ruth replied, "Wherever you go, I will go." "We are forbidden to seclude ourselves in private with a strange man." "Where you lodge, I will lodge." "We are commanded [to fulfill] 613 commandments." "Your people shall be my people." "Idolatry is forbidden to us." "And your God [shall be] my God" (Yev. 47b).

Noting that Orpah kissed Naomi when she left her mother-in-law, but Ruth "clung to her" (Ruth 1:14), R. Isaac related that God said: "May the descendants of the one who kissed [Goliath and his brothers, who were sons of Orpah] fall at the hands of the one who clung [David, the grandson of Ruth]" (Sot. 42b).

When Naomi and Ruth arrived in Bethlehem, "the whole city buzzed with excitement over them." Naomi was so much changed by poverty and affliction that the women who had known her exclaimed, "Can this be Naomi?" She replied, "Do not call me Naomi ['pleasantness']; call me Mara ['bitterness']" (Ruth 1:19–20). The *aggadah* relates that previously Naomi traveled in covered carriages, but now walked. Rather than being clothed in garments of silk, she now was clad in rags. And her face, previously ruddy from food and drink, now was sallow from hunger (Ruth R. 3:7).

When Naomi showed Ruth's child to her female neighbors, they excitedly exclaimed, "A son is born to Naomi!" (Ruth 4:16–17). The Talmud asks, "Was it then Naomi who bore him? Surely it was Ruth who bore him! But Ruth bore him and Naomi raised him; therefore, he was called after her [Naomi's] name" (Sanh. 19b). *See also* Boaz.

Naphtali, sixth son of Jacob, and the second son of Bilhah, the maidservant of Rachel.

Naphtali's name was given by Rachel: "A fateful contest [*naftalin*] I waged with my sister; yes, and I have prevailed" (Gen. 30:8). The flag of the tribe of Naphtali was of a color described as clarified red wine (Num. R. 2:8) embroidered with a deer, based on the verse, "Naphtali is a hind let loose" (Gen. 49:21). The *aggadah* relates the second half of the verse, "who delivers beautiful sayings," to the story about the death of Jacob. When his sons were preparing to bury him in the Cave of Machpelah, Esau tried to stop them by asserting that as the firstborn he had a prior claim to the last remaining gravesite. When Esau demanded that they "produce a document [of sale] for me!" the fleet Naphtali ran like a deer to Egypt and brought back the deed (Sot. 13a).

After the conquest of Canaan, the tribe of Naphtali was allotted territory north and west of the Sea of Galilee (Josh. 19:32–39).

Nathan, prophet who played a prominent role in three events at the court of King David.

In a prophetic vision (1 Chron. 17:4–27), Nathan was commanded to inform David that he would not build the Temple. Instead, this task would be postponed until the reign of David's son, Solomon, because David had shed blood and thus could not erect a house to honor God's name. Nathan consoled David by noting that God would build a "house" for David, the unconditional assurance that the Davidic dynasty would endure forever.

The second prophecy was his rebuke of David concerning his adultery with Bathsheba, compounded by the king ordering the killing of her innocent husband, Uriah, to cover his crime (2 Sam. 12:1–15). In his third and final appearance (1 Kings 1:11–40), Nathan responded to Adonijah's proclamation that he would succeed to the throne of his aging father by persuading Bathsheba to approach the ailing David and urging him to fulfill his solemn oath pledging that Solomon would reign after his death. David was convinced by her words, ordering Solomon be crowned king even while David was still alive.

According to the Talmud, "Samuel wrote the book that bears his name . . . [but] it was completed by Gad the seer and Nathan the prophet" (BB 15a). *See also* Bathsheba.

Nehemiah, son of Hacaliah, and the rebuilder of the walls of Jerusalem after the Babylonian Exile.

Literally meaning "God has consoled," Nehemiah was a cupbearer to the Persian King Artaxerxes I (465–424 B.C.E.). When he learned of the poor condition of the exiles who had returned from Babylonia to Jerusalem, he obtained a commission from the Persian ruler to serve as governor of Judah in order to help his fellow Jews. One of Nehemiah's first tasks was to provide protection for the people by rebuilding the walls of Jerusalem. To repopulate the city, he ordered that one of every ten Jews should take up residence in the capital. Together with Ezra the scribe, Nehemiah rectified social injustices, including restoration to their original owners of lands taken for debt by the wealthier members of the community. They enforced observance of the Sabbath and festivals and the prohibition of mixed marriages, which preserved the identity and continuity of the Jewish people.

According to the Rabbis, Nehemiah completed the Book of Chronicles, which was written by Ezra the scribe (BB 15a).

Nethanel, son of Zuar and chieftain of the tribe of Issachar.

Nethanel made the second of the twelve identical offerings for the dedication of the Tabernacle in the wilderness (Num. 7:18–23).

Nimrod, son of Cush, grandson of Ham, and the great-grandson of Noah.

Labeled a "mighty hunter" (Gen. 10:9), Nimrod was depicted as having established a great empire that included Babylon, one of the major cities of the ancient world. The *aggadah* describes Nimrod as having introduced the eating of meat by humans and being the first to wage war against others. The Rabbis considered Nimrod, whose Hebrew name comes from the root *mered* (rebel), as having instigated the building of the Tower of Babel as an act of rebellion against God (Hul. 89b).

According to legend, the source of Nimrod's power was the garment of glory that God had made for Adam and was taken by Noah into the ark. When they disembarked onto dry land, Noah's son Ham took the garment and bequeathed it to Nimrod. Whenever Nimrod wore it, all the cattle, beasts, and fowl would come and prostrate themselves before him. Thinking that this adoration reflected Nimrod's own strength, the people of the land made him king over them, and he appointed Terah, the father of Abraham, as his minister. Then Nimrod said to his subjects, "Come, let us build a city and a tower with its top in the heavens"—the biblical Tower of Babel (Gen. 11:4). According to the *aggadah*, Nimrod was slain by Esau, who was jealous of his success as a hunter and coveted his magic garment (PdRE 24).

A *midrash* relates that, just before the birth of Abraham, astrologers warned Nimrod that a child would be born who would challenge his authority and put an end to idolatry. Therefore, Nimrod ordered the killing of all male newborn babies. However, Abraham's mother escaped into the fields and gave birth secretly. When Abraham rejected the idolatry of his father, Terah, the future patriarch was brought before Nimrod, who commanded: "Since you do not worship images, you should worship fire." Abraham replied, "We should rather worship water, which extinguishes fire." When Nimrod agreed that the worship of water was acceptable, Abraham said: "We should rather worship the cloud that carries water." The argument continued with the "wind that disperses the cloud" and "the human being that carries the wind [in the breath of the body]," until it eventually arrived at what the philosophers call a "First Cause"—the ultimate Creator (Gen. R. 38:13).

Noah, son of Lamech, and the father of Shem, Ham, and Japheth.

The name Noah, which derives from a Hebrew root meaning "rest," was given because "this one will provide us relief from our work and from the toil of our hands, out of the very soil which the Lord placed under a curse" (Gen. 5:29). The *aggadah* (Tanh. Bereshit 11) explains that Noah received his name after having invented the plow and other farm implements (scythe, hoe), which greatly enhanced the production of food crops and effectively alleviated the curse meted out to the recently deceased Adam (Gen. 3:18–19). A different legend relates that Methusaleh, who was a great scholar, warned Lamech not to call Noah by his correct name lest the wicked people living at the time kill him through sorcery, which was effective only if the correct name were used. So Methusaleh told Lamech that in public he always should call the boy Menachem, meaning "this one will comfort us" (Yalkut Shimoni, Bereshit 42).

The description of Noah as "a righteous man; he was blameless in his generation; Noah walked with God" (Gen. 6:9) was interpreted by some Rabbis as words of praise. If Noah was such a moral person that he was not adversely affected by the corruptness of his generation, how much more virtuous would he have been if surrounded by upright individuals. Others took a different approach, arguing that Noah was righteous only in comparison to the extremely wicked men around him, and that he would have been no better than average in a more moral age. Other sages provided colorful illustrations of these different opinions. To support the first view, one likened the situation to a "vial of [fragrant] spikenard oil lying amid excrement; if it is fragrant where it is, how much more so if it were amidst spices." The contrary position was suggested by an image of a barrel of wine lying in a cellar filled with vats of vinegar. "Its odor is fragrant [by comparison with the vinegar], but elsewhere it would not be" (Sanh. 108a).

The Bible notes that "Noah walked with God" (Gen. 6:9). Explaining this verse, the Rabbis (Gen. R. 30:10) presented the parable of a king who had two sons, one grown and the other still a child. To the child he said, "Walk *with* me"; but to the grown son he said, "Walk *before* me." Thus when God later addressed Abraham, a paragon of spiritual strength, He said: "Walk before me and be perfect" (Gen. 17:1).

Because of the rampant lawlessness and immorality on earth, God decided to send a great Flood to destroy the entire human race, with the exception of Noah (Gen. 6:11ff). He ordered Noah to build an ark into which he would bring his family, a male and female of every "unclean" species of living creature (to allow for their regeneration) (Gen. 6:20), and seven of each type of "clean" animal (needed for sacrifices after the Flood) (Gen. 7:2). From the phrase "Make *for yourself* an ark," the Rabbis deduced that Noah was to build the ark himself over 120 years. When the curious would ask what he was doing, Noah was to reply that God was about to bring a flood on the world because of the sins of humanity. This was designed as a stern warning to spur the people to repent, a quintessential concept in Judaism. However, the contemporaries of Noah were irredeemably corrupt and merely mocked his efforts (Gen. R. 30:7).

Noah regarded himself as responsible for the welfare of the animals in the ark and the preservation of all animal species. Consequently, he and his sons provided each animal with its usual diet at its usual mealtime, thus sleeping neither during the day nor at night (Sanh. 108b). "He took in branches for the elephants, tasty shrubs for the deer, and glass beads for the ostriches," as well as vine, fig, and olive shoots for future plantings (Gen. R. 31:14). Once Noah was late feeding the lion, which clawed at him so that Noah came away limping (Tanh. Noah 9).

After Noah entered the ark (at age 600), "The rain fell on the earth forty days and forty nights" (Gen. 7:12) and the mountains were covered with water, and every living thing not sheltered in the ark perished from the earth. After 150 days, the waters began to recede; eventually "the ark came to rest on the mountains of Ararat" (Gen. 8:4). Noah sent out a dove from the ark, but it returned when it "could find no resting place for its foot" (Gen. 8:8). A week later, the dove was sent out again, but this time it returned to the ark with an olive leaf (traditionally plucked from the Mount of Olives in Jerusalem) in its mouth, indicating to Noah that the waters had subsided enough for life to reappear on the earth.

After leaving the ark, Noah erected an altar to God and sacrificed one of every species of clean animal. In accepting this offering, God promised never again to send a universal flood, symbolizing this covenant with the rainbow. Compromising the vegetarian ideal of the Garden of Eden, God now permitted human beings to eat animals for food, though they were strictly prohibited from consuming their blood. The shedding of human blood was forbidden as a crime punishable by death (Gen. 9:3–6).

In a classic legend, when Noah prepared to plant a vineyard after emerging from the ark following the Flood (Gen. 9:20), Satan volunteered to assist him. He brought a sheep, a lion, a pig, and a monkey and slew them under the vine, allowing their blood to drench the soil. That is why "before a man drinks wine he is simple like a sheep and quiet like a lamb in front of its shearers. When he is drunk in moderation, he is strong like a lion and declares that there is none his equal in the world. When he has drunk more than enough, he becomes like a pig wallowing in filth. When he is intoxicated, he becomes like a monkey dancing about, uttering obscenities before all and ignorant of what he is doing" (Tanh. Noah 13).

"Noah drank of the wine and became drunk, and [losing control of himself] he uncovered himself within his tent" (Gen. 9:20–21). His eldest son, Ham, saw his father and derisively reported his condition to his brothers, Shem and

Japheth, who respectfully covered Noah with a cloth, "walking backwards . . . so that they did not see their father's nakedness" (Gen. 9:22–24). Recovering his senses, Noah blessed Shem and Japheth but cursed Ham, through his son Canaan (Gen. 9:25–27). Noah died at age 950, the second progenitor (after Adam) of the human race, since only his descendants survived the Flood.

The Rabbis derived seven basic laws that were binding on all human beings and constituted the fundamental precepts required for the establishment of a civilized society. Termed the "Noahide laws," they were to be observed by all people on earth, whom the Torah described as descended from the three sons of Noah (Gen. 9:19). These laws included (1) the establishment of courts of justice, and the prohibition of (2) idolatry, (3) blasphemy, (4) murder, (5) incest and adultery, (6) robbery, and (7) eating flesh cut from a live animal. Although Israelites in the Land were obliged to carry out all of the Torah commandments, only observance of the seven Noahide laws was required of non-Jews who lived among the Israelites or attached themselves to the Jewish community.

Obadiah, fourth of the minor prophets.

Obadiah was the author of the shortest book in the Bible, containing a single chapter with only twenty-one verses. It predicts the destruction of Edom, who not only exulted at the humiliation of the inhabitants of Judah when Jerusalem fell in 586 B.C.E., but also actively assisted their Babylonian enemies by intercepting the fugitives and occupying the Negev. The final five verses describe the reestablishment of the children of Jacob in their homeland, when Mount Zion will rule over Mount Esau (Edom).

The Rabbis identified Obadiah the prophet with the man of the same name who lived during the time of Ahab, considering him an Edomite convert. God deemed Obadiah the perfect person to prophesize against Edom: "Let one who lived with two wicked persons [Ahab and Jezebel], but did not learn from their bad deeds, come and prophesy against the wicked Esau [father of Edom], who lived with two righteous persons [Isaac and Rebecca] and yet did not learn from their good deeds" (Sanh. 39b).

Obadiah, "governor of the house" of King Ahab.

Obadiah "feared the Lord greatly" and protected some of the prophets of Israel from the murderous actions of Queen Jezebel (1 Kings 18:3–7), who was attempting to kill them all. Obadiah "took one hundred prophets, hid them by fifties in a cave, and fed them with bread and water" (Sanh. 39b).

Obed-Edom, Gittite who watched over the Ark of the Covenant after the death of Uzza.

The Ark remained there for three months (before being brought up to Jerusalem), "and the Lord blessed Obed-Edom and his entire household" (2 Sam. 6:11–12). According to the *aggadah*, this blessing was children; his wife and eight daughters-in-law either bore children twice during each of the three months that the Ark remained with him (Num. R. 4:20), or each bore six children at once (Ber. 63b). Taking Obed-Edom's name, which comes from two Hebrew words—*obed* (the servant [who obeys God in the right way]) and *edom* (red [or one who causes to blush])—the *aggadah* relates it to the shame that David felt when, after being initially afraid to receive the Ark, he saw Obed-Edom take it into his house without hesitation (Num. R. 4:21).

Og, Amorite king of Bashan in Transjordan.

Described as the last of the Rephaim (antediluvian giants), Og was said to have slept on an iron bedstead nine cubits long and four cubits wide (about 13.5 by 6 feet) (Deut. 3:11). According to the Talmud, Og was not destroyed by the Flood, either because the waters only came up to his ankles or because he sat on a rung of the ladder outside the ark, receiving his food each day through a hole made in the side of the vessel after he had sworn to be a slave to Noah and his children (Nid. 61a). Soon after defeating Sihon, the Israelites conquered the armies of Og and took possession of his territory (Num. 21:33–35).

Oholiab, craftsman who assisted Bezalel in constructing the Tabernacle and its furnishings.

Son of Ahisamach and a prince of the tribe of Dan, Oholiab (with Bezalel) was described in the Bible as "endowed with the skill to do any work—of the carver [engraver]; the designer; the embroiderer in blue, purple, crimson yarns, and in fine linen; and of the weaver—as workers in all crafts and as makers of designs" (Exod. 35:34–35). Noting that Oholiab, who came from the lowliest tribe of Dan, was the major assistant of Bezalel, who belonged to the aristocratic tribe of Judah, the Rabbis interpreted this as teaching that before God "the great and the lowly are equal" (Exod. R. 40:4).

Onan, second son of Judah, brother of Er, and husband of Tamar.

After the death of his elder brother, Onan refused to fulfill the terms of a levirate marriage with his sister-in-law, Tamar. Known as *yibbum*, this was an obligation of the brother of a childless widow to produce a son who would be considered the dead man's heir. "But Onan, knowing that the seed would not count as his, let it go to waste [lit., 'he let it spill on the ground'] whenever he joined with his brother's wife, so as not to provide offspring for his brother" (Gen. 38:9). As punishment for this action, God also took Onan's life (Gen. 38:10).

Othniel, son of Kenaz, younger brother of Caleb, and the first judge of Israel.

After eight years of oppression by a Mesopotamian king, "the people of Israel cried out to the Lord, [and] the Lord raised up a deliverer [Othniel] to save them." Othniel led the Israelites in a successful campaign against Cushan-Rishathaim, king of Aram, and subsequently "the land had peace for forty years" (Judg. 3:9–11).

P

Pagiel, son of Ochran and chieftain of the tribe of Asher.

Pagiel made the eleventh of the twelve identical offerings for the dedication of the Tabernacle in the wilderness (Num. 7:72–77).

Pinchas, son of Eleazar, and the grandson of Aaron.

At the height of the idolatrous reveling and debauchery at Shittim, Pinchas killed an Israelite man (Zimri) and a Midianite woman (Cozbi), who were engaging in flagrantly immoral behavior in the sight of Moses and the entire community (Num. 25:7–8). This zealous act ended the plague that had broken out among the people as punishment for their wanton conduct in engaging in the orgiastic cult of Baal-Peor (Num. 25:8–9). It also earned for Pinchas a Divine "covenant of peace" (to protect him from any revenge by Zimri's clan), and for his family the "eternal priesthood" (so that his descendants, later called the Zadokites, would be the sole priests officiating in the Temple service)—"because he took impassioned action for his God, thus making expiation for the Israelites" (Num. 25:12–13). In a subsequent war against the Midianites, Moses equipped Pinchas with sacred utensils and sent him to serve as priest in the campaign (Num. 31:1–6).

Were the actions of Pinchas justified? The psalmist (106:30–31) and most rabbinic commentators praised his courage in taking prompt measures to slay a prince of Israel who was profaning the Name of God, for in this way he prevented the Divine slaughter of countless lives ("so that I did not wipe out the Israelite people in My passion") (Num. 25:11). According to the tradition, moral threats imperil national survival more than physical threats. Consequently, the Israelites were commanded not to hate the Egyptians and the Edomites, who threatened their physical existence, but to exterminate the Midianites, who attempted to undermine Israel's moral standing. The Talmud states that a person who saw Pinchas in a dream would have a miracle performed for him (Ber. 56b). However, Pinchas's zealous actions have appeared to many postbiblical commentators as simple vigilantism, a fanatic response that set a dangerous precedent. Some have argued that the impulsive actions of Pinchas merely reflected a generational shift in the Israelite leadership. According to this view, "Just as the stern and demanding Moses was balanced by Aaron, who avoided quarrel and confrontation, the more moderate Joshua was balanced by the fervor of Pinchas as high priest" (*Etz Hayim* 918).

Pinchas, younger son of Eli, who officiated as a priest in the sanctuary at Shiloh. *See also* Hophni.

Piram, king of Jarmuth.

He joined the coalition of five Amorite kings that was defeated by Joshua at Gibeon (Josh. 10:3). *See also* Adoni-Zedek.

Potiphar, Egyptian officer who was in charge of the royal prison.

Potiphar purchased Joseph as a slave from the Ishmaelites and eventually made him head of his household. However, when Potiphar's wife unsuccessfully attempted to seduce Joseph, she accused him of attempted rape. When Potiphar heard this story, "he was furious" and had Joseph put in prison (Gen. 39:19–20). The *aggadah* asked whether Potiphar's anger was really directed at Joseph or at his wife, whom he may have suspected of having fabricated her story (Gen. R. 87:9). Had Potiphar believed his wife, he could have had Joseph killed rather than placed in a royal prison for high-ranking officials. Moreover, the Hebrew text noted that Potiphar "took him" to the prison, providing a personal escort, which indicated his high esteem for the Hebrew servant.

The Talmud embellishes the story, relating that every day the wife of Potiphar endeavored to entice the virtuous Joseph with words. In addition, "the garments she put on for him in the morning, she did not wear in the evening; those she had put on in the evening, she did not wear in the morning." When he rebuffed her advances and she threatened to put him in prison, Joseph retorted: "The Lord releases the bound" (Ps. 146:7). Potiphar's wife then boasted that she would "bend your proud stature [humiliate him with slave labor]," but Joseph noted, "The Lord raises up those who are bowed down" (Ps. 146:8). In response to her threat to blind his eyes, Joseph replied: "The Lord opens the eyes of the blind" (Ps. 146:8; Yoma 35b). Elsewhere, Rav stated that the phrase "He bought him for himself" meant that Potiphar was inflamed by Joseph's beauty and purchased him for "immoral purposes." However, the angel Gabriel came and castrated Potiphar, a deduction that he based on the fact that the Hebrew word for "officer" used to describe Potiphar also means "eunuch" (Sot. 13b).

When Joseph became the viceroy of Egypt, second in command only to Pharaoh, he was given as a wife Asenath, whom the Bible described as the daughter of Poti-Phera, priest of On (Gen. 41:45). A *midrash* identifies her as the daughter of Dinah (and thus Joseph's niece), who was later adopted by

Potiphar (PdRE 38), so that Potiphar became the father-in-law of Joseph. *See also* Asenath; Joseph.

Puah, one of the two Hebrew midwives in Egypt.

Along with Shiphrah, Puah bravely refused to obey Pharaoh's order to kill all the newborn Israelite boys (Exod. 1:15–21). *Midrashic* tradition has identified Puah as Miriam, the sister of Moses (Sot. 11b). The *aggadah* related that she was given this name (from a Hebrew root meaning "to open the mouth") because she used to put in her mouth bubbles (*nofa'at*) of wine to amuse the infant while Shiphrah attended to the mother; or revive (*mefiah*) the infant by artificial respiration when people said it was dead. From the word *hophiah* (lift), the Rabbis explained that Puah "lifted Israel up to God" or "lifted up her face against Pharaoh [uttering an angry rebuke] and turned up her face against him," defying the ruler and frustrating his plans (Exod. R. 1:13).

Interpreting the biblical verse "They gave life to the children" (Exod. 1:17), a *midrash* relates that the midwives performed good deeds for them. For example, they collected water and food from the houses of rich women and gave it to poor women, who thus were able to provide for their children. Moreover, they prayed that the poor emerge unblemished and God heeded their voices (Exod. R. 1:15).

R

Rachel, younger daughter of Laban, second wife of Jacob, mother of Joseph and Benjamin, and the fourth matriarch of Israel.

After first meeting Rachel at a well near Haran as he fled Canaan to escape the wrath of his brother Esau, Jacob fell instantly in love with her and agreed to serve Laban for seven years as a bride price—"and they seemed to him but a few days because of his love for her" (Gen. 29:9–20). After a gala wedding feast and consummating the marriage, Jacob realized that Laban had tricked him into taking Rachel's elder sister, Leah. When Jacob berated Laban for his duplicity, his father-in-law calmly replied: "It is not the practice in our place to marry off the younger before the older." However, Laban agreed to give Rachel to Jacob, as long as he would promise to serve him seven more years (Gen. 29:22–27).

According to a *midrash*, Rachel warned Jacob that her cunning father would try to substitute her older unmarried sister Leah in her place. Jacob confidently retorted, "I am his brother in deceit," and they agreed on a sign by which he would recognize Rachel on their wedding night. When Laban sent Leah into the bridal chamber, Rachel disclosed the sign to her sister, lest she be put to shame. As a reward for this selfless act, the Talmud stated that Rachel earned the merit to be the ancestress of King Saul (Meg. 13b).

The Bible describes Rachel as "shapely and beautiful" (Gen. 29:17) and beloved by Jacob, but she was barren. Jealous of her "unloved" sister Leah, who had given birth to four sons, Rachel cried to Jacob: "Give me children, or I shall die" (Gen. 30:1). Rachel gave Jacob her handmaiden, Bilhah, as a concubine so that she might gain children through her. After Leah had borne two more sons, "God remembered Rachel . . . and opened her womb" (Gen. 30:22). She named her son Joseph, praying that God "add [*yosef* in Hebrew] another son for me" (Gen. 30:24), but also implying that God had taken away (*asaf*) her disgrace at being childless. She also may have feared that, if she had remained barren, Laban would have permitted only Leah to accompany Jacob to the Land of Israel and kept the childless wife in her father's house (Gen. R. 73:3). According to a *midrash*, Rachel's words were evidence that she was a prophetess. Knowing that Jacob was destined to have only twelve sons and noting that Joseph was the eleventh, she prayed that she be granted one more son. This caused Leah's seventh child, which at the time of conception was a son, to be transformed into a daughter (Dinah), for otherwise Rachel would have been the mother of only one son (Gen. R. 72:6).

When Jacob eventually decided to return to Canaan and face Esau, he consulted with Rachel and Leah about his plan and received their consent. Without her husband's knowledge, before they left, Rachel stole the household idols (*teraphim*) of her father, hid them in the camel cushion, and sat upon them (Gen. 31:19). This act usually has been considered as either an attempt to turn her father away from idolatry (Gen. R. 74:5) or her reluctance to totally break with the family religion. However, comparative studies of ancient Near Eastern religions indicate that Rachel may have had another underlying motive, since the possessor of the household gods and the spirits of the dead (*teraphim*) was considered to have the primary claim on the family inheritance. According to the *aggadah*, Jacob's unintentional curse when Laban accused him of stealing his property—"With whomever you find your gods, he shall not live" (Gen. 31:22)—led to Rachel's premature death (Gen. R. 74:4). The curse would have taken effect at once had it not been destined that Rachel would bear Jacob his youngest son (PdRE 36).

As the favored wife, Jacob placed Rachel and her son in the most protected location at the rear of the column as he prepared to face the wrath of his estranged brother, Esau (Gen. 33:2). While traveling from Bethel to Ephrat (now Bethlehem), Rachel died giving birth to her second son, whom she called "Ben-oni" (son of my sorrow), but Jacob named him Benjamin (Gen. 35:16ff). Rather than bury Rachel in the ancestral family vault in the Cave of Machpelah, the heartsick Jacob buried her along the road, and the ancient site of her tomb remains revered as an important religious shrine to this day. According to a *midrash*, Jacob buried Rachel on the road because he foresaw that the Israelites, when driven from Jerusalem to exile in Babylonia, would need her intercession with God on their behalf (Gen. R. 82:10). Jeremiah poignantly described Rachel at that moment, "weeping for her children [and] refusing to be comforted" (Jer. 31:15).

Although the younger, Rachel is always mentioned first whenever the two sisters are listed together in the Bible. Rachel is also named first in the parental blessing recited over daughters on the Sabbath eve. The same sequence occurs in the blessing for brides on their wedding day, as was given to Ruth when she married Boaz: "The Lord make the woman who is coming to your house like Rachel and Leah, the two who built the house of Israel" (Ruth 4:11). *See also* Benjamin; Bilhah; Dan; Joseph; Naphtali.

Rahab, a woman of Jericho who sheltered the two spies sent by Joshua to scout out the land.

Rahab hid the spies in her house, which was situated within the city wall and had a window facing the outside. Rahab was described as a *"zonah,"* meaning "harlot," but is sometimes translated as "innkeeper" (derived from the Hebrew root *zun*, meaning to "provide food") (Josh. 2). According to the *aggadah*, Rahab was a prominent prostitute, who had relations with every prince and ruler and thus knew what was occurring outside the walls of her town (Zev. 116b). Informed that spies had entered her house, the king of Jericho ordered Rahab to hand them over. Instead, Rahab hid the spies on the roof under some stalks of flax and asserted that the two men had come and gone without her knowing their identity. After she gratuitously added, "Quick, go after them, for you can overtake them," the servants of the king "pursued them in the direction of the Jordan." Rahab then spoke to the spies, indicating that she knew how God had miraculously dried up the waters of the Sea of Reeds for the Israelites and delivered Sihon and Og into their hands. Before letting the two spies leave through the window in the wall, Rahab asked them to reward her kindness by sparing her and her family when the Israelites inevitably defeated Jericho. The spies swore to do as she requested, ordering her to "tie this length of crimson cord to the window through which you let us down. Bring your father, your mother, and all your family together in your house. If anyone ventures outside the doors of your home, his blood will be on his head and we shall be innocent. But if a hand is laid on anyone who remains in the house with you, his blood shall be on our hands." When Joshua conquered Jericho, he commanded the two spies to rescue Rahab and her family, whose descendants resided in Israel from then on (Josh. 6:22–23, 25).

According to the *aggadah*, Rahab was one of the four most beautiful women in the world (Meg. 15a). After the Israelites conquered Jericho, Rahab became a convert and married Joshua, becoming the ancestress of eight priests who also were prophets (including Jeremiah) and the prophetess Huldah (Meg. 14b).

Rebecca, daughter of Bethuel, wife of Isaac, mother of Jacob and Esau, and the second matriarch of Israel.

Seeking a wife for his son, Isaac, and not wanting him to marry a local Canaanite woman, Abraham sent his servant Eliezer in search of a suitable bride for his family in Haran (Gen. 24:1–59). Arriving at a well, Eliezer prayed that God would send an appropriate young woman who would offer to draw water both for his camels as well as for himself. The compassionate Rebecca was the chosen one. According to the *aggadah*, Eliezer immediately realized the greatness of Rebecca when the water of the well rose to greet her as she came near (Gen. R. 60:5). Eliezer first obtained the consent of her mother and brother, Laban. Then the future bride agreed to go with him to Canaan (Gen.

24:1–59), from which the Rabbis deduced that a fatherless maiden may not be given in marriage without her consent (Gen. R. 60:12).

Seeing a handsome man from afar and learning from Eliezer that it was his master, Rebecca immediately covered herself with a veil and got down from her camel (Gen. 24:65). This is one reason given for Jewish brides wearing this symbol of female modesty during the marriage ceremony. "And Isaac brought her into his mother Sarah's tent" (Gen. 24:67). According to the *aggadah*, "As long as Sarah lived, a cloud [signifying the Divine Presence] hung over her tent, the doors were open wide, her dough was blessed, and a lamp burned [in the tent] from one Sabbath eve to the next. When Sarah died, all these ceased; but when Rebecca arrived, they all returned. So when Isaac saw Rebecca following in his mother's footsteps, separating her dough offering in purity, she became his wife" (Gen. R. 60:16).

Prior to their departure, Rebecca's family blessed her: "O sister! May you grow into thousands of myriads; may your offspring seize the gates of their foes" (Gen. 24:60). However, the Rabbis believed that the "blessings" of her mother and brother were not sincere. Deemed the "blessings of the impious, which are curses," they caused Rebecca to remain barren for twenty years (Gen R. 60:13). Isaac fervently prayed to God, "Let all the children You will grant me be from this righteous woman" (Gen. R. 63:5). Only then did Rebecca finally conceive twins. As the Rabbis noted, "Two women [Rebecca and Tamar] covered themselves with a veil and gave birth to twins" (Gen. R. 60:15). "But the children struggled in her womb," prompting Rebecca to seek Divine guidance at the academy of Shem and Eber. This led the Rabbis to state, "To visit a sage is like visiting the Divine Presence" (Gen. R. 63:6). Rebecca received the following reply: "Two nations are in your womb, two separate peoples shall issue from your body; one people shall be mightier than the other, and the older shall serve the younger" (Gen. 25:23). According to a *midrash*, the respective characters of the two brothers were revealed before they were born. Whenever Rebecca passed a pagan house of worship, Esau struggled to get out; whenever she passed a synagogue or house of study, Jacob eagerly moved within her (Gen. R. 63:6). For the first thirteen years, both children went to school. However, once they reached maturity, one went to houses of study and the other to shrines of idolatry (Gen. 63:10). As the twins grew, each was preferred by one of the parents—"Isaac favored Esau [a skillful hunter] because the patriarch had a taste for game; but Rebecca favored Jacob" (Gen. 25:28). As the *aggadah* observes, "The more Rebecca heard his [Jacob's] voice [engaged in study], the stronger grew her love for him" (Gen. R. 63:10). When the couple was forced by famine to settle among the Philistines, Isaac resorted for protection to the same stratagem as his father, Abraham, pretending that his beautiful wife, Rebecca, was actually his sister (Gen. 26:7).

When Isaac was on his deathbed, he asked Esau to hunt and prepare venison stew before bestowing his blessing upon him. Overhearing her husband's words, Rebecca contrived a plot to allow Jacob to receive the paternal blessing intended for Esau (Gen. 27:1–29). Of course, this was consistent with the previously noted Divine promise, as transmitted to Rebecca before the birth of the twins, that the "older shall serve the younger." Seeing Esau's fury when he returned and learned that he had to be content with the lesser blessing, Rebecca convinced Jacob to flee to her brother Laban to escape Esau's murderous wrath. As a pretext, she used her disgust over Esau's marriage to a local woman and her determination that Jacob marry within the family (Gen. 27:41–48). Like Isaac and his parents, Rebecca was buried in the Cave of Machpelah (Gen. 49:31). *See also* Eliezer.

Rehoboam, first ruler of the Southern Kingdom of Judah (931–914 B.C.E.).

The son of Solomon and the Ammonitess Naamah, after the death of his father, Rehoboam traveled to the sacred northern city of Shechem to be crowned the new king (2 Chron. 10). Before formally agreeing to submit themselves to his rule, the leaders of the ten northern tribes requested that Rehoboam agree to ease the burden of taxation and forced labor that had been imposed by his father. The old advisers, who had seen the evils of Solomon's rule, urged Rehoboam to be conciliatory: "If you would be kind to this people, if you would please them and speak good words to them, they will be your servants forever." However, Rehoboam rejected this wise counsel, instead siding with his younger contemporaries who had enjoyed the material luxuries of Solomon's court and its never-ending need for additional revenues: "Whereas my father put a heavy yoke upon you, I will put more to your yoke; my father chastised you with whips, but I will chastise you with scorpions." Furious at these words, the ten northern tribes seceded and established the Kingdom of Israel under the rule of Jeroboam. Rehoboam planned to attack Israel and try to conquer it by force, but abandoned this effort after hearing the prophecy of Shemaiah: "Thus said the Lord, You shall not set out to make war on your kinsmen, the people of Israel. Let every man return home, for this thing has been brought about by Me" (1 Kings 12:24).

Rava interpreted the biblical verse, "Your wonders and Your thoughts are for *us* [rather than 'me']" (Ps. 40:6) as meaning that as Rehoboam (his grandson) sat on his lap, David said to him: "These two Scriptural verses were said for the benefit of *both of us*" (i.e., permitting Ammonite and Moabite women in marriage, since this ruling allowed him [a descendant of Ruth, a Moabitess] and Rehoboam [the son of Naamah, an Ammonitess] to enter into the assembly of Israel) (Yev. 77a).

According to a *midrash*, Joseph had collected a vast treasure when all the countries in the world came to Egypt to purchase grain during the great famine. When the Israelites left Egypt during the Exodus, they carried this treasure with them (Exod. 12:36). The treasure remained with the Israelites until the time of Rehoboam, when "Shishak, king of Egypt, came up against Jerusalem and took away the treasures of the house of the Lord, and the treasures of the king's house" (1 Kings 14:25). *See also* Shemaiah.

Reuben, firstborn son of Jacob and Leah.

The simplest explanation for Reuben's name is that it derives from two Hebrew words [*r'u ben*], literally meaning "See, a son!"—a joyful exclamation by Leah and Jacob at the time of his birth. The Bible, however, states that Leah named him Reuben because "the Lord has seen my affliction [*ra-ah b'onyi*]. . . . Now my husband will love me" (Gen. 29:32).

The red flag of the tribe of Reuben was embroidered with a mandrake, for once "at the time of the wheat harvest, Reuben came upon some mandrakes in the field and brought them to his mother, Leah" (Gen. 30:14). In exchange for this aphrodisiac, the childless Rachel agreed to allow Jacob to spend an extra night with her less-favored sister (Gen. 30:15). Soon afterward, Rachel conceived her first child, Joseph.

Although the firstborn and entitled to the birthright, priesthood, and kingship, Reuben lost these privileges to Joseph, Levi, and Judah, respectively. He earned Jacob's wrath by impetuously lying with Bilhah, Rachel's handmaid and his father's concubine—"for when you went up upon your father's bed, you brought disgrace" (Gen. 49:4). The patriarch accused his eldest son as being "unstable as water," acting irresponsibly and without moral restraint, just like a rushing torrent. In view of contemporaneous custom in the ancient Near East, many scholars view Reuben's seemingly impetuous act as having a political rather than licentious purpose. It was a regular practice for an heir apparent to take possession of his father's wife to assert his right to the throne and to become identified with the ruler's personality in the eyes of the people. Thus Reuben's deed was a claim of leadership rather than lust. The Rabbis attempted to minimize Reuben's transgression and rejected the idea that he was guilty of incest (Shab. 55b). As a *midrash* explains, "For as long as Rachel lived, her bed stood near that of the patriarch Jacob [in the place of honor in his private quarters]. When Rachel died, Jacob took Bilhah's bed and placed it at his side. [Reuben said,] 'Is it not enough for my mother [Leah] to be jealous during her sister's lifetime, but must she also be so after her death?' [i.e., Reuben saw this as a slight upon his mother's honor, and his sin consisted solely in removing Bilhah's bed]" (Gen. R. 98:4). Moreover, "Reuben was not ashamed to confess [his sin]" and thus was worthy of life in the World to Come (Sot. 7b). As the *aggadah* (Gen. R. 84:19) observed, "Just as you were the first to repent, so your descendant [the prophet Hosea] will be the first to urge others to repent"—"Return, O Israel, unto the Lord your God" (Hos. 14:2).

As raisers of cattle and sheep, the tribe of Reuben, with Gad and half the tribe of Manasseh, was permitted to settle on the east side of the Jordan, on the condition that they help in the conquest of Canaan (Josh. 13:8). *See also* Bilhah.

Ruth, Moabite woman who married Mahlon, the son of Elimelech and Naomi.

Ten years after the death of her Israelite husband, Ruth decided to join her mother-in-law, Naomi, who was planning to return to her family home in Bethlehem. Although Naomi tried to convince her daughter-in-law to remain in Moab and find a new husband in her homeland, Ruth unequivocally rejected this alternative: "Do not urge me to leave you. . . . For wherever you go, I will go; wherever you lodge, I will lodge; your people shall be my people, and your God my God" (Ruth 1:16).

Arriving in Bethlehem, Ruth gleaned in the fields of Boaz, Elimelech's kinsman, who married Ruth and redeemed the estate of her father-in-law. Their child, Obed, became the father of Jesse and the grandfather of King David (Ruth 4:22).

The Talmud states that Ruth's name comes from a Hebrew root meaning "replenish," because "she was privileged to be the ancestress of David, who replenished the Holy One, blessed be He, with songs and hymns" (Ber. 7b, BB 14b). The Zohar (1:188b) says that the line of Judah was built from two women—Tamar and Ruth—from whom issued King David, King Solomon, and the Messiah. After their husbands died, both women made positive efforts to continue the family line. They both acted properly for the sake of kindness for the dead by bearing children who would perpetuate their memory. As an *aggadah* relates, "God once said to Abraham, I have two excellent shoots [belonging to idolatrous nations] to graft upon the stock of Israel—Ruth from Moab [ancestress of David] and Naamah from Ammon [mother of Rehoboam and his distinguished descendants Asa, Jehoshaphat, and Hezekiah]" (Yev. 63a). And because of these two good "doves," God had mercy on two great nations (Moab and Ammon) and did not destroy them (BK 38b). *See also* Boaz; Naomi.

S

Samson, son of Manoah of the tribe of Dan, brave and powerful warrior, and judge over Israel for twenty years.

Samson was a Nazirite—a man consecrated to God who was forbidden to partake of alcohol and whose supernatural strength lay in his unshorn hair. Single-handedly, he fought guerrilla actions against the Philistines. Samson once caught 300 foxes, attached torches to their tails, and released them to burn up the Philistine fields of grain (Judg. 15:4–5). On another occasion, a Philistine army demanded that the men of Judah bind Samson and hand him over to them. But "the spirit of the Lord came mightily upon him," so that the new ropes on his arms "became as flax that was burned with fire, and his bands melted from his hands." Picking up the jawbone of an ass, he slew 1,000 Philistines with it (Judg. 15:12–16).

The Philistines tried unsuccessfully to capture and kill Samson. However, when they learned that the hero of Israel had fallen in love with the beautiful Delilah, they saw their opportunity. For a price, Delilah agreed to ascertain the source of Samson's strength. After three unsuccessful attempts, she finally induced Samson to divulge his secret. Telling the Philistines to lie in wait by her bedchamber, Delilah rocked Samson to sleep, with his head on her lap, whereupon a man came and shaved off all of Samson's hair. Blinded and deprived of his strength, Samson was imprisoned in Gaza and forced to grind corn like an animal by turning a huge millwheel.

Some time later, the Philistines gathered in their temple for a religious festival and led Samson out in chains, roaring with laughter at his misery. They did not realize that his hair had grown back, and with it his strength. Feigning weariness, Samson asked his guards for permission to lean against the temple pillars and rest for a few moments. Uttering a final prayer for vengeance, Samson seized the pillars with all his might and bent them so that the roof came crashing down, killing himself and the 3,000 worshipers. Thus, in his death, Samson killed more Philistines than he had during his life (Judg. 16:21–30).

Samson was incredibly strong and large. The *aggadah* relates that "there were sixty cubits [ninety feet] between Samson's shoulders," though "he was lame in both legs" (Sot. 10a). When the Holy Spirit rested on him, his stride spanned the distance between Zorah and Eshtaol, two great mountains that he uprooted and ground together as if they were pebbles (Sot. 9b; JT Sot. 1:8). When the patriarch Jacob saw Samson in a prophetic vision, he was convinced that this was the Messiah who would redeem Israel (Gen. R. 98:14). Yet, like the mighty Goliath, Samson eventually failed because he did not use his gift for its God-given purpose. By sinning, his strength was no longer considered a gift from God but rather a mere physical attribute that was not guaranteed to protect him (Num. R. 22:7). According to the Talmud (Sot. 9b), "Samson went after the desire of his eyes, and therefore the Philistines captured him and put out his eyes" (Judg. 16:21). *See also* Delilah; Manoah.

Samuel, son of Elkanah and Hannah.

Samuel was the last of the judges and the first of the major prophets, who anointed the first two kings of Israel, Saul and David. His barren mother, Hannah, had vowed that if granted a son she would dedicate him to the service of God. When her prayers were answered, Hannah left her home in Ramah and brought Samuel to Shiloh, where he "entered the service of the Lord under the priest Eli" (1 Sam. 2:11). The two sons of Eli, Hophni and Pinchas, were "scoundrels and paid no heed to the Lord" (1 Sam. 2:12), and Samuel served God in their stead. At a time when "the word of the Lord was rare and prophecy was not widespread" (1 Sam. 3:1), God appeared to Samuel and informed him that the sons of Eli would be killed and, with their deaths, the house of Eli would cease. "Samuel grew up and the Lord was with him and did not leave any of Samuel's predictions unfulfilled. All Israel, from Dan to Beersheba, knew that Samuel was trustworthy as a prophet of the Lord" (1 Sam. 3:19–20).

While Samuel was a child at Shiloh, the Philistines decisively defeated the Israelites and began twenty years of oppression over Israel. When Samuel had become a well-respected prophet, he assembled all Israel at Mitzpeh, where he organized their forces and conquered the Philistines. Samuel served as a judge of Israel, each year making a circuit of Bethel, Gilgal, and Mitzpeh, before returning to his home in Ramah. When he grew old, Samuel appointed his sons over Israel, but they "did not follow his ways; they were bent on gain, they accepted bribes, and they subverted justice" (1 Sam. 8:3). The people called upon Samuel to "make us a king to judge us like all the nations" (1 Sam. 8:4–5). Despite Samuel's solemn warnings of how this would work to their disadvantage, the people continued to demand a king. So Saul was selected as the first king of Israel and anointed by Samuel (1 Sam. 10:1).

Although Saul fought many battles against the enemies of Israel and won numerous victories, his failure to obey the Divine command to totally destroy the Amalekites and dispose of their possessions led to a public rebuke by Samuel, who prophesied that God had rejected Saul as king (1 Sam. 15).

Before his death, God commanded Samuel to invite Jesse and his family to a sacrificial feast, where "you shall anoint for Me the one I point out to you." Jesse presented seven of his sons to Samuel, but the prophet declared, "The Lord has not chosen any of these." Finally, Jesse brought forth his youngest son, who was tending the flock. When David came before him, God said: "Rise and anoint him, for this is the one." Therefore, Samuel anointed David in the presence of his brothers, "and the spirit of the Lord gripped David from that day on" (1 Sam. 16:3–13). After Samuel's death, Saul went to the Witch of En Dor to communicate with the spirit of Samuel beyond the grave, but received only a prediction of his imminent doom (1 Sam. 28).

According to the Rabbis, when Jesse brought forth his youngest son, Samuel saw that David was "ruddy-cheeked" (1 Sam. 16:12). According to a *midrash*, Samuel feared that this might indicate that he was a murderer like the wicked Esau. However, God reassured him that David also had "beautiful eyes." This meant that "Esau killed on his own impulse, whereas David would kill [his foes] only on the sentence of the Court [i.e., the advice of the Sanhedrin—'the eyes of the congregation' (Num. 15:24)]" (Gen. R. 63:8). The Talmud states that Samuel was very wealthy (Ned. 38a) and wrote the Books of Judges and Ruth, as well as those bearing his own name (BB 14b). *See also* Eli; Hannah; Saul.

Sarah, wife of Abraham, mother of Isaac, and the first matriarch of Israel.

Initially known as Sarai, God changed her name to Sarah (both meaning "princess") after the formal covenant with Abraham that was sealed by the rite of circumcision (Gen. 17:15). As a tribute to their pious behavior, both Sarai and Abram had added to their names the Hebrew letter *hei*, half of the two-word name of God. Daughter of his brother Haran, and therefore Abraham's niece, Sarah was called "Iscah" (Gen. 11:29) from a root meaning "to see," either because she had prophetic visions or because her beauty attracted general attention and admiration (Meg. 14a). This created problems when she and Abraham were forced to travel to Egypt to escape the famine in Canaan. As Abraham stated, "I know what a beautiful woman you are. If the Egyptians see you and think, 'She is his wife,' they will kill me and let you live. Please say that you are my sister, that it may go well with me because of you, and that I may remain alive thanks to you" (Gen. 12:11–13). As predicted, Sarah was taken into Pharaoh's harem. "But the Lord afflicted Pharaoh and his household with mighty plagues on account of Sarai, the wife of Abram" (Gen. 12:17). A similar incident occurred later with Abimelech (Gen. 20:2–13).

Unable to conceive, Sarah gave Abraham her handmaiden, Hagar (Gen. 16). However, when the servant became pregnant and claimed equality with her mistress, Sarah drove her away. Hagar later returned and gave birth to Ishmael. Almost ninety years old and despairing of ever bearing a child, Sarah was dumbfounded when, eavesdropping at the entrance of the tent, she overheard an angel of the Lord informing Abraham: "At the same season next year, Sarah shall have a son" (Gen. 18:9–14).

Because Sarah laughed with incredulity at the news, they named their son Isaac (*Yitzhak* in Hebrew, meaning "he will laugh"), for "God has brought me laughter. Everyone who hears will laugh with me" (Gen. 21:6). "On the day Isaac was weaned, Abraham made a great banquet, but all the peoples of the world derided him. 'Have you seen that old man and woman, who brought a foundling from the market and now claim him as their son, even making a great banquet to establish their claim!' So Abraham invited all the great men of the age and Sarah invited their wives. Each one brought along her child without a wet nurse. Then a miracle occurred, and the breasts of Sarah opened like two fountains and she nursed them all. Yet they still scoffed, saying, 'Granted that Sarah could give birth at the age of ninety, but could Abraham sire a child at the age of one hundred?' Immediately, the appearance of Isaac's face changed and became like Abraham's, causing all to cry out, 'Abraham sired Isaac'" (BM 87a).

When Sarah saw Ishmael "mocking" Isaac (or "making sport with"; lit., "playing with" him and interpreted in a *midrash* as cruelty and possibly even sexual molestation) (Gen. R. 53:11), she urged Abraham to "cast out that slave-woman and her son" (Gen. 21:9). This reflected her fear of Ishmael's corrupting influence and her conviction that Ishmael was unworthy to be the heir of her husband ("for the son of that slave shall not share in the inheritance with my son Isaac"). God commanded the reluctant Abraham to comply with his wife's wishes, comforting Abraham with the assurance, "I will make a nation of him, too, for he is your seed" (Gen. 21:11–13).

Sarah died in Hebron at the age of 127, which the *aggadah* interprets as meaning that she preserved the innocence of a 7-year-old when she was 20, and the beauty of a 20-year-old when she was 100 (Gen. R. 58:1). Legends connect Sarah's death with her son Isaac's narrow escape at the *Akedah* (binding of Isaac), because it immediately followed the conclusion of that narrative. According to one version, Sarah died instantly upon being misinformed that Isaac had perished. Sarah was buried in the Cave of Machpelah, which Abraham had purchased as her gravesite from Ephron the Hittite (Gen. 23:3–20). *See also* Abraham; Hagar; Isaac; Ishmael.

Saul, first king of Israel (c. 1030–1010 B.C.E.).

The son of Kish and a brave warrior of the tribe of Benjamin, Saul was described as the tallest and most handsome man in the land (1 Sam. 9:2).

After many years of periodic attacks by the Philistines, the elders came to Samuel and said: "Behold, you are old, and your sons do not walk in your ways; now make us a king to judge us like all the nations" (1 Sam. 8:4–5). The Bible relates two different versions of how Saul was selected as the first king of Israel. In the first, "pro-monarchial" account, Saul was vainly searching for his father's lost donkeys when he sought out the "man of God," Samuel, for assistance (1 Sam. 9–10). At the command of God, Samuel anointed Saul as "captain over His inheritance" (king of Israel) in a private ceremony in Ramah. The second, "anti-monarchial" version emphasizes that Samuel strongly opposed the people's demand for a king, considering it a repudiation of the sovereignty of God (1 Sam. 8:6–8). However, God urged Samuel to "listen to their voice," but to "solemnly warn them [of] the customary practice of the king who shall reign over them." Samuel stressed that a king would force their sons to join his army and work his lands, take their daughters "to be perfumers, cooks, and bakers," and expropriate a tenth of their seed, vineyards, and sheep—"And you shall cry out in that day because of your king which you shall have chosen; and the Lord will not hear you" (1 Sam. 8:11–18). Nevertheless, the people continued to demand a king. Samuel eventually relented and presided over the public anointing of Saul in Mitzpeh, with the people enthusiastically proclaiming, "Long live the king!" (1 Sam. 10:24–25).

Saul fought many battles against the enemies of Israel and won numerous victories. On one occasion, the prophet Samuel relayed God's command that Saul destroy the Amalekites and dispose of their possessions (1 Sam. 15). However, Saul failed to comply with this order, sparing Agag, the Amalekite king, and acceding to the people's request to save the best of the captured herds to make a sacrifice to the Lord. Furious, Samuel said to Saul: "Do you think the Lord delights more in sacrifices than in obedience to His words? . . . Because you have rejected the word of the Lord, He has also rejected you as king." Publicly rebuked by the prophet, Saul suffered from depression, which could only be relieved by the beautiful music of David. However, when David became increasingly popular among the people because of his unexpected victory over the Philistine giant Goliath (1 Sam. 17) and other military exploits, Saul developed such a blind hatred for the young man that David was forced to flee for his life. In Saul's last battle with the Philistines, the Israelite forces were badly defeated. With his sons slain by the enemy, Saul fell upon his sword and killed himself (1 Sam. 31:6).

The Rabbis listed Saul's virtues: "He was so humble that he ate even ordinary unhallowed food only when ritually pure. He spent his own money freely, but protected the money of Israel. And he set the honor of his servant equal to his own" (Num. R. 11:3). Moreover, Saul "supplied all the poor daughters of Israel with dowries" (Mish. R. Eliezer 10). Citing the verse, "Saul was a year old when he reigned" (1 Sam. 13:1), one Rabbi explained that when Saul became king he was "like a one year old who had never tasted sin" (Yoma 22b). Ironically, the Talmud declares that the kingdom of Saul did not endure "because no reproach rested on him [i.e., there was no flaw in his ancestry, so that his descendants would have become arrogant]." From this the Rabbis concluded that a person should not be appointed leader of a community unless he "carried a basket of reptiles/vermin on his back. If he ever assumed haughty airs, the king could be told to look behind him" (Yoma 22b), implying that there was some skeleton in his family that would dispel his unwarranted arrogance.

From the life of Saul, the Rabbis deduced that power can become intoxicating. As R. Joshua ben Perahiah said, "At first whoever would say to me, 'Take up the honor' [of becoming president of the Sanhedrin], I would bind him and put him in front of a lion; but now whoever would say to me, 'Give up the honor,' I would pour over him a kettle of boiling water. For [we see that] Saul [at first] shunned [the throne], but after he had taken it he sought to kill David" (Men. 109b). *See also* Agag; Ahimelech; En Dor (Witch of); Jonathan; Samuel.

Seth, third son of Adam and Eve.

Born after Cain had murdered Abel, Eve named him Seth because "God has provided [*shat*] me with another offspring in place of Abel" (Gen. 4:25), with the Hebrew root meaning "to place, put, or set." Born when Adam was 130 years old, Seth lived to the age of 912 (Gen. 5:8).

According to legend, by killing Abel and incurring the death penalty, Cain would have returned the world to its primordial state of "*tohu va'vohu*" (complete emptiness). If not for the birth of Seth, the human race would have ceased to exist (Gen. R. 2:3).

Shamgar, son of Anath and a judge of Israel.

Shamgar "slew 600 Philistine men with an ox goad; and he also saved Israel" (Judg. 3:31). However, the judgeship of Shamgar was not a peaceful time, for "the highways were unoccupied, and the travelers walked through crooked back roads" (Judg. 5:6).

Sheba (Queen of), monarch of a wealthy state near the southern tip of the Arabian peninsula.

Hearing of Solomon's wealth and wisdom, the Queen of Sheba came to Jerusalem "with a large retinue, camels that carried spices, and much gold and precious stones" (1 Kings 10). After exchanging costly presents with

Solomon and amazed that the king's immense fame did not do him justice, she returned to her own land.

The Midrash and Targum literature relate numerous riddles posed by the Queen of Sheba to test the wisdom of King Solomon. "What is a well of wood, a pail of iron which draws up stones and pours out water?" Solomon answered, "A tube of cosmetic." "What is that which comes from the earth as dust, the food of which is dust, which is poured out like water, and which looks toward the house?" Solomon answered, "Naphtha." "What precedes all, like a general; which cries loudly and bitterly; the head of which is like a reed; which is the glory of the rich and the shame of the poor, the glory of the dead and the shame of the living; the joy of the birds and the sorrow of the fishes?" Solomon answered, "Flax." Other riddles include: "Seven issue, nine enter; two pour, one drinks." Solomon answered, "Seven days of a woman's menstrual impurity, nine months of pregnancy; two breasts of the mother at which the child is nourished" (Mid. Prov. [Buber ed.] 1). "How can a woman say to her son, 'Your father is my father, your grandfather my husband; you are my son; I am your sister?'" Solomon answered, "The mother is one of the daughters of Lot [who became pregnant by their father and bore sons]."

Shechem, son of Hamor the Hivite, who was chief of the city-state of the same name.

Shechem was "strongly drawn to Dinah, daughter of Jacob." He "saw her, and took her, and lay with her by force" (Gen. 34:2). After raping Dinah, Shechem was "in love with the maiden" and asked his father to make arrangements for him to marry her. Her outraged brothers seemed to agree to the proposed marriage, though the text notes that they "were speaking with guile because he [Shechem] had defiled their sister, Dinah." As a precondition, however, they insisted that Shechem and all the men of the city be circumcised. On the third day after the procedure, when all were in intense pain, Shimon and Levi, two of Dinah's full brothers, "took each his sword, came upon the [defenseless] city unmolested, and slew all the males." Jacob feared that this savage act might cause the neighboring tribes to exact revenge. In his final blessing to his sons, the dying Jacob censured their behavior: "Cursed be their anger so fierce, and their wrath so relentless" (Gen. 49:7).

Shelah, youngest son of Judah and his Canaanite wife, known as the "daughter of Shua" (Gen. 38:5).

After the death of his older brothers, Er and Onan, who had married Tamar, Judah refused to permit Shelah to enter into a levirate marriage with his sister-in-law. Known in Hebrew as *yibbum*, this was the obligation of a surviving brother to marry the widow of his brother if he died without having sired children (Deut. 25:5–6). As an excuse, Judah pointed to Shelah's young age (Gen. 38:11). However, even when Shelah was grown, Judah feared for his safety and refused to permit him to marry Tamar. Consequently, Tamar devised an elaborate scheme to secure an heir by having relations with her father-in-law (Gen. 38:14–19).

Shelomith, daughter of Dibri of the tribe of Dan, and the wife of an Egyptian.

Shelomith was the mother of an unnamed man who blasphemed the Name of God and was ordered by Moses to be stoned to death by the entire community (Lev. 24:10–15). It was unclear whether the "blasphemer cursed God, cursed someone else using the name of God, or simply pronounced God's name without due reverence." Although the name of the guilty party was never mentioned, Rashi maintained that his mother and tribe are cited to indicate that one who sins brings shame not only upon himself but also on his parents and tribe.

Shelumiel, son of Zurishaddai and chieftain of the tribe of Shimon.

Shelumiel made the fifth of the twelve identical offerings for the dedication of the Tabernacle in the wilderness (Num. 7:36–41).

Shem, youngest of the three sons of Noah.

Shem is always mentioned first among the sons of Noah in the biblical account, "because they are listed in the order of their wisdom rather than age" (Sanh. 69b). Shem is traditionally known as the father of the Semitic peoples and the ancestor of the patriarchs of Israel. His descendants, along with those of his brothers, Ham and Japheth, populated the entire earth after the Flood (Gen. 9:18–19). Rather than joining Ham in mocking the drunken Noah who lay sleeping in his tent, Shem and Japheth covered him with a garment while "their faces were turned the other way, so that they did not see their father's nakedness" (Gen. 9:21–23). Because the verb in the phrase "took a garment" is in the singular, the Rabbis maintained that only Shem initiated this praiseworthy act; as a reward, his descendants (the Jews) were rewarded with the mitzvah of the fringed garment (*tallit* with *tzitzit*). When Noah awoke and learned what had transpired, he said: "Blessed be the Lord, the God of Shem; let Canaan [son of Ham] be his servant. May God enlarge Japheth, and let him dwell in the tents of Shem; and let Canaan be a slave to them" (Gen. 8:26–27).

According to the *aggadah*, Shem, later joined by his great-grandson Eber, established a *bet midrash* (school for Torah study) where Jacob studied (Gen. R. 63:10). In the World to Come, Torah scholars will be privileged to study at the Heavenly Academy of Shem, Eber, and other heroes of Israel.

Shemaiah, prophet who lived during the reign of Rehoboam (tenth century B.C.E.).

Shemaiah convinced Rehoboam, the son of Solomon and first king of Judah, not to wage war against Jeroboam and the breakaway Kingdom of Israel, stating that it was God's will that the ten northern tribes form an independent state (1 Kings 12:22–24). Later, Shemaiah warned Rehoboam that the invading armies of Shishak, king of Egypt, would be victorious because "the princes of Judah . . . have forsaken Me" (2 Chron. 12:5). However, after the leaders humbled themselves and repented, "the wrath of the Lord turned from him [Rehoboam]" (2 Chron. 12:12). *See also* Rehoboam.

Shephatiah, fifth son of King David, born in Hebron to Abital (2 Sam. 3:4).

Shimei, son of Gera of the tribe of Benjamin, and "a man of the family of the house of Saul."

When David fled Jerusalem during the revolt of his son, Absalom, Shimei cursed the king: "Get out, get out, you criminal, you villain. The Lord is paying you back for all your crimes against the family of Saul, whose throne you have seized. The Lord is handing over the throne to your son, Absalom, your son; you are in trouble because you are a criminal" (2 Sam. 16:5–8). According to the *aggadah*, Shimei not only called David insulting names, but also taunted him about his Moabite descent from Ruth and his adultery with Bathsheba (Shab. 105a). After putting down the rebellion, David formally forgave the repentant Shimei (2 Sam. 19:17–23). However, in his dying words, David commanded his son Solomon to avenge the insult and punish Shimei (1 Kings 2:8–9). Solomon ordered Shimei to build a house in Jerusalem and remain there, warning that he would be killed if he ever dared to leave the city. When Shimei disobeyed, traveling to Gath to bring back two runaway slaves, Solomon had him executed upon his return. "Thus the royal power of Solomon was securely established" (1 Kings 2:36–46).

According to the *aggadah*, Shimei was a teacher of Solomon. As long as he lived, Solomon did not marry the daughter of Pharaoh, out of respect for his teacher, and took only Jewish wives (Ber. 8a). Shimei pleaded that David accept his sincere apology for wronging him, just as Joseph forgave his brothers (Yalkut Shimoni, Samuel 151). "If you treat me kindly and accept me, all the people of Israel will come forward and make peace with you" (Mid. Ps. 3:3).

Shimon, second son of Jacob and Leah.

Shimon's name came from a Hebrew root meaning "to hear," as Leah explained: "This is because the Lord heard that I was unloved and has given me this one also" (Gen. 29:33). The green flag of the tribe of Shimon was embroidered with a castle, representing the fortress of Shechem.

After the rape of their sister Dinah by Shechem, the son of Hamor the Hivite, Shimon and Levi avenged her honor by attacking the city and killing its inhabitants (Gen. 34). This murderous deed earned them a stinging rebuke by Jacob on his deathbed—"Cursed be their anger so fierce, and their wrath so relentless" (Gen. 49:6). Moreover, "I will divide them in Jacob"—descendants of Shimon would be scribes in the synagogues, while those of the tribe of Levi would be students and teachers of the Mishnah, engaged in the study of the Torah in the houses of study. Therefore, by their professions they would be scattered and prevented from living together in large numbers.

When the sons of Jacob journeyed to Egypt to buy corn during the famine, Shimon was imprisoned by Joseph as a guarantee that Benjamin, the youngest brother, would be brought to him (Gen. 42:24). A *midrash* explains that this was because it was Shimon who had pushed Joseph into the pit. Moreover, separating Shimon from Levi would prevent them from conspiring against him. As his brothers were about to return home without him, Shimon said to them: "What you did to Joseph, you wish to do to me?" The brothers replied that they had no choice: "Are the members of our households to die of famine?" "Do as you will," Shimon told them. "Now I will see who will [have the power to] put me in prison!" Joseph asked Pharaoh to send seventy of his mightiest warriors to throw his brother into prison, but when they approached and Shimon shouted at them, they fell on their faces and their teeth broke. Immediately, Joseph ordered his son Manasseh to accomplish this task. With one blow he succeeded in throwing Shimon into prison and putting him in chains (Gen. R. 91:60).

The tribe of Shimon settled in Canaan in the territory south of Judah, which included the city of Beersheba (Josh. 19:1–9). However, they never produced either a judge or a king because of Zimri's sin of immorality (Num. 25:7–8; Yalkut Shimoni, Exodus 42). Eventually, the tribe of Shimon merged with the dominant tribe of Judah to its north. *See also* Levi.

Shiphrah, one of the two Hebrew midwives in Egypt.

Along with Puah, Shiphrah bravely refused to obey Pharaoh's order to kill all the newborn Israelite males (Exod. 1:15–21). Described as "fearing God" (Exod. 1:17), the midwives explained to Pharaoh that the Hebrew women were not like their Egyptian counterparts: "Before the midwife can come to them, they have given birth" (Exod. 1:19). *Midrashic* tradition has identified Shiphrah as Jochebed, the mother of Moses (Sot. 11b).

According to the *aggadah*, Shiphrah was named because she cleansed (*mishaperet*) the child when he was born covered with blood; the people of Israel multiplied (*peru*) at her hand; her deeds were pleasant (*shaphru*) before God; and she appeased (*mishaperet*) Pharaoh for her daughter's harsh words, saying: "Why do you pay attention to her. She is [only] a child; she has no understanding" (Exod. R. 1:13). *See also* Jochebed.

Sihon, king of the Amorites.

Sihon ruled the land east of the Jordan from the Arnon River in the south to the Jabbok River in the north. His capital was Heshbon, which he had captured from the king of Moab (Num. 21:26). During the travels of the Israelites in the wilderness, Sihon refused their request for permission to pass through his land, even though they assured him that they would "not turn off into fields or vineyards" or "drink water from wells," but would "follow the king's highway until we have crossed your territory" (Num. 21:21–22). Sihon would not even sell the Israelites food and water (Deut. 2:28–30), instead mounting an army to fight them. However, the Israelites defeated his forces and took possession of his land (Num. 21:24–25).

According to the *aggadah*, Sihon was the brother of Og, and both were grandsons of the fallen angel, Shamhazai (Nid. 61a).

Sisera, commander of the army of Jabin, the Canaanite king of Hazor.

Sisera subjugated the Israelites until his army was defeated by the forces of Deborah and Barak (Judg. 4:2–16). Sisera fled alone on foot until he reached the tent of Jael, who offered him milk to drink and shelter. However, after Sisera had fallen asleep, Jael killed him by taking a hammer and driving a tent peg through his head (Judg. 4:21).

According to the tradition, the Rabbis decided that on Rosh Hashanah there should be 100 shofar blasts, equal to the number of sobs of Sisera's mother or the number of letters in her lament for her son as recounted in the Song of Deborah (Judg. 5:28). This was designed to show that, just as Jews were sensitive to the tears of the mother of an archenemy, so too they hoped God would be sensitive to their tears and judge them mercifully on the High Holy Days.

Solomon, son of David and Bathsheba, and the third king of Israel.

Solomon's long reign (970–931 B.C.E.) was generally one of peace, as befitted his name (derived from the Hebrew word *shalom*). After Absalom's rebellion was crushed, the question of a successor arose as David lay dying. As the eldest of David's surviving children, Adonijah impetuously tried to have himself proclaimed king while David was still alive (1 Kings 1). Bathsheba (Solomon's mother), the prophet Nathan, and other influential royal advisers succeeded in convincing the aged and feeble David to fulfill his pledge to make Solomon heir to the crown. Solomon quickly solidified his position by eliminating all potential claimants to the throne (Adonijah, Abiathar the priest, Joab the commander of the army, and Shimei, who had cursed David).

One evening after Solomon had made 1,000 burnt offerings in Gibeon, God appeared in a dream and offered to give the king whatever he wished (1 Kings 3). Solomon asked only for "an understanding heart to judge your people, so that I may discern between good and bad." This choice of wisdom—rather than long life, wealth, honor, or the destruction of his enemies—greatly pleased the Lord, who also granted the king these as well. Solomon immediately had an opportunity to display his great wisdom. Two women who had recently given birth came before the king, each claiming that the live baby was hers and the dead infant belonged to the other. Solomon called for his sword and ordered the living child divided in two, so that each woman would receive half and be satisfied. "No!" shrieked the first woman, "Let her have the living child, but do not kill it." However, the second woman approved of Solomon's compromise: "Let it be neither mine nor yours, but divide it." The king promptly awarded the child to the first woman, certain that she was the true mother since she loved the baby so much that she would rather part with him than have him killed. This story led the Rabbis to observe, "One who sees Solomon in a dream can look forward to wisdom" (Ber. 57b).

In the fourth year of his reign, Solomon began building a Temple for the Lord in Jerusalem. Constructed with the finest cedar wood from Lebanon and huge blocks of stone, it was decorated with gold and rich carvings and fronted by two great bronze pillars. According to the *aggadah*, the building of the Temple was miraculous, with the large, heavy stones rising to and settling in their respective places by themselves (Exod. R. 52:3). Because it was forbidden to use iron tools, which were considered implements of war, to construct the House of God, the Rabbis maintained that the stones were hewn by the *shamir*, one of the ten miraculous things created at twilight on the sixth day of Creation (Avot 5:8), a magical worm whose mere touch could cut any substance. After seven years the building was finished, and Solomon dedicated the imposing edifice as the House of the Lord. Solomon also built palaces, roads, and aqueducts. However, the price of Solomon's luxury was high taxation. His many political marriages to the daughters of neighboring kings introduced idol worship into the land. Popular resentment and unrest led to internal conflict, and after Solomon's death the kingdom split apart into two rival states—Israel (Ephraim) in the north and Judah in the south.

R. Isaac asked, "Why were the reasons for [most] biblical laws not revealed? Because in two verses reasons were revealed, and they caused the greatest in the world to stumble" (Sanh. 21b). This referred to King Solomon, who although considered the wisest man of his time, disobeyed two commandments for which reasons were given. The Torah commanded that a king "shall not have many wives lest his heart go astray" (Deut. 17:17). Although Solomon was convinced that this would not affect him, "in his old age, his wives turned his heart toward other gods" (1 Kings 11:4). Similarly, Solomon disobeyed the commandment against a king keeping many horses or causing the people to return to Egypt (Deut. 17:16), even though this eventually led to the Israelites frequently going to Egypt to trade in the great horse market in this country (1 Kings 10:29).

During the reigns of David and Solomon, no potential converts of Judaism were accepted (Av. Zar. 3b), because it was suspected that such individuals might be converting only for financial gain. Similarly, no converts will be accepted in the days of the Messiah, when Israel will be prosperous and universally respected and prospective converts may merely be motivated by selfish considerations (Yev. 24b).

When Solomon erected the Temple, he built two gates: one for bridegrooms and the other for mourners. On the Sabbath, the inhabitants of Jerusalem would gather and go up to the Temple Mount and sit between the two gates in order to perform acts of kindness—gladdening the bridegrooms and consoling those in mourning (PdRE 17).

According to the Rabbis, "When Solomon married Pharaoh's daughter, the archangel Gabriel descended from heaven and stuck a reed in the sea, around which accumulated a sand-bank on which was ultimately built the great city of Rome" (Sanh. 21b). This indicates that it was this moral weakness of the king that laid the foundations of a hostile world, symbolized in the Talmud as Rome, which overthrew Israel. On her wedding night, Pharaoh's daughter brought him 1,000 musical instruments, explaining how each was played to honor a different idol, yet Solomon did not forbid it (Shab. 56b). Then she spread over his bed a tapestry studded with diamonds and pearls that shone like stars in the sky. When he thought it time to awaken, he saw the "stars" and, thinking it was still night, went back to sleep until the fourth hour of the morning. This greatly distressed the people, for although it was the joyous day of the dedication of the Temple, the daily sacrifice could not be offered because the keys to the Temple were under Solomon's head and they were afraid to wake the king (Lev. R. 12:5; Num. R. 10:4).

According to tradition, Solomon is considered the author of three books of the Bible: Song of Songs, Proverbs, and Ecclesiastes. The Song of Songs was written during his youth, Proverbs in middle age, and Ecclesiastes when Solomon had become old and believed in the futility of the material world (Song. R. 1:11). Perhaps the most difficult work to gain acceptance was the Song of Songs. Some Rabbis argued that it was merely a love idyll, while others viewed it as an allegory of the love between God and Israel. R. Akiva sided with the latter camp and had the last word: "The whole world is not as worthy as the day on which the Song of Songs was given to Israel. For all the Writings are holy, but the Song of Songs is the Holy of Holies" (Yad.

3:5). Solomon and David composed the blessing for Jerusalem in the Grace after Meals: David introduced the words, "For Israel, Your people, and for Jerusalem, Your city," while Solomon added the words, "For the great and holy House" (Ber. 48b). *See also* Benaiah; Hiram; Jeroboam; Sheba (Queen of); Shimei.

T

Tamar, daughter-in-law of Judah.

After the death of his two older sons, Er and Onan, both of whom had married Tamar, Judah sent his daughter-in-law "to stay as a widow in your father's house until my son Shelah grows up" (Gen. 38:11) and could fulfill the levirate obligation to marry the childless widow. When Shelah reached maturity but did not marry her, because of Judah's fear that his third son would suffer the same fate as the other two, Tamar decided to take matters in her own hands to secure an heir for her late husband (Gen. 38:14–23). Extremely modest, Tamar had always covered her face in the house of her father-in-law, so that Judah did not recognize her (Meg. 10b). Disguising herself as a prostitute sitting by the side of the road, she offered her services to the recently widowed Judah, who did not realize it was his daughter-in-law and unwittingly fulfilled the levirate obligation when he impregnated her. As a guarantee that he would pay her a kid from his flock, Judah gave Tamar his seal, wrap, and staff, all of which were sufficiently distinctive to identify its owner.

Three months later when her pregnancy was discovered, Judah ordered Tamar to be burned to death as punishment for her unchastity. Tamar then confronted her father-in-law with the pledges he had given her: "I am with child by the man to whom these belong." Faced with incontrovertible evidence that he was the father, Judah admitted his actions: "She is more right than I, inasmuch as I did not give her to my son Shelah." After Judah confessed, a *bat kol* (heavenly voice) called out, "You saved Tamar and her two sons from fire. In your merit, I will save three of your descendants from fire—Hananiah, Mishael, and Azariah" (Sot. 10b). Tamar gave birth to twins—Zerah and Perez—with the latter being the ancestor of King David (Ruth 4:18–22).

As R. Ulla observed, "Both Tamar and Zimri committed an immoral act. Tamar [with her father-in-law Judah, intending to do a righteous deed] gave birth to kings and prophets [David and his descendants were of the tribe of Judah, as traditionally were the prophets Amos and Isaiah]; Zimri [with Cozbi, intending to commit a sin] led to the death of many tens of thousands of Israel [in a plague; Num. 25:9]" (Naz. 23b). *See also* Rebecca.

Tamar, daughter of King David, and the sister of Absalom.

Her half-brother Amnon, who as David's eldest son was heir-apparent to the throne, fell passionately in love with the beautiful Tamar and was "so tormented that he fell sick" for her (2 Sam. 13). His "cunning" friend Jonadab suggested to Amnon: "Lay down on your bed and make yourself sick. When your father visits, ask him to 'let my sister Tamar come, give me bread, prepare the food in my sight, that I may see it and eat it from her hand.'" The ruse succeeded and Amnon seized the opportunity to overpower Tamar and rape her. However, he soon tired of his half-sister and callously drove her away. Weeping uncontrollably, Tamar fled to her brother Absalom, who sheltered her in his house and promised to avenge her violated honor. Two years later, he had Amnon killed.

According to the *aggadah*, Tamar was the daughter of David by a captive whom he married after she had renounced her pagan religion. Because of her "illegitimacy," it would have been lawful for Tamar to marry Amnon, the son of David. Therefore, when threatened by Amnon she said, "I beg you, speak to the king; for he will not withhold me from you" (2 Sam. 13:13). This meant that if Amnon had only asked for Tamar as his wife, David would have granted his request (Sanh. 21a).

Terah, father of Abraham, Nahor, and Haran (Gen. 11:26).

According to legend, when Abraham was born, a star rose in the east and swallowed four stars in the corners of heaven. Interpreting this miraculous occurrence, Nimrod's magicians warned the king that the descendants of this son of Terah would inherit both this world and the World to Come. They recommended that Nimrod give Terah a house full of silver and gold on the condition that his newborn son be killed. However, Terah diplomatically refused this offer by relating a parable. Once a horse was told that if he would agree to have his head cut off, he would be given a barn full of barley. The horse replied, "You fools! If you cut off my head, who will eat the barley?" Terah explained, "So if you kill my son, who will make use of the silver and gold?"

With his three sons, Terah emigrated from Ur of the Chaldees to Haran, where he died (Gen. 11:32). According to a *midrash*, Terah manufactured and sold idols. One day, Terah went out from the shop and left Abraham to sell the idols in his place. When a man asked to buy one, Abraham asked his age. Learning that he was fifty years old, Abraham incredulously replied, "You are fifty years old and worship a day-old object!" At that the man became ashamed and departed. On another occasion, a woman came with a plateful of flour and asked Abraham to give it to the idols. So Abraham took a stick, smashed several idols, and put the stick in the hand of the largest one. When his father returned, demanding, "What have you done to them?" Abraham replied: "I cannot conceal anything from you. A woman came with a plateful of fine meal and requested me to offer it to them. One [idol] claimed, 'I must eat first,' while another said, 'I must eat first.' Then the largest idol took the stick and smashed them." Terah exclaimed that this was impossible: "They are made of stone. There is no soul or spirit in them." Thereupon Abraham challenged his father: "Then why do you worship them?" In another version of this tale, Terah complained about his son to Nimrod, the mighty warrior, who ordered Abraham thrown into a fiery furnace and burned to death, but the patriarch miraculously emerged unharmed (Gen. R. 38:13).

Timna, royal princess (Gen. 36:22) who wanted to convert to Judaism.

According to a *midrash*, Timna came to Abraham, Isaac, and Jacob, but they refused to accept her as a proselyte. So Timna became a concubine of Eliphaz, the son of Esau, saying: "I had rather be a servant to this people [the descendants of the God-fearing Abraham, Isaac, and Jacob] than a mistress of another nation." Timna gave birth to Amalek, the archenemy of the Jewish people. "Why was it so? Because they [the patriarchs] should not have repulsed her [but rather should have converted her]" (Sanh. 99b). *See also* Amalek.

Tola, son of Puah of the tribe of Issachar, and judge in Israel.

Tola became judge in Israel after the death of Abimelech. He lived in Shamir on Mount Ephraim and judged Israel for twenty-three years (Judg. 10:1–2).

Tubal-cain, son of Lamech and descendant of Cain.

Tubal-cain "forged all implements of copper and iron" (Gen. 4:22), thus developing the skill of working with metals. The name "Tubal" derived from Akkadian and Sumerian words meaning "metalworker," while the word "*kayin*" meant a "smith" in several Semitic languages (*Etz Hayim* 28). Tubal-cain had a sister named Naamah, an interesting parallel to the Greek smith-god, Hephaestus, and his sister, Aphrodite. According to the *aggadah*, Naamah was the wife of Noah, but this idea has been rejected by most biblical commentators. Another taught that, by providing human beings more efficient tools to kill, Tubal-cain "perfected" (Hebrew, *tibbel*) their ability to repeat the sin of his ancestor, Cain (Gen. R. 23:3).

U

Uriah, Hittite husband of Bathsheba.

When Bathsheba became pregnant with David's child, the king summoned Uriah (one of David's thirty "mighty men") back to Jerusalem, ostensibly to see "how the war prospered." However, his real motive was to have him cohabit with Bathsheba, so that it would appear that the child was his (2 Sam. 11). Uriah thwarted the royal scheme by sleeping at the door of the king's house with all the servants, explaining: "The Ark, Israel, and Judah remain in tents. My lord Joab and his servants are encamped in the open fields; how can I go home and eat and drink and sleep with my wife?" David dispatched a secret letter to Joab, the commander of his army: "Place Uriah in the front line where the fighting is fiercest; then fall back so that he may be killed." After Uriah's death, David married Bathsheba, which earned him a bitter rebuke in a parable spoken by Nathan the prophet (2 Sam. 12). Although the child Bathsheba carried died soon after birth, she and David later were the parents of Solomon.

The Rabbis tried to mitigate the sinfulness of David's actions toward Bathsheba and Uriah. Some Talmudic authorities even asserted that David did not commit adultery, for at that time all women obtained a conditional writ of divorce (*get*) from their husbands who went to war. Otherwise, if a soldier died in battle but no one could attest to seeing the body, his wife would become an *agunah* (chained woman) and be unable to remarry. The Rabbis also attempted to blame the victim, arguing that David should not be blamed for Uriah's death since the latter had committed the capital crime of refusing to obey the royal command to return home to the bed of his wife (Shab. 56a; Kid. 43a).

Uzza, son of Abinadab.

For twenty years, the Ark of the Covenant remained in Uzza's house in Kiryat Jearim (1 Sam. 7:1–2). When David assembled 30,000 chosen men of Israel to escort the Ark of the Covenant to Jerusalem, it was placed on a new cart led by Uzza and his brother, Ahio (2 Sam. 6). The gala ceremonial procession was accompanied by men playing "on all manner of instruments made of cypress wood, and on lyres, lutes, tambourines, rattles, and cymbals." However, when they came to the threshing floor of Nachon, the ox pulling the cart stumbled. Fearing that the Ark would fall, Uzza reached out his hand to steady it. Immediately, "the anger of the Lord was kindled against Uzza; God struck him there for his error and he died by the Ark of God."

The Rabbis subsequently offered unconvincing attempts to explain the seemingly excessive punishment that befell Uzza for what appeared to be his innocent and instinctive act. As an example, "The Holy One, blessed be He, said to him, 'Uzza, [the Ark] carried its bearers; must it not all the more [be able to carry] itself!'" (Sot. 35a).

Uzziah, ninth king of Judah (771–736 B.C.E.).

Ascending the throne at age sixteen following the murder of his father, Amaziah, Uzziah's long reign was described in historical sources (especially in Chronicles) as one of the golden eras of the kingdom. According to the Bible (2 Chron. 26:16–21), Uzziah was struck with "leprosy" after he had entered the Temple of God and tried to burn incense on the altar, thus usurping a prerogative of the priests (Sot. 9b). This action probably reflected an attempt by Uzziah to demonstrate his authority in the struggle between the monarchy and the priesthood for supremacy over the Temple ritual. As a result of his affliction, Uzziah was forced to live "in a house set apart," while his son Jotham acted as regent.

V

Vashti, wife of King Ahasuerus, and the banished Queen of Persia in the Purim story.

Vashti hosted a banquet for the women of the kingdom separate from the weeklong drunken celebrations that Ahasuerus held for his princes, nobles, and servants. On the seventh day of the banquet, when the king's heart was "merry with wine," he ordered seven eunuch attendants to summon Vashti to come before him and his guests to display her beauty, wearing nothing but her royal crown. When Vashti refused to obey this command, Ahasuerus became angry and asked his courtiers the appropriate punishment for her disobedience. Memucan urged Ahasuerus to banish Vashti from the court and find another queen, since Vashti had wronged not only the king but, by extension, all Persian husbands, since her actions might encourage other wives to be disobedient to their husbands. Ahasuerus agreed and, after a royal beauty contest, selected Esther as his new queen (Esth. 1).

According to the *aggadah*, Vashti was the daughter of the wicked Nebuchadnezzar of Babylonia, who had destroyed the First Temple and exiled the Jews from the Land of Israel (Meg. 10b). With Athaliah, Jezebel, and Semiramism (the wife of Nebuchadnezzar), Vashti was described as one of the women who "wielded the scepter" (i.e., ruled) in the world (Esth. R. 3:2). *See also* Ahasuerus.

Z

Zadok, high priest during the reign of King David.

The son of Ahitub, Zadok's lineage was traced back to Eleazar, the third son of Aaron (1 Chron. 6:1–8). When David fled with the Ark of the Covenant during Absalom's rebellion, the king begged both Zadok and Abiathar to remain in Jerusalem, where they and their sons could keep him informed about what was happening in the capital (2 Sam. 15:24–35). However, as David was dying, the two priests supported different claimants for the throne—Abiathar favored Absalom, while Zadok championed the cause of Solomon (1 Kings 1:7–8). After Zadok anointed Solomon as the new king (1 Kings 1:39), he was rewarded for his loyalty by being named high priest (1 Kings 2:35). This position remained in the family of Zadok until the rise of the Maccabees.

Zebulun, tenth son of Jacob, and the sixth born to him by Leah.

Zebulun's name derived from Leah's exclamation: "God has given me a choice gift [*zebadani*]; this time my husband will exalt me [*yizbeleini*] for I have borne him six sons" (Gen. 30:20). The flag of Zebulun was white embroidered with a ship, based on the verse: "Zebulun shall dwell by the seashore; he shall be a haven for ships" (Gen. 49:13).

The territory of Zebulun, a tribe of sea-faring merchants, spanned the land from the Sea of Galilee to the Mediterranean. It extended to Sidon, the Phoenician port city that became the northernmost limit of the empire during David's reign. The tribe of Zebulun played a major role in the victorious military campaigns of Deborah and Barak over Sisera (Judg. 4:6, 10) and of Gideon over the Midianites (Judg. 6:35).

Zebulun was closely connected with the tribe of Issachar, both geographically in southern Galilee (Josh. 19:10–23) and in the blessings of Jacob (Gen. 49:13–15) and Moses (Deut. 33:18–19). Based on the *aggadic* description of the economic activities of Zebulun enabling his older brother Issachar to devote his life to study (Gen. R. 99:9), it became an honored tradition in Judaism for wealthy individuals to support Torah scholars. However, this model was vehemently opposed by Maimonides: "Whoever deliberately sets out to devote himself to the Torah and not work for a living, but be dependent on charity, has thereby desecrated the Divine name, brought the Torah into disrepute, extinguished the light of religion, brought evil upon himself, and forfeited the World to Come."

The Talmud relates that Zebulun complained to God (concerning his future portion in the Land of Israel): "To my brothers You have given fields and vineyards, but to me You have given hills and mountains; to my brothers You have given lands, but to me You have given lakes and rivers." God replied, "They will all require your *hilazon* [a small shellfish from which was extracted the purple color (*techeilet*) used for dying the fringes of the *tallit*]." But Zebulun was not satisfied and asked, "Who will inform me [i.e., can You ensure that I will be paid for this service]?" God replied, "Whoever takes [the *hilazon*] from you without payment will not prosper in his business" (Meg. 6a). *See also* Eleazar; Issachar.

Zechariah, eleventh of the minor prophets.

Zechariah lived in Jerusalem after the return from Babylonian exile (c. 520 B.C.E.). His writing is filled with mystic visions replete with symbolic figures. The portion of the Book of Zechariah read on the Sabbath of Hanukkah opens, "Shout for joy, Fair Zion! For lo, I come; and I will dwell in your midst" (Zech. 2:14), and it contains the vision of a Golden Menorah (Zech. 4:1). Lest Jews be smug about their military accomplishments on this holiday commemorating their victory over the Syrian-Greeks, they were warned by the words of a prophet who lived almost four centuries before the Maccabees: "Not by might, nor by power, but by My spirit said the Lord of Hosts" (Zech. 4:6). Zechariah called for rebuilding the Temple and prophesied the coming of the Messianic age, when all the nations will recognize the universal kingdom of God in Jerusalem—"And the Lord shall be King over all the earth; in that day the Lord shall be one and His Name one" (Zech. 14:9)—which is recited as the concluding verse of the *Aleinu* prayer.

According to the Talmud, "After the death of the last prophets—Haggai, Zechariah, and Malachi—the Holy Spirit [of prophecy] departed from Israel" (Yoma 9b).

Zedekiah, nineteenth and last king of Judah (597–586 B.C.E.).

Originally named Mattaniah, this youngest son of Josiah was placed on the throne by Nebuchadnezzar after the Babylonian ruler captured Jerusalem and exiled Jehoiachin (2 Kings 24:10–17). However, the people did not accept the concept of a ruler appointed by a foreign sovereign and continued to regard Jehoiachin as their legitimate king (Jer. 37:1). Zedekiah's weakness and inexperience prevented him from withstanding the nationalist currents that urged rebellion against Babylonia. After a siege lasting one and a half years, the walls of Jerusalem were breached and the city fell. In the confusion, Zedekiah and his entourage escaped, but they were captured near Jericho. Tried for treason, his sons were killed before his eyes. Zedekiah himself was blinded before being carried captive to Babylonia and imprisoned until his death (Jer. 52:9–11). With the fall of Jerusalem and the destruction of the Temple, the Kingdom of Judah ceased to exist as an independent nation.

According to the *aggadah*, when Nebuchadnezzar exiled Jehoiachin, the Babylonian conqueror had compassion for the Israelites and asked whether there was any descendant of Josiah he should appoint as their king. Consequently, Zedekiah was soon crowned as king of Jerusalem. Nebuchadnezzar ordered Zedekiah, "Swear to me that you will not rebel against me," and Zedekiah replied, "I swear by my soul." However, this did not satisfy Nebuchadnezzar, who demanded, "I will accept only an oath on the Torah that was given at Mount Sinai." He brought a Torah scroll, placed it on Zedekiah's knees, and made him swear never to rebel. Yet before Nebuchadnezzar had returned to Babylonia, Zedekiah rebelled against him (Pes. Rab. 26).

Zedekiah also was not faithful to his word when he once saw Nebuchadnezzar eating a live (raw) rabbit. The embarrassed Babylonian ruler exclaimed, "Swear to me that you will never reveal this matter and bring scorn upon me." Although Zedekiah swore, he later regretted his action, had his oath annulled by a sage, and broke his promise by relating to everyone what had happened, much to Nebuchadnezzar's chagrin (Ned. 65a).

Eventually, Zedekiah was punished for his unfaithfulness. When Jerusalem fell and Zedekiah saw the Temple in flames, he tried to escape with his ten sons through a tunnel extending from his house to Jericho. According to Rashi, God sent a deer into the Babylonian camp, and as the soldiers pursued the animal, they reached the opening of the tunnel just as Zedekiah was leaving it (2 Kings 25:4). When Nebuchadnezzar saw the potential escapees, he rhetorically asked what punishment the rebel ruler deserved. "By what law should I judge you? If by the law of your God, you must be slain for swearing falsely in His Name. If by the laws of the kingdom, you must die for rebelling against the king" (Pes. Rab. 26). Despite the cruelty of his punishment, Jeremiah's prophecy that Zedekiah would "die in peace" (Jer. 34:5) was fulfilled in that he outlived Nebuchadnezzar for a short period (MK 28b), presumably as a reward for having "had Jeremiah lifted from the mire" (Jer. 38:12).

The Talmud noted that God acted charitably toward Israel by having the exile of Zedekiah (and the bulk of the Jewish people, in 586 B.C.E.) to Babylonia at a time when the people of Jehoiachin's exile (i.e., the sages) were still alive, so that they could teach Torah to the newcomers (Git. 88a).

Zelophehad, son of Hepher, and the great-grandson of Manasseh.

After their father's death in the wilderness, the five unmarried daughters of Zelophehad (Mahlah, Noah, Hoglah, Milcah, and Tirzah) came before Moses to claim their inheritance, even though the law at the time stated that only men could inherit because the tribes were perpetuated through the male line. The daughters argued that their father did not participate in any of the rebellions against Moses, "but died for his own sin" (see below). Although Zelophehad left no sons, "Let not our father's name be lost to his clan just because he had no son! Give us a holding among our father's kinsmen!" (Num. 27:1–5). When Moses "brought their case before the Lord," God agreed with the daughters' plea and even added a new law to the Torah: "If a man dies without leaving a son, you shall transfer his property to his daughter" (Num. 27:5–8). However, the leaders of Zelophehad's tribe of Manasseh objected to this decision, because if the women were to marry outside their tribe, their land would pass over to the tribes of their husbands. Agreeing that this plea also was just, Moses made a creative compromise—the daughters had a right to inherit, but they must marry within their own tribe, as they eventually did by marrying their cousins (Num. 36:1–12).

According to the Talmud, both Zelophehad and his father were among those whom Moses had led out of Egypt. Consequently, Zelophehad himself was entitled to three portions in the Land of Israel—two as the firstborn of his father, and one in his own right—and his daughters claimed all these portions when their father died (BB 116b). R. Akiva identified Zelophehad as the man who was executed for gathering wood on the Sabbath (Num. 15:32–36). Other Rabbis reproved him for this statement: "If you are right, the Torah shielded him [i.e., if the Torah did not reveal his name, why do you do so?]; and if not [i.e., if he was innocent of the crime], you cast a stigma on a righteous man" (Shab. 96b). R. Nathan maintained that this episode demonstrated that the tenacity of women was stronger than that of men. When the men rejected Moses and Aaron and said, "Let us appoint a leader and return to Egypt" (Num. 14:4), this indicated that they were willing to give up the Land of Israel. In contrast, the daughters of Zelophehad demanded, "Give us a possession [of the Land]" (Num. 27:4; Sifrei Num. 133).

Zephaniah, ninth of the minor prophets.

Living in Jerusalem during the reign of King Josiah (640–609 B.C.E.), Zephaniah prophesied the downfall of Nineveh and the Assyrian empire. He warned the people of a cataclysmic "Day of the Lord" (Zeph. 1:12–18), when they would be punished for their evil deeds. Eventually, however, salvation would come to Israel and to the entire world. His statement that God "will search Jerusalem with candles" (Zeph. 1:12) is reflected in the ceremony of searching for leaven (*hametz*) by candlelight on the night before the Passover seder.

Zillah, one of the two wives of Lamech, and the mother of Tubal-cain and Naamah (Gen. 4:19, 22).

According to the Jerusalem Talmud, she was named Zillah because she dwelled in the shadow (*zeil*) of her children (JT Yev. 6:5). *See also* Adah.

Zilpah, handmaid of Leah, and the mother of Gad and Asher.

After giving Jacob three sons (Reuben, Shimon, Levi), Leah "saw that she had stopped bearing." Sensing that her husband wanted more children, she "gave her [Zilpah] to Jacob as a concubine" (Gen. 30:9). In this way, any children Zilpah bore would be treated as Leah's own.

Zimri, son of Salu and "chieftain of an ancestral house of the tribe of Shimon" (Num. 25:14).

When God sent a devastating plague and ordered a public execution to punish the Israelites who were "profaning themselves by whoring with the Moabite women" and worshiping Baal-Peor, the people wept for Divine forgiveness at the entrance of the Tent of Meeting. Zimri brazenly brought Cozbi, a Midianite princess, and had sexual intercourse with her "in the sight of Moses and of the whole Israelite community." In a zealous rage, Pinchas, a grandson of Aaron, seized a spear, followed the couple into Zimri's tent, and "stabbed both of them, the Israelite and the woman, through the belly. Then the plague against the Israelites was checked" (Num. 25).

The *aggadah* expands upon the story. When Moses ordered the Israelites to slay all of their brethren who had profaned themselves with the Moabite women, the leaders of the tribe of Shimon went to Zimri and said to him: "Capital punishment is being meted out, yet you sit silent [i.e., inactive]?" So Zimri arose and assembled 24,000 Israelites, went to Cozbi, and said to her, "Surrender yourself to me!" She replied, "I am the daughter of a king, and my father has instructed me to yield only to the greatest man among you." Zimri replied, "I also am the prince of a tribe; moreover, I am greater than [Moses], for I am from the second tribe [Shimon, the second son of Jacob] while he is from the third [Levi]." Then Zimri seized Cozbi by her hair and brought her to Moses. "Son of Amram, is this woman forbidden or permitted? If you say 'forbidden,' who permitted Jethro's daughter to you?" At that moment, Moses forgot the *halachah* concerning intimacy with a heathen woman, since he had married Zipporah before the giving of the Torah and she had become Jewish by the time the Torah was given (Rashi). But Pinchas "saw it" (i.e., remembered the *halachah* and the command that an Israelite who cohabited with a heathen woman was punished by zealots) and raced to slay Zimri to save Israel from shame (Sanh. 82a). Entering Zimri's tent, he found that God had stuck Cozbi and Zimri together so that they could not separate, and thus he killed both of them together (Exod. R. 33:5). The Talmud adds, "If Zimri had forsaken his mistress (i.e., separated from her) before Pinchas killed him, Pinchas would have been executed for this action," for the zealot may slay only when the perpetrator is engaged in the commission of the offence. "And had Zimri turned around and killed Pinchas, he would not have been executed. Since Pinchas was a pursuer" seeking to take his life, Zimri was permitted to defend himself (Sanh. 82a).

In another version, Zimri said to Moses, "You, the faithful one of the Torah of whom God boasts, have taken a wife [Zipporah] who is forbidden to you. [Cozbi] is a Midianite and [Zipporah] is a Midianite; [Cozbi] is the daughter of a king and [Zipporah] is the daughter of an idolatrous priest" (Exod. R. 33:5).

Zipporah, wife of Moses.

One of the seven daughters of Jethro, priest of Midian (Exod. 2:16), Zipporah bore Moses two sons, Gershom and Eliezer (Exod. 2:22; 18:3–4). When God was about to kill Moses for failing to circumcise his son, Zipporah averted the imminent death of her husband by circumcising Gershom with a flint (Exod. 4:24–26). According to a *midrash*, Moses had not circumcised the baby by order of his father-in-law (Yalkut Shimoni, Exodus 168). When Zipporah saw that an angel had swallowed Moses from his head until the place of circumcision, she realized that he was being attacked because of failure to perform this ritual act (Exod. R. 5:8). Zipporah then returned with her children to her father's home in Midian, rejoining Moses at Mount Sinai after the Exodus from Egypt (Exod. 18:1–6).

Why was Zipporah called "the Cushite" (Num. 12:1)? A *midrash* explains that just as the Cushite woman was distinguished from other women by the color of her skin, so too was Zipporah distinguished from other women by her beauty. When Miriam saw that Zipporah did not adorn herself with women's ornaments, she realized that Moses was abstaining from marital relations with his wife (Sifri Beha'alotcha 99). After the appointment of the elders of Israel, everyone lit candles and rejoiced for them. When told by Zipporah the reason for this celebration, Miriam remarked: "How fortunate are the wives who see their husbands rise to high position!" However, the long-suffering Zipporah sadly said, "Woe to them, since from now on their husbands will separate from them" (Yalkut Shimoni, Beha'alotcha).

Appendix
Chronological Listing of Figures
according to First Biblical Appearance

Adam	Gen. 2:19
Eve	Gen. 3:20
Cain	Gen. 4:1
Abel	Gen. 4:2
Enoch	Gen. 4:17
Lamech (Cain line)	Gen. 4:18
Zillah	Gen. 4:19
Adah (wife of Lamech)	Gen. 4:19
Jabal	Gen. 4:20
Jubal	Gen. 4:21
Tubal-cain	Gen. 4:22
Seth	Gen. 4:25
Enosh	Gen. 4:26
Methusaleh	Gen. 5:21
Lamech (Seth line)	Gen. 5:25
Noah	Gen. 5:29
Japheth	Gen. 5:32
Ham	Gen. 5:32
Shem	Gen. 5:32
Canaan	Gen. 9:18
Nimrod	Gen. 10:8
Eber	Gen. 10:24
Nahor	Gen. 11:22
Terah	Gen. 11:24
Abraham	Gen. 11:26
Haran	Gen. 11:26
Lot	Gen. 11:27
Sarah (Sarai)	Gen. 11:29
Melchizedek	Gen. 14:18
Eliezer (servant of Abraham)	Gen. 15:2
Hagar	Gen. 16:1
Ishmael	Gen. 16:11
Moab	Gen. 19:37

Ammon	Gen. 19:38
Abimelech (of Gerar)	Gen. 20:2
Isaac	Gen. 21:3
Bethuel	Gen. 22:23
Ephron	Gen. 23:8
Rebecca	Gen. 24:15
Laban	Gen. 24:29
Keturah	Gen. 25:1
Esau	Gen. 25:25
Jacob	Gen. 25.26
Rachel	Gen. 29:6
Leah	Gen. 29:16
Zilpah	Gen. 29:24
Bilhah	Gen. 29:29
Reuben	Gen. 29:32
Shimon	Gen. 29:33
Levi	Gen. 29:34
Judah	Gen. 29:35
Dan	Gen. 30:6
Naphtali	Gen. 30:8
Gad (son of Jacob)	Gen. 30:11
Asher	Gen. 30:13
Issachar	Gen. 30:18
Zebulun	Gen. 30:20
Dinah	Gen. 30:21
Joseph	Gen. 30:24
Hamor	Gen. 34:1
Shechem	Gen. 34:2
Benjamin	Gen. 35:18
Adah (wife of Esau)	Gen. 36:2
Eliphaz	Gen. 36:4
Amalek	Gen. 36:12
Timna	Gen. 36:12
Potiphar	Gen. 37:36
Er	Gen. 38:3
Onan	Gen. 38:4
Shelah	Gen. 38:5
Tamar (daughter-in-law of Judah)	Gen. 38:6
Asenath	Gen. 41:45
Manasseh (son of Joseph)	Gen. 41:51
Ephraim	Gen. 41:52
Gershon	Gen. 46:11

Og	Num. 21:33
Balak	Num. 22:2
Balaam	Num. 22:5
Pinchas (high priest)	Num. 25:7
Zimri	Num. 25:14
Cozbi	Num. 25:15
Zelophehad	Num. 26:33
Rahab	Josh. 2:1
Achan	Josh. 7:1
Adoni-Zedek	Josh. 10:1
Debir	Josh. 10:3
Hoham	Josh. 10:3
Japhia	Josh. 10:3
Piram	Josh. 10:3
Othniel	Judg. 3:9
Ehud	Judg. 3:15
Shamgar	Judg. 3:31
Deborah	Judg. 4:4
Barak	Judg. 4:6
Jael	Judg. 4:17
Gideon	Judg. 6:11
Abimelech (son of Gideon)	Judg. 8:31
Tola	Judg. 10:1
Jair	Judg. 10:3
Jephthah	Judg. 11:1
Manoah	Judg. 13:2
Samson	Judg. 13:24
Delilah	Judg. 16:4
Elkanah	1 Sam. 1:1
Hannah	1 Sam. 1:2
Eli	1 Sam. 1:3
Hophni	1 Sam. 1:3
Pinchas (son of Eli)	1 Sam. 1:3
Samuel	1 Sam. 1:20
Saul	1 Sam. 9:2
Jonathan	1 Sam. 13:2
Michal	1 Sam. 14:49
Abner	1 Sam. 14:50
Ahinoam (wife of Saul)	1 Sam. 14:50
Agag	1 Sam. 15:8
Jesse	1 Sam. 16:1
David	1 Sam. 16:13

Goliath	1 Sam. 17:4
Ahimelech	1 Sam. 21:2
Doeg	1 Sam. 21:8
Achish	1 Sam. 21:11
Gad (seer)	1 Sam. 22.5
Abiathar	1 Sam. 22:20
Abigail	1 Sam. 25:3
Nabal	1 Sam. 25:3
Ahinoam (Jezreelite woman)	1 Sam. 25:43
Abishai	1 Sam. 26:6
En Dor (Witch of)	1 Sam. 28:7
Ishbosheth	2 Sam. 2:8
Joab	2 Sam. 2:13
Asahel	2 Sam. 2:18
Amnon	2 Sam. 3:2
Absalom	2 Sam. 3:3
Chileab	2 Sam. 3:3
Adonijah	2 Sam. 3:4
Shephatiah	2 Sam. 3:4
Ithream	2 Sam. 3:5
Abital	2 Sam. 4:3
Uzza	2 Sam. 6:3
Obed-Edom	2 Sam. 6:10
Nathan	2 Sam. 7:2
Zadok	2 Sam. 8:17
Benaiah	2 Sam. 8:18
Bathsheba	2 Sam. 11:3
Uriah	2 Sam. 11:3
Hiram	2 Sam. 11:5
Solomon	2 Sam. 12:24
Tamar (daughter of David)	2 Sam. 13:1
Ahithophel	2 Sam. 15:12
Ahimaaz	2 Sam. 15:27
Hushai	2 Sam. 15:32
Shimei	2 Sam. 16:5
Amasa	2 Sam. 17:25
Abishag	1 Kings 1:3
Sheba (Queen of)	1 Kings 10:1
Jeroboam	1 Kings 11:26
Rehoboam	1 Kings 11:43
Shemaiah	1 Kings 12:22
Asa	1 Kings 15:8

Jehoshaphat	1 Kings 15:24
Ahab	1 Kings 16:28
Jezebel	1 Kings 16:31
Elijah	1 Kings 17:1
Obadiah (servant of Ahab)	1 Kings 18:3
Elisha	1 Kings 19:16
Naboth	1 Kings 21:1
Zedekiah	1 Kings 22:11
Ahaziah	1 Kings 22:40
Jehoram	1 Kings 22:51
Gehazi	2 Kings 4:12
Athaliah	2 Kings 8:26
Jehoash	2 Kings 12:1
Amaziah	2 Kings 12:22
Jotham	2 Kings 15:5
Ahaz	2 Kings 15:38
Hezekiah	2 Kings 16:20
Jehoahez	2 Kings 19:35
Manasseh (king)	2 Kings 21:1
Amon	2 Kings 21:18
Josiah	2 Kings 21:24
Hilkiah	2 Kings 22:4
Huldah	2 Kings 22:14
Jehoiakim	2 Kings 23:34
Jehoiachin	2 Kings 24:6
Gedaliah	2 Kings 25:22
Isaiah	Isa. 1:1
Jeremiah	Jer. 1:1
Baruch	Jer. 32:12
Ezekiel	Ezek. 1:3
Hosea	Hos. 1:1
Gomer	Hos. 1:3
Joel	Joel 1:1
Obadiah (prophet)	Obad. 1:1
Jonah	Jon. 1:1
Habakkuk	Hab. 1:1
Haggai	Hag. 1:1
Zephaniah	Zeph. 1:1
Micah	Mic. 1:1
Nahum	Nah. 1:1
Malachi	Mal. 1:1
Asaph	Ps. 50:1

Job	Job 1:1
Eliphaz	Job 2:11
Elimelech	Ruth 1:2
Naomi	Ruth 1:2
Ruth	Ruth 1:4
Boaz	Ruth 2:1
Ecclesiastes (Kohelet)	Eccles. 1:1
Ahasuerus	Esth. 1:1
Vashti	Esth. 1:9
Mordechai	Esth. 2:5
Esther	Esth. 2:7
Haman	Esth. 3:1
Azariah	Dan. 1:6
Daniel	Dan. 1:6
Hananiah	Dan. 1:6
Mishael	Dan. 1:6
Ezra	Ezra 7:1
Nehemiah	Neh. 1:1
Bithiah	1 Chron. 4:18
Abijah	2 Chron. 11:20
Uzziah	2 Chron. 26:1

Glossary

Abba. Familiar form of the Hebrew word for "father."

Aggadah. Nonlegal rabbinic writings in the Talmud and Midrash that include statements of major moral and ethical principles (often elucidated by the use of parables and anecdotes), stories about biblical heroes and the great Rabbis, and Jewish folklore. Unlike *halachah*, *aggadah* is not legally binding. It serves to explain and clarify Jewish laws and customs and accentuate the ethical ideas of the Torah.

Agunah (chained woman). One whose marriage has in fact ended, but who legally remains a married woman (bound to a husband who no longer lives with her) and thus is unable to remarry. The *halachah* prescribes that a marriage can only be dissolved by divorce, with a valid divorce document (*get*) delivered by the husband to the wife, or the death of either spouse.

Akedah (binding of Isaac). Hebrew term for the biblical account of the Divine command to Abraham to offer his son Isaac as a sacrifice to test the patriarch's loyalty and faith (Gen. 22).

Aleinu (It is our duty). Opening word and name for a prayer proclaiming the sovereignty and unity of God, which is found near the end of every prayer service.

Aliyah. Literally meaning "ascent," the Hebrew word used to describe the honor of being called up to read a portion from the Torah.

Am ha'aretz. Literally "people of the land," a Hebrew phrase used in the Bible to refer to the Jewish masses. In Talmudic times, this term was applied to the common people who did not observe rabbinic ordinances.

Amidah (standing [prayer]). Referred to in the Talmud as simply *Ha-Tefillah* (The Prayer) and now known popularly as the *Shemoneh Esrei* (18 [blessings], though there actually are 19), the *Amidah* has been the core of the prayer service since the destruction of the Second Temple.

Amora (explainer). Teacher of Jewish law in the Land of Israel and Babylonia after the redaction of Mishnah by Judah the Prince (c. 200 C.E.). The discussions of the *amora'im* (200–500 C.E.), who interpreted the Mishnah and applied it to case law, form the Gemara, which together with the Mishnah constitute the Babylonian Talmud and the Palestinian Talmud.

Apocrypha. Literally meaning "hidden books," the collective name for Jewish books written in the Hellenistic and Roman periods that were included in the Septuagint (Greek translation of the Bible) but not accepted into the normative Hebrew canon.

Arachin (Ar.). Fifth tractate of Kodashim (holy things) in the Mishnah, it deals with the laws of valuations of people, houses, fields, and objects vowed to the Sanctuary.

Aramaic. Ancient Semitic tongue that was the official language of the Persian Empire and became the vernacular of the Israelites who were exiled to Babylonia after the destruction of Jerusalem in 586 B.C.E.

Ark of the Covenant. Oblong portable cabinet of acacia wood, inlaid with pure gold both inside and outside, which contained both the shattered first tablets and the intact second tablets of the Ten Commandments. It was carried by the Levites during the Israelites' trek through the wilderness as a visible reminder of the covenant between God and the people, providing assurance that the Divine Presence was always with them on their journey.

Av bet din. Literally "father of the law court," the Hebrew title of the vice president of the Supreme Court (Sanhedrin) in Jerusalem during the Second Temple period.

Avodah Zarah (Av. Zar.). Eighth tractate of Nezikin (damages) in the Mishnah, it deals with laws concerning the prohibition of idolatry.

Avot. *See Pirkei Avot*.

Avot de-Rabbi Natan (ARN). Minor tractate of the Talmud, a commentary on the Mishnah tractate Avot. It has traditionally been ascribed to R. Nathan, the second-century son of a Babylonian exilarch, who moved to Palestine and was the chief *halachic* adversary of Judah the Prince.

Babylonian Talmud. Compendium of the wide-ranging discussions and elaborate interpretations of the Mishnah by scholars known as *amora'im* in the great academies of learning in Babylonia.

Bar. Hebrew term meaning "son of" used in Babylonia during the Talmudic period.

Baraita. Aramaic word meaning "outside," a piece of legal, historic, or *aggadic* tradition that was not included in the Mishnah of Judah the Prince. *Baraitot* are attributed to rabbinic teachers who lived in the Land of Israel at or before the time of the Mishnah.

Bat kol. Literally "daughter of the voice," this Hebrew expression was commonly used in the Talmud to denote a heavenly voice or the voice of God, which was heard by individuals or groups of people. Distinct from a prophetic communication, it often functioned in the context of giving approval to a *halachic* decision.

Bava Batra (BB). Third section of the first tractate of Nezikin (damages) in the Mishnah, it deals with property law (real estate, inheritance, sales, and partnerships) and such issues as beautification and protection of the environment and honest business practices.

Bava Kamma (BK). First section of the first tractate of Nezikin (damages) in the Mishnah, it deals with torts (damages to person and property). It requires wrongdoers to ask for forgiveness and injured parties to grant it.

Bava Metzia (BM). Second section of the first tractate of Nezikin (damages) in the Mishnah, it deals with civil law (lost and found property, fraud, usury, bailments, relations with workers).

B.C.E. (acronym for "Before the Common Era"). This neutral term is used by Jews and biblical scholars to denote the period traditionally labeled "B.C." (before [the birth of] Christ) by Christians.

Bechorot (Bek.). Fourth tractate of Kodashim (holy things) in the Mishnah. Literally meaning "firstlings," it deals with the laws relating to firstborn children and animals.

Beitzah (Betz.). Seventh tractate of Mo'ed (festivals) in the Mishnah, it deals with general laws regarding the festivals.

Ben. Hebrew term meaning "son of" used in the Land of Israel during the Talmudic period.

Berachot (Ber.). First tractate in Zera'im (seeds) and the initial tractate in the entire Mishnah, it deals with blessings and prayers, illustrating the central role these play in Jewish life.

Bet Midrash. Literally "house of study," in Talmudic times this Hebrew term was used to describe an academy for the study of Jewish religious texts that was presided over by a legal scholar. Today, it refers to an independent religious school or one located in a synagogue.

Bikurim (Bik.). Eleventh and final tractate of Zera'im (seeds) in the Mishnah, it deals with the ceremony and laws relating to the offering of the first fruits at the Temple.

Birthright. Privilege of the firstborn son in ancient Israel to lead the family and receive a double share of the inheritance.

C.E. (acronym for "Common Era"). This neutral term is used by Jews and scholars to denote the period traditionally labeled "A.D." (*anno Domini*; in the year of the Lord [i.e., Jesus]) by Christians.

Cubit. Biblical measurement of length, based on the distance between the elbow and the tip of the middle finger, which in an average man equals about 18 inches (1.5 feet or 45 cm).

Demai (Dem.). Third tractate in Zera'im (seeds) in the Mishnah, it deals with the requirements for tithing produce when there is doubt whether proper tithes have been given.

Deuteronomy Rabbah (Deut. R.). *See* Midrash Rabbah.

Ecclesiastes Rabbah (Eccles. R.). *See* Midrash Rabbah.

Eduyot (Eduy.). Seventh tractate of Nezikin (damages) in the Mishnah, it primarily deals with various rabbinic teachings (testimonies, *eduyot* in Hebrew) of later sages on the legal controversies and rulings of earlier authorities, such as those between Bet Hillel and Bet Shammai.

Ephod. Ornamented long vest worn by the high priest over the blue robe. Attached to the ephod was the breastplate containing the *Urim* and *Thumim.*

Eruv. Literally meaning "blending" or "intermingling," a rabbinically permitted way to overcome the restrictions on carrying and travel on the Sabbath while preserving the sanctity of the day. The establishment of an *eruv* takes advantage of the legally mandated permission to carry inside a private domain by converting a large public area into a huge "private domain."

Eruvin (Er.). Second tractate of Mo'ed (festivals) in the Mishnah, it deals with the permissible limits for carrying on the Sabbath.

Esther Rabbah (Esth. R.). *See* Midrash Rabbah.

Exilarch. Political head of the Jewish community in Babylonia from the first through the thirteenth centuries.

Exodus Rabbah (Exod. R.). *See* Midrash Rabbah.

Gehenna. Greek form of the Aramaic "*Gehinnom*" (the Valley of [the sons of] Hinnom), the ravine in the southern part of ancient Jerusalem. Although translated as "Hell," the traditional rabbinic view of *Gehenna* was a purgatory, where even the worst of sinners would spend only a year.

Gehinnom. See Gehenna.

Gematria. Interpretive device whereby words are understood through the numerical value of their letters (numerology).

Genesis Rabbah (Gen. R.). *See* Midrash Rabbah.

Get. Talmudic term for a formal divorce document that is signed by the husband and then delivered to his wife. Just as a Jewish marriage is entered into by a contract between husband and wife (see *ketubah*), it can be terminated only by a legal document nullifying the original contract.

Gittin (Git.). Sixth tractate of Nashim (women) in the Mishnah, it deals with the laws of divorce.

Golem. Legendary creature made of dust and clay by human hands in a magical, artificial way to serve its creator. The most famous *golem* legend involved the sixteenth-century Rabbi Judah Loew of Prague, who created one to protect the Jews of his city against a false charge of blood libel.

Haftarah. Literally meaning "concluding portion," a selection from the Hebrew prophets that is read after the Torah reading on Sabbaths, major festivals, and fast days.

Haggadah. Literally meaning "telling" (of the Exodus), a collection of prayers and blessings, stories, legends, commentaries, psalms, and songs that are traditionally recited at the Passover seder.

Hagigah (Hag.). Twelfth tractate in Mo'ed (festivals) in the Mishnah, it deals with the special sacrifices for the three pilgrimage festivals.

Halachah. Literally meaning "walking," the all-inclusive term for the body of law (rules, prohibitions, requirements) that governs every aspect of Jewish life and constitutes the essence of Jewish religious and civil practice.

Hallah (Hal.). Ninth tractate of Zera'im (seeds) in the Mishnah, it deals with the dough offering to the priests.

Hametz. Hebrew term for leavened products, which are explicitly prohibited on Passover. The Rabbis deemed that this characteristic applied to the five species of grain indigenous to the Land of Israel—wheat, barley, oats, rye, and spelt.

Hanukah. Eight-day festival, beginning on the twenty-fifth of Kislev (December), which commemorates the victory of Judah Maccabee and his followers over the army of the Syrian ruler, Antiochus Epiphanes, and the rededication of the defiled Temple (165 B.C.E.).

Hanukiah. Eight-branched candelabrum, also called a "Hanukah menorah," which is lit as the major ritual associated with the festival.

Havdalah. Literally meaning "separation," an ancient ritual ceremony that marks the conclusion of the Sabbath (or a festival).

Hazzan. Synagogue official who leads the congregation in prayer and song.

Hermeneutics. Method of biblical interpretation developed by the Rabbis of the Talmudic period.

Holy of Holies. Innermost portion of the Temple, which housed the Ark of the Covenant. A windowless ten-meter cube, the Holy of Holies was entered only once a year, by the high priest on Yom Kippur.

Horayot (Hor.). Tenth tractate of Nezikin (damages) in the Mishnah, it deals with erroneous decisions (*horayot*) made by the court on matters of religious law (and how to correct them).

Hullin (Hul.). Third tractate of Kodashim (holy things) in the Mishnah, it deals with the ritual slaughter of animals and the dietary laws.

Intercalation. Addition of an extra month seven times in every nineteen years. This was necessary because the Jewish lunar calendar is approximately eleven days shorter than the solar year. Without any adjustments, the festivals would "wander" and shift from their appointed seasons of the year.

Judge. Title for the twelve leaders of the Israelites after the death of Joshua until the beginning of the monarchy. Well-known judges include Deborah, Gideon, Jephthah, and Samson.

Kavanah. Hebrew word meaning "devotion, intent, or conscious purpose," which describes the state of mind required for praying or performing a *mitzvah*.

Keriah. Ritual tearing of a garment as a sign of grief, which is a traditional Jewish mourning custom.

Keritot (Ker.). Seventh tractate of Kodashim (holy things) in the Mishnah, it deals with the biblical punishment of *karet* (punishment "at the hands of Heaven") and lists the offenses to which it was applied.

Ketubah. Literally meaning "written document," the Jewish marriage contract. Written in Aramaic, it stipulates the obligations of the husband toward his wife, including his duty to "maintain, honor, and support her as it is fitting for a Jewish husband to do."

Ketubot (Ket.). Second tractate in Nashim (women) in the Mishnah, it deals with the mutual rights between husband and wife as detailed in the marriage contract (*ketubah*).

Kiddushin (Kid.). Seventh tractate in Nashim (women) in the Mishnah, it deals with the laws of betrothal and marriage (including prohibited marriages).

Kilayim (Kil.). Fourth tractate in Zera'im (seeds) in the Mishnah, it deals with prohibitions against "diverse kinds"—crossbreeding and mingling of varied species of plants, animals, and clothing. *See also Sha'atnez*.

Kippah. Head covering worn by Jews in modern times. Also known by its Yiddish equivalent *yarmulke* (skullcap), it has become a universally recognized symbol of Jewish identity.

Kohen. Member of the hereditary priestly caste (*kohanim*), the male descendants of Aaron. They were to be shown honor and deference because they were consecrated to God and offered the sacrifices to the Lord.

Lag ba'Omer. Thirty-third day of the counting of the *omer*. According to tradition, the terrible "plague" that afflicted the students of R. Akiva ceased on that day.

Lamentations Rabbah (Lam. R.). *See* Midrash Rabbah.

Lashon ha-ra. Literally "evil speech" but translated as "gossip," the term refers to any derogatory or damaging statements against an individual, even when the slanderous or defaming remarks are true, which if publicized to others would cause the subject physical or monetary damage, anguish, or fear.

Levirate marriage (*yibbum*). Obligation of a surviving brother to marry the widow of his brother, if he died without having sired children.

Levites (*levi'im*). Descendants of the tribe of Levi (third son of Jacob and Leah), who were consecrated by Moses to serve in the Tabernacle and Temple as gatekeepers, musicians, teachers, and assistants to the priests (*kohanim*).

Leviticus Rabbah (Lev. R.). *See* Midrash Rabbah.

Lulav. Branch of the date palm that is part of the four species used on Sukkot. The four species are often collectively called *lulav*, since it is their largest member.

Machoza. Town in Babylonia, on the shores of the Tigris, which was an important Jewish center and site of a major talmudic academy after the destruction of Nehardea in 259. In the early fourth century, many scholars from the academy of Pumbedita moved to Machoza, but this center of learning was destroyed in 363.

Major prophets. The three prophets—Isaiah, Jeremiah, and Ezekiel—whose writings are substantially longer than the combined output of the twelve so-called "minor" prophets.

Makot (Mak.). Fifth tractate in Nezikin (damages) in the Mishnah, it deals with the rules governing flogging, false witnesses, and the cities of refuge.

Mamzer. Often mistranslated as "bastard," this Hebrew word does not refer to someone born out of wedlock. Instead, a *mamzer* is the child of a sexual relationship between a man and woman whose marriage could never be valid under Jewish law. Examples include a child born to a married woman by some man other than her lawful husband; a child born of a woman who had remarried without having obtained a valid divorce (*get*) from her first husband; a child of an incestuous relationship. According to the Bible, a *mamzer* and all of his or her descendants may never marry a Jew, though a marriage between two *mamzerim* is permitted.

Manna. Food that nourished the Israelites during their forty years of wandering in the wilderness.

Masoretes. Textual scholars of the sixth through ninth centuries who determined and preserved the authentic (masoretic) text of the Torah.

Matzah. Unleavened bread that is made from flour and water and is the quintessential symbol of Passover.

Mechilta. *Halachic midrash* on the Book of Exodus.

Megillah. Hebrew word for "scroll," usually used for the Book of Esther (*Megillat Esther*), the reading of which is the main feature of the festival of Purim.

Megillah (Meg.). Tenth tractate of Mo'ed (festivals) in the Mishnah, it deals with the reading of the Scroll of Esther on Purim.

Menahot (Men.). Second tractate in Kodashim (holy things) in the Mishnah, it deals with the preparation of meal offerings, *tzitzit*, and *tefillin*.

Menorah. Seven-branched candelabrum that once stood in the Jerusalem Temple. One of the most beloved and enduring symbols of Judaism, the menorah is the emblem of the modern State of Israel.

Mezuzah. The distinctive mark of a Jewish home and a reminder of the Divine Presence, it consists of a piece of parchment with biblical verses that is affixed at an angle to the upper third of the doorpost on the right side of the outside door, as well as to the doorpost of every living room in the house (excluding bathrooms, storerooms, and kitchen).

Midrash. Deriving from a Hebrew root meaning "to search out," the word can refer to either the process of interpreting the Bible or to the genre of rabbinic literature that has collected these interpretations. Midrash fills in the gaps of the terse biblical narrative, which provides little information as to the thoughts and feelings of the characters or the motivations behind their actions.

Midrash Rabbah. Literally "The Great Midrash," a ten-part collection of *aggadic midrashim* on the Five Books of Moses and the five *megillot* (Song of Songs, Ruth, Lamentations, Ecclesiastes, Esther), which were written by different authors, in different locales, and in different historical eras (from the fifth to the twelfth centuries).

Mikva'ot (Mik.). Sixth tractate in Tohorot (purity) in the Mishnah, it deals with the regulations concerning the *mikveh*.

Mikveh. Literally a "collection [of water]," the Hebrew term for a ritual bath. Immersion in the *mikveh* is indispensable in the conversion of both male and female non-Jews to Judaism.

Minor prophets. Collective term for twelve prophets—Hosea, Joel, Amos, Obadiah, Jonah, Micah, Nahum, Habakkuk, Haggai, Zephaniah, Zechariah, and Malachi. The popular epithet "minor" has solely a quantitative connotation and is not necessarily an indication of relative importance.

Minyan. Literally "number," the term for the quorum of ten necessary for congregational worship and certain other religious ceremonies.

Mishnah. Literally meaning "repetition" or "teaching" in Hebrew, the earliest major rabbinic book and the basis for the Talmud. It was compiled in the early third century by Judah ha-Nasi, who sifted through, evaluated, and edited the vast number of legal opinions constituting the Oral Law that had been expressed over the centuries in the academies of learning, primarily in the Land of Israel.

Mishneh Torah. Massive fourteen-volume legal code compiled by Maimonides in the twelfth century.

Mitzvah (pl., *mitzvot*). Derived from a Hebrew root meaning "to command," the term is applied to a religious obligation. In common usage, *mitzvah* has also come to mean a "good deed." The 613 *mitzvot* in the Torah are traditionally divided into 248 positive requirements and 365 negative prohibitions.

Mo'ed Katan (MK). Literally meaning "little festival," this eleventh tractate of Mo'ed (festivals) in the Mishnah deals with the nature of work permitted during the intermediate days of Passover and Sukkot, as well as mourning on holy days.

Molech. Canaanite fire deity to whom pagans offered their young children as sacrifices.

Musaf. Literally "additional," the service added after the morning service on those days when an additional sacrifice was offered in the Temple—Sabbath, New Moon, the three pilgrimage festivals (Passover, Shavuot, Sukkot), New Year (Rosh Hashanah), and the Day of Atonement (Yom Kippur).

Nasi (prince). Talmudic title for the president of the Sanhedrin, who served as the spiritual head of the Jewish people and later was also recognized as their political leader (patriarch) by the Roman government.

Nazir. Fourth tractate of Nashim (women) in the Mishnah, it deals with the vows of the Nazirite.

Nazirite. Literally meaning either one who was "separated" (from the temptations of the environment) or "consecrated" (to God), a person who voluntarily assumed restrictions beyond the obligatory commandments in order to reach an elevated state of holiness. The Nazirite vowed to allow the hair to remain uncut during the period of the vow; abstain from grapes or grape products such as wine; and avoid any contact with a human corpse. The most famous Nazirite was Samson.

Nedarim (Ned.). Third tractate in Nashim (women) in the Mishnah, it deals with the making and annulling of vows.

Nehardea. City in Babylonian and site of a famous talmudic academy, which was destroyed in 259.

Niddah (Nid.). Seventh tractate in Tohorot (purity) in the Mishnah, it deals with family purity (menstruation and the monthly period of separation between husband and wife) and the ritual uncleanness related to childbirth.

Numbers Rabbah (Num. R.). *See* Midrash Rabbah.

Omer period. Seven weeks from the second day of Passover until the festival of Shavuot. For the ancient Israelites, the Omer period was the critical time when the success of the harvest was determined. Except for the thirty-third day of the Omer (*Lag ba-Omer*), the Omer period is observed as a time of semimourning, during which traditional Jews do not get haircuts, celebrate weddings, or attend concerts.

Oral Law. Body of rabbinic discussions, expositions, and commentaries on the Torah (Written Law) that deals with all aspects of existence from the most trivial to the sublime. According to tradition, it was part of the Revelation given to Moses and subsequently transmitted faithfully by the leaders of each generation to their successors. The Oral Law consists of two major divisions: *halachah* and *aggadah*.

Passover. Spring pilgrimage festival, also known as the "Feast of Unleavened Bread," which commemorates the redemption of the Jewish people from bondage and the Exodus from Egypt.

Patriarchate. Administration under the Sanhedrin, whose president (*nasi*, or "patriarch" as he was called in the outside world) became officially recognized as the representative of the Jewish people in its relations with the Roman authorities. The most famous patriarch was Judah the Prince, who compiled the Mishnah.

Pe'ah. Second tractate in Zera'im (seeds) in the Mishnah, it deals with the setting aside of the corners of the field for the poor, as well as other duties owed them.

Pesachim (Pes.). Third tractate in Mo'ed (festivals) in the Mishnah, it deals with regulations regarding Passover (*hametz*, *matzah*, paschal sacrifice).

Pesikta de-Rav Kahana (PdRK). Collection of *midrashic* homilies on the scriptural readings in synagogues for special Sabbaths and holidays, written in the fifth century in the Land of Israel.

Pesikta Rabbati (Pes. Rab.). Medieval *midrash* on the Scriptural readings in synagogues for special Sabbaths and holidays.

Pharisees. One of the three major sects in Israel before the destruction of the Second Temple in 70 C.E., its teachings formed the basis of rabbinic Judaism.

Pirkei Avot (Ethics of the Fathers). Portion of the Mishnah that has no legal content and consists of the moral and practical teachings of some sixty sages whose lives spanned nearly five centuries.

Pirkei de-Rabbi Eliezer (PdRE). *Aggadic midrash* on the biblical narrative, written in the eighth century and named for the Talmudic sage, Eliezer ben Hyrcanus.

Pumbedita. Site of the one of the two major Talmudic academies in Babylonia. Founded in the third century after the destruction of Nehardea and rivaled only by the academy at Sura, Pumbedita remained a center of Jewish learning for almost 800 years.

Purim. Hebrew word literally meaning "lots," the joyous festival on the fourteenth of Adar that celebrates the deliverance of the Jews from the plot of the Persian villain Haman to kill them. The main feature of Purim is the synagogue reading of the Book of Esther.

Rabban. Variant of the title "rabbi." During the Mishnaic period, it was used as an honorary title, especially for heads of the Sanhedrin.

Rabbi. Literally "my master" or "my teacher" in Hebrew, this title was originally used during the first century C.E. to identify those Torah scholars who had been properly ordained as graduates of the Talmudic academies in the Land of Israel. (The alternative title in Babylonia was *rav*.)

Rav. Literally "great" or "teacher," an alternative title in Babylonia for "rabbi."

Rosh Hashanah. Literally "head of the year," the first and second days of the month of Tishrei (September) that are celebrated as the beginning of the Jewish New Year and the anniversary of the Creation of the world.

Rosh Hashanah (RH). Eighth tractate of Mo'ed (festivals) in the Mishnah, it deals with the laws concerning the sanctification of the New Moon, fixing the months and years, the blowing of the shofar, and the order of prayers on Rosh Hashanah.

Rosh Hodesh. Literally "head of the month," the first day of the month that correlates with the sighting of the crescent of the new moon.

Ruth Rabbah (Ruth R.). *See* Midrash Rabbah.

Sabbath. The seventh day of the week and a time of rest and spiritual renewal, which begins at sunset on Friday evening and ends on Saturday evening when three stars are visible in the sky.

Sabbatical year. In Hebrew *shemitah* (lit., "release"), every seventh year in which all the land of Israel was to lie fallow and it was forbidden to cultivate the soil, water, and prune trees. Owner, servants, gentile laborers, the poor, the stranger, and even wild and domesticated animals had equal rights to the produce.

Sadducees. One of the three major sects of Judaism in the late Second Temple period, a predominantly aristocratic group, many of whom were priests officiating in the Temple.

Sages. Collective term for the *tanna'im* and *amora'im*, the Rabbis of the Talmudic era cited in the Mishnah and Gemara.

Sanhedrin. Supreme judicial, religious, and political body in the Land of Israel during the Roman and Byzantine periods.

Sanhedrin (Sanh.). Fourth tractate in Nezikin (damages) in the Mishnah, it deals with courts of justice, judicial procedure, and criminal law.

Satan. Rather than a demonic creature who is the personification of evil and the enemy of God, the biblical word *satan* is merely a common noun that means "adversary," "accuser," or "hinderer." The role of Satan is to make things difficult for human beings, so that they can overcome temptations and their evil inclinations.

Savora'im. Literally "reasoners" and the disciples of the last *amora'im*, the *savora'im* probably completed the final editing of the Babylonian Talmud in the mid-sixth century (after the work of Rav Ashi and Ravina).

Se'ah. Biblical measurement of volume, thought to be equal to about five gallons.

Seder. Literally "order," the home celebration held on the first night of Passover (also the second in the Diaspora) that fulfills the biblical injunction that parents tell their children about the miraculous deliverance of their ancestors from Egypt.

Sefer Yetzirah. Literally "Book of Creation/Formation," widely regarded as the first classic text of Kabbalah.

Semichah. Literally meaning "laying (of hands)," the traditional ordination required before a rabbi can decide practical questions of Jewish law.

Sha'atnez. Literally meaning "mixture," this Hebrew term refers specifically to a fabric made of a mixture of wool and linen (flax) that is explicitly forbidden in the Torah.

Shabbat (Shab.). First tractate in Mo'ed (festivals) in the Mishnah, it deals with the rules governing the observance of the Sabbath, including the thirty-nine categories of prohibited work.

Shavuot. The second of the pilgrimage festivals, it occurs fifty days after Passover. Initially a harvest festival, during the Talmudic period Shavuot was transformed into the anniversary of the giving of the Torah on Mount Sinai.

Shechinah. Translated as "Divine Presence," one of the rabbinic names for God.

Shekalim (Shek.). Fourth tractate in Mo'ed (festivals) in the Mishnah, it deals with the half-shekel tax that was used to maintain the worship services during the Second Temple period.

Shema. Declaration of faith of the Jewish people in the Unity and Oneness of God and their acceptance of the yoke of the Kingdom of Heaven (Deut. 6:4).

She'ol. Dwelling place of the dead according to the Bible.

Sheva Brachot. Literally "seven blessings," the seven benedictions recited at the wedding ceremony under the *huppah* after the bridegroom places the ring on the finger of his bride.

Shevarim. One of the three sounds of the shofar, a series of three short broken notes that resemble a sobbing sound, in recognition of the sins we have committed.

Shevu'ot (Shev.). Sixth tractate of Nezikin (damages) in the Mishnah, it deals with different types of oaths.

Shiloh. Capital of Israel during the time of the judges, situated north of Bethel in the mountains of the territory of Ephraim.

Shirat ha-Yam (Song at the Sea). Victory hymn using powerful poetic metaphors and celebrating the mighty acts of God, which Moses and the Israelites sang after crossing the Sea of Reeds to escape the pursuing Egyptians (Exod. 15:1–18).

Shivah. Literally "seven," the most intense period of mourning, which is observed for father, mother, wife, husband, son, daughter, brother, and sister (including half-brother and half-sister).

Shofar (ram's horn). Ancient musical instrument that is the most recognizable symbol of Rosh Hashanah.

Showbread. Twelve large flat, oblong loaves of wheat flour (corresponding to the number of the tribes of Israel) that were placed on the Table in the Sanctuary each Sabbath. They were left there until the next Sabbath, when they were removed (miraculously still fresh) and eaten by the priests.

Sifra. Halachic midrash on the Book of Leviticus, probably written in the second or third century.

Sifrei. Halachic midrash on the Books of Numbers and Deuteronomy (third century).

Song of Songs Rabbah (Song. R.). *See* Midrash Rabbah.

Sopherim (Soph.). Literally "scribes," a post-Talmudic treatise on the mode of writing the books of the law.

Sotah (Sot.). Fifth tractate in Nashim (women) in the Mishnah, it deals with the woman suspected of adultery.

Sukkah. Hastily constructed, insubstantial structure that Jews erect as part of the observance of the fall Festival of Sukkot.

Sukkah (Suk.). Sixth tractate of Mo'ed (festivals) in the Mishnah, it deals with the laws concerning the Festival of Sukkot and the four species.

Sukkot. Last of the three agricultural pilgrimage festivals. Also known as Tabernacles, this fall festival of thanksgiving celebrates the joy of the harvest and commemorates the temporary shelters (*sukkot*) in which the Israelites dwelled as they wandered through the wilderness.

Sura. Ancient city in southern Babylonia and the site of one of the two major Talmudic academies, which was founded in the early third century by Rav. In the fourth and fifth centuries, the Talmud was edited by Rav Ashi and Ravina in Sura, which remained a center of Jewish learning for 700 years.

Ta'anit (Taan.). Ninth tractate in Mo'ed (festivals) in the Mishnah, it deals with the fast days other than Yom Kippur.

Tallit. Traditional prayer shawl worn during daily morning prayers and all services on Yom Kippur. Ritual fringes (*tzitzit*) are attached to each of the four corners of the *tallit* in accordance with biblical law.

Talmud. In general use, the term "Talmud" refers to the Babylonian Talmud, though there is also a much smaller Jerusalem Talmud. The Babylonian Talmud is a compendium of the extensive discussions and interpretations of the Mishnah in the great academies of learning, by scholars known as *amora'im*, from the first half of the third century (Rav and Samuel) to the editing by Rav Ashi and Ravina around 500.

Tamid (Tam.). Ninth tractate in Kodashim (holy things) in the Mishnah, it deals with the regulations for the daily burnt offerings in the Temple as well as the general organization of that institution.

Tanach. Hebrew term for the Bible, the acronym *Ta-Na-Kh* (or *Tanach*) is derived from the initial letters of the names of its three major divisions—Torah; *Nevi'im* (Prophets); and *Ketuvim* (Writings).

Tanhuma. *Aggadic midrash* on each section of the Torah, attributed to Tanhuma bar Abba, a fourth-century *amora* and prolific *aggadist* in the Land of Israel.

Tanna. Literally "repeater" in Aramaic, the initial teachers of the Mishnah in the first and second centuries. Because of the prohibition against writing down the Oral Law, the *tanna'im* acted as "living books" in transmitting the teachings of the Mishnah to their disciples. The classical period of the *tanna'im* began with the death of Hillel and Shammai and ended with the generation after Judah ha-Nasi, the editor of the Mishnah.

Targum Onkelos. Official Aramaic translation of the Bible (second century), which is printed next to the Torah text in most rabbinic Bibles.

Tashlich (You will cast). From the verse in Micah (7:19), "You will cast (*v'tashlich*) all our sins into the depths of the sea," the ceremony on the afternoon of the first day of Rosh Hashanah in which Jews recite special penitential prayers and psalms and throw crumbs or small pieces of bread into a body of water (river, lake, or ocean) to symbolically cast away their sins.

Techeilet. Thread of blue put with seven white ones on each corner of the *tallit*. This blue was made from a rare dye that was extracted from a sea snail (*hilazon*) by a few families on the Mediterranean coast.

Tefillah. Talmudic word for the *Amidah*, the core of the prayer service since the destruction of the Second Temple.

Tefillin. Two small black leather boxes that are bound by black leather straps to the forehead and arm. Also known as phylacteries, they contain parchments on which are written the four sets of biblical verses that mention the commandment to wear them as "a sign upon your hand and as frontlets between your eyes."

Tekiah. One of the three sounds of the shofar, a long sustained blast.

Ten Lost Tribes of Israel. The tribes of the North Kingdom of Israel that, after the Assyrian conquest in 721 B.C.E., were scattered throughout the empire, assimilated, and lost to history. Over the centuries, various groups have claimed that they are the descendants of these lost tribes.

Ten Martyrs. Renowned sages executed by the Romans following the unsuccessful Bar Kochba revolt (132–135 C. E.) for defying Emperor Hadrian's prohibition, under penalty of death, against the observance and study of Jewish law. Although their identity is uncertain, they probably were among these eleven rabbis: Akiva ben Joseph, Ishmael ben Elisha, Elazar ben Dama, Hanina ben Teradyon, Judah ben Bava, Hutzpit the Interpreter, Yeshevav the Scribe, Eleazar ben Shammua, Hanina ben Hakhinai, Shimon ben Gamaliel I, and Ishmael the high priest.

Ten Plagues. Afflictions suffered by the Egyptians because of Pharaoh's refusal to allow the enslaved Israelites to leave Egypt. The ten plagues were: (1) blood; (2) frogs; (3) vermin (lice); (4) wild beasts; (5) pestilence (disease of the flocks); (6) boils; (7) hail; (8) locusts; (9) darkness; and (10) slaying of the firstborn.

Teruah. One of the three sounds of the shofar, a blast of at least nine staccato notes that has been interpreted as symbolic of wailing.

Terumah. From a Hebrew root meaning "life up from," a generic term for the various offerings given to the *kohanim*. The *terumah* could be eaten only by a ritually clean *kohen* and members of his household, including his Israelite wife and gentile slaves.

Tetragrammaton. Greek for "four-letter word," the holiest name of God and the one that is most distinctly Jewish.

Tisha b'Av. Ninth day of the month of Av (July/August), the saddest day in the Jewish calendar. This major fast day marks the anniversary of the destruction of the First Temple by the Babylonians in 586 B.C.E. and the Second Temple by the Romans in 70 C.E.

Torah (1). The first five books of the Bible. Also known as the Pentateuch, the Torah begins with Creation and ends with the death of Moses, as the Israelites are poised to cross the Jordan River into the Promised Land.

Torah (2). Inclusive term used for all of Jewish law and learning—both the Written Law and the Oral Law, as well as all the commentaries and *responsa* produced during the subsequent centuries to the present day.

Tosefta. In Hebrew *tosafah*, a collection of *beraitot* arranged according to the order of the Mishnah. About four times larger than the Mishnah itself, the Tosefta (meaning "supplement") is an independent work that contains versions of *halachot* that supplement but sometimes contradict the Mishnah.

Tractate (*masechet*). Individual volumes into which each order of the Mishnah is divided.

Twelve Tribes of Israel. Founders of the Jewish people, listed in two ways in the Bible. Jacob had twelve sons with his wives, Leah and Rachel, and his concubines, Bilhah and Zilpah—Reuben, Shimon, Levi, Judah, Dan, Naphtali, Gad, Asher, Issachar, Zebulun, Joseph, and Benjamin. However, for purposes of settling the Promised Land, Joseph received a double share that was passed on to his sons, Ephraim and Menasseh. The postsettlement listing of the Twelve Tribes of Israel excludes Levi, because this tribe inherited the priesthood rather than any of the tribal lands and was scattered among the people. Jews today are the descendants of the two southern tribes (Judah and Benjamin) plus the Levites, since the ten northern tribes were lost after the Assyrian conquest.

Tzara'at. Although often translated as "leprosy," the signs described in the Torah and the reversibility of this skin condition make it doubtful that it refers to that incurable disease. The Rabbis regarded *tzara'at* as Divine punishment for slander or tale-bearing (see *lashon ha-ra*), indicating that such a person is a "moral leper" who must be excluded from the camp of Israel.

Tzitzit. Ritual fringes that are attached to each of the four corners of the *tallit* in accordance with biblical law.

Urim and **Thumim**. Typically translated as "lights and perfections" or "revelation and truth," an oracular device sanctioned by the Bible for determining the will of God on specific issues that were beyond human ability to decide.

Written Law. The Five Books of Moses.

Yeshivah. From a Hebrew root meaning "to sit," an academy of intensive higher learning in Babylonia and the Land of Israel during the Talmudic period and beyond.

Yetzer ha-ra and *Yetzer ha-tov*. Literally the "inclination toward evil" and the "inclination toward good," these Hebrew terms reflect the rabbinic concept that within each person there are opposing natural drives continually in conflict.

Yevamot (Yev.). First tractate in Nashim (women) in the Mishnah, it deals with levirate marriage and prohibited marriages.

Yom Kippur (Day of Atonement). Major fast day, ten days after Rosh Hashanah, which is devoted to individual and communal repentance and is the most solemn day in the Jewish calendar.

Yoma. Fifth tractate in Mo'ed (festivals) in the Mishnah, it deals with the Temple service on the Day of Atonement as well as the regulations concerning the Yom Kippur fast and the significance of atonement and repentance.

Zevachim (Zev.). First tractate in Kodashim (holy things) in the Mishnah, it deals with the sacrificial system in the Temple.

Zohar. Known as the "Book of Splendor," the principal *kabbalistic* book that is the basis for all subsequent Jewish mystical works. Although attributed to the second-century rabbinic authority Shimon bar Yochai and his colleagues and disciples, scholars now believe that the Zohar was written in the late thirteenth century by Moses de Leon.

Zugot. Literally "pairs," the Hebrew term for the pairs of sages in the Land of Israel who for five generations (second century B.C.E. to first century C.E.) were the leaders of rabbinic Judaism. In each pair, one was the *nasi* (president of the Sanhedrin) and the other was designated as the *av bet din* (head of the religious court). The *zugot* were: Jose ben Yo'ezer and Jose ben Yochanam; Joshua ben Perachyah and Nittai of Arbela; Judah ben Tabbai and Shimon ben Shetach; Shemaiah and Avtalyon; and Hillel and Shammai.

Bibliography

ArtScroll Siddur. Brooklyn: Mesorah Publications, 1986.

Bialik and Ravitsky. Sefer ha-Aggada. In *Nature of Aggada in Midrash and Literature* (eds. Geoffrey H. Harman and Sanford Budick). New Haven, CT: Yale University Press, 1986.

Etz Hayim. Senior editor David Lieber. Philadelphia: Jewish Publication Society, 2001.

Friedman, Richard Elliott. *Who Wrote the Bible?* New York: Doubleday, 1987.

Gordon, Cyrus H. *Before the Bible: The Common Background of Greek and Hebrew Civilizations*. Plainview, NY: Books for Libraries Press, 1973.

Isaacs, Ronald. *The Jewish Book of Numbers*. Northvale, NJ: Aronson, 1996.

JPS Hebrew-English Tanakh. Philadelphia: Jewish Publication Society, 2001.

Kadden, Barbara Binder, and Bruce Kadden. *Teaching Jewish Life Cycle*. Denver: A. R. E. Publishing, 1997.

Maimonides, Moses. *Mishneh Torah*. Trans. Philip Birnbaum. New York: Hebrew Publishing, 1974.

Millgram, Abraham. *Sabbath, the Day of Delight*. Philadelphia: Jewish Publication Society, 1959.

Schottenstein Edition of the Babylonian Talmud. Brooklyn: Mesorah Publications, 2005.

Schottenstein Edition of the Jerusalem Talmud. Brooklyn: Mesorah Publications, 2005.

Soncino Talmud. Chicago: Davka, 2005.

Stone Chumash. Brooklyn: Mesorah Publications, 1994.

Weissman, Moshe. *The Midrash Says: Deuteronomy*. Brooklyn, NY: Benei Yaakov, 1980.

About the Author

Ronald L. Eisenberg is a professor of radiology at Harvard Medical School and on the faculty at Beth Israel Medical Center in Boston. Dr. Eisenberg has been awarded master's and doctoral degrees in Jewish studies from Spertus Institute in Chicago and has published six critically acclaimed books on Jewish topics, including *The Jewish World in Stamps* (Schreiber, 2003), *The JPS Guide to Jewish Traditions* (Jewish Publication Society, 2004), *The 613 Mitzvot* (Schreiber, 2005), *Dictionary of Jewish Terms* (Schreiber, 2008), and *What the Rabbis Said* (Praeger, 2010). He has authored more than twenty books in his medical specialty and is also a nonpracticing attorney.